Intergroup Behavior

Intergroup Behavior

Edited by

JOHN C. TURNER *and* HOWARD GILES

The University of Chicago Press

The University of Chicago Press, Chicago 60637

Basil Blackwell Publisher Ltd, Oxford OX4 1JF

© 1981 by Basil Blackwell Publisher Limited

All rights reserved. Published 1981
Printed in Great Britain by
The Camelot Press, Southampton

ISBN: 0-226-81726-1

Library of Congress Catalog Card No.: 81-52768

CONTENTS

CONTRIBUTORS

Rupert J. Brown, Social Psychology Research Unit, University of Kent at Canterbury

Howard Giles, Department of Psychology, University of Bristol

Patricia Johnson, Department of Psychology, University of Bristol

David Milner, School of the Social Sciences and Business Studies, The Polytechnic of Central London

Geoffrey M. Stephenson, Social Psychology Research Unit, University of Kent at Canterbury

Henri Tajfel, Department of Psychology, University of Bristol

John C. Turner, Department of Psychology, University of Bristol

PREFACE AND ACKNOWLEDGEMENTS

This book is an introduction to and survey of *the social psychology of intergroup behaviour*. It attempts to describe and evaluate the important research themes in the field. Thus it should be useful to researchers, teachers and students of social psychology, whether interested in specific aspects of the topic or simply wishing to familiarize themselves with a core area of the discipline. It should also be useful to other social scientists interested in intergroup behaviour.

Some good books have appeared recently on this topic. The present volume differs from these in several ways, but perhaps primarily in that we have tried to produce a survey of the research literature that is both more concise and also more comprehensive of current trends than are the others. We have divided the field into large bodies of work united by a common theme that seemed to us to represent the major lines of current research and asked contributors to these areas to review them in a single chapter. The contributors were also encouraged not merely to catalogue research results, but to assess the progress that has been made (or not) and discuss theoretical issues relevant to the direction of research. Needless to say, 'comprehensive' does not mean 'exhaustive'. There is much interesting work that cannot be included in a survey of this kind. Doubtless, too, we have excluded topics that some readers will consider important. This is practically inevitable in a field that is both disparate and very large. However, the result of our approach is a series of reviews that provide, we think, a unique coverage: of the six major research traditions presented here, for example, not more than two or three altogether are discussed in more than passing in any other recent book. Thus this book comprises critical discussions of specific areas and through them a bird's eye view of the whole field.

Howard Giles and Pat Johnson are grateful to Miles Hewstone, W. Peter Robinson, Donald M. Taylor and John Turner for their extremely valuable comments on earlier drafts of chapter 7.

Geoffrey Stephenson wishes to thank the Social Science Research Council for financial support, Jennie Williams for her comments on an earlier draft of chapter 6, and the editors for their valuable suggestions on the same.

John Turner wishes to acknowledge the value of discussions with Mike Hogg on social categorization and group cohesiveness, Penny Oakes on stereotyping, social cognition and the salience of group membership, Steve Reicher on crowd psychology, and Margaret Wetherell on group polarization, which have contributed to the ideas expressed in chapters 1 and 3; he is also grateful to the Social Science Research Council for financial support for related research.

Finally, as editors, John Turner and Howard Giles would like to thank all the contributors for their work, patience and ready acceptance of suggestions, Charles Husband for his moral support, useful comments on the book, and especially valuable points about social identity theory, some of which have been incorporated into chapter 1, the Social Psychology Section of the British Psychological Society for their aid and encouragement in organizing the conference (on the social psychology of intergroup behaviour at the University of Bristol in 1978) which gave us the idea for the present book, and Alma Foster, Jean Britton, Hilda Barrow and Anne Merriman for their excellent and careful typing of much of the manuscript.

JOHN C. TURNER
HOWARD GILES

CHAPTER 1

Introduction: The Social Psychology of Intergroup Behaviour

JOHN C. TURNER and HOWARD GILES

1 Preamble

This book is intended as a comprehensive review of the social psychology of intergroup behaviour. It comprises separate surveys of the important research traditions or themes in the field. We have identified these (in chapter order) as: (1) individualistic theories of intergroup relations (for example, belief congruence theory); (2) intergroup cooperation and competition; (3) racial prejudice; (4) social stereotyping; (5) intergroup negotiation and bargaining; and (6) the role of language in intergroup relations. These six themes overlap in some respects and differ markedly in others; they demonstrate the extraordinary breadth of social psychological research, from the analysis of basic processes in the experimental laboratory to the elucidation of concrete events and problems in macrosocial contexts. We believe that together they are a faithful representation of the general currents in the field.

Chapter 2 is somewhat different from the others. Its primary aim is to discuss the fundamental and thorny issue of whether there is a psychological distinction between interpersonal and intergroup behaviour and so to make explicit the working perspective of the book. However, it also describes empirical research. It includes thorough presentations and critiques of belief congruence theory and the contact hypothesis and a briefer consideration of the frustration–aggression hypothesis (see also chapter 4).

This introductory chapter discusses the definition of intergroup behaviour and the role and history of intergroup research in social psychology, outlines the contents of the chapters following and considers some general themes or issues in the field. These last two sections can also be reread to serve as a conclusion to the book.

2 *Defining intergroup behaviour*

What is intergroup behaviour? Concrete examples are not difficult to recognize. Any daily newspaper provides plenty. For example, on just one day in 1980 (19 September) the British*Daily Telegraph* carried headlines which included: 'Iran and Iraq nearer to war', 'Israeli raid on Lebanon', 'Peace formula lifts dock strike threat', 'Electronics firms fear Japanese . . . competition', 'West Berlin link cut by strike', and so on. In fact, most of the political, economic and international news had to do in one way or another with intergroup relations. Nor is intergroup behaviour just to do with 'bad' news. There were just as many examples in the sports pages. Nearly all team games (football, rugby, cricket, baseball, etc.) are examples of pure intergroup behaviour. Indeed, this is a large part of their attraction for both players and spectators: to identify with one's own team or the representatives of one's own institution, area or country, empathize with their struggles and share vicariously in the emotions of victory or defeat.

These examples illustrate that much intergroup behaviour (such as international diplomacy or the class struggle) can be usefully and is sometimes most sensibly analysed at a macrosocial level; it can be discussed in political, sociological, economic, historical or some other terms. It needs to be stressed at the outset therefore that this book is concerned with its *social psychological* and not *macrosocial* or *biological* component. This does not deny that a comprehensive understanding of intergroup behaviour ultimately requires an interdisciplinary approach. This may be taken for granted. However, such an approach demands the complementary efforts of different sciences working at their own problems, and at their own levels of analysis. This book aims to present the specific contribution of social psychology to the analysis of intergroup behaviour.

What, then, is intergroup behaviour from a social psychological perspective? There are two kinds of answers. Firstly, intergroup behaviour as a research field is defined by the topics investigated within it. The chief problems described in the present book include the effects of frustration, social contact and differences in beliefs on intergroup attitudes, the determinants of social conflict and ethnocentrism, the development of racial prejudice and the impact on its victims, the perception of individuals as members of social categories rather than as individual personalities, collective bargaining, and the role of language as a symbol of ethnic identity.

Common to these topics are three themes. Intergroup behaviour has to do with:

1   the division of human society into different social groups and their interrelations: the actions of members of one social group (their ingroup) towards or in relation to the members of other social groups (their outgroups),
2   the collective actions of large numbers of people; and
' 3   the conflicts, tensions, antipathies and 'pathologies' in society related to group membership.

These themes help to indicate the character of the issues studied in the field.

Secondly, there is intergroup behaviour as a psychological phenomenon. This is a theoretical and empirical matter to be resolved ultimately through research. The object here can only be to provide a provisional, working definition. Such a definition should be reasonably consistent with our 'naive' experience and recognition of intergroup behaviour, and also suggest testable ideas about its psychological determinants. To begin with, we can consider what might seem to be the obvious first step.

It might seem that intergroup behaviour could simply be defined as social interaction between members of different 'social groups'. To define a 'social group' one could then select the most popular conceptualization current in social psychology. In other words, perhaps we should be wise and save ourselves much work if we were to build upon the results of past research into the structure and dynamics of group functioning. This is a sound approach in principle but not very satisfactory in practice.

Sherif (1967, p. 12), for example, tried it. Very reasonably he considered it necessary to formulate an adequate definition of a group before embarking on the investigation of intergroup relations. He adopted, after consideration, the following definition:

a social unit that consists of a number of individuals (1) who, at a given time, have role and status relationships with one another, stabilized in some degree and (2) who possess a set of values or norms regulating the attitude and behaviour of individual members, at least in the matters of consequence to them. Shared attitudes, shared sentiments, shared aspirations and goals that characterize the

closely identified members are related to these properties, especially
to the common values or norms of the group.

He went on to state that 'intergroup relations' refers to the
relations between groups thus defined (1967, p. 62). However,
when he attempts to be more specific in his description of intergroup behaviour, the above definition seems to play little or no
role: 'Whenever individuals belonging to one group interact, collectively or individually, with another group or its members *in
terms of their group identification*, we have an instance of intergroup
behaviour'. (1967, p. 12)

Here what seems to matter is not the characteristics of social
groups as such but their role as subjective or perceptual determinants of social interaction. There is no necessary connection
between the two as conceptualized by Sherif. For example, we
can suppose from his standpoint two opposed armies that have
ceased to be unitary psychological groups. They may be conscript
armies fighting an unpopular war, characterized by dissent over
goals, ideological and political conflicts and open rebellion and
mutiny in the ranks – in other words, they have lost their internal
structure and normative consensus. We can also imagine a chance
meeting between deserters from the respective armies. In the
heat of the moment and solely on the basis of their mutual identification of each other as members of opposed groups through
recognition of their uniforms, the deserters might flee, hide or
attack each other. It is plain that some event could take place
which we should naturally call intergroup behaviour and which
would meet Sherif's criterion despite the fact that the armies are
apparently no longer social groups.

Thus, in describing intergroup behaviour Sherif in fact tends to
move away from the carefully selected (and insightful) definition
of a social group. The general point is not that conceptualizations
of the social group and intergroup behaviour are independent of
each other. The problem is that the former have tended in the
main to be elaborated in the context of intragroup rather than
intergroup relations. In consequence and also for methodological
reasons, social psychology has been preoccupied with the
dynamics of small face-to-face groups and has tended in its
theories to emphasize their special features.

To illustrate we can list the six main approaches to concep-
tualizing the social group outlined by Shaw (1976, pp. 6–11):

1   in terms of *perception*: that individuals share a collective per-
    ception of themselves as a social unit or define themselves
    as a group,
2   in terms of *motivation*: that individuals associate with each
    other to satisfy their needs, because their affiliation is
    mutually rewarding,
3   in terms of *goals*: that individuals associate or cooperate to
    achieve common objectives and purposes,
4   in terms of *organization* (social structure): that the relations
    between individuals are organized and regulated by a sys-
    tem of roles and shared norms (the definition emphasized
    by Sherif),
5   in terms of *interdependence*: that individuals are in some
    respect interdependent, for example in social interaction,
    for need-satisfaction, or as parts of a 'dynamic' social
    system,
6   in terms of *interaction*: that individuals are in regular or
    some degree of face-to-face contact, communication or
    social interaction with each other.

Shaw (1976) argues that there is overlap between these
theories (group structure, for instance, is a consequence of
interdependent social relationships), and that they all refer to the
same basic concept. He summarizes the concept of a group as
'two or more persons who are interacting with one another in
such a manner that each person influences and is influenced by
each other person' (1976, p. 11). This makes it very plain that the
theories are largely products of research into groups sufficiently
small that members can interact with each other on a personal
basis. Shaw in fact is explicit about the bias in social psychology
in this respect. He subtitles his book *Group Dynamics*, a comprehensive survey of the social psychology of group processes,
The Psychology of Small Group Behaviour. He defines a small group
as one comprising 20 or fewer members and more usually less
than five.

Thus, the social psychology of intragroup relations has largely
studied the functioning of small face-to-face groups. This inevitably emphasizes the role of interpersonal relationships in the
formation, maintenance and activities of social groups. Intergroup relations, however, is not primarily about such groups but
the relations between members of large-scale social categories,

such as nations, races, classes, the sexes, religions, occupations (and perhaps even armies), and so on.

These social categories may fail to meet most of the theoretical criteria but there is no doubt that they can function as psychological groups. The 'French', for example, are such a group. It is not an emergent group which developed out of interpersonal relationships; on the contrary it is an historical and cultural given, which precedes and conditions the interpersonal relations between its members. To a large extent the group is imposed upon its members by social consensus, whether or not it satisfies their individual needs. The members do not cooperate as one entity to achieve common goals, but are divided by many issues both relevant and irrelevant to being French. They are not integrated into one unified and consensual system of roles and norms, but divided into numerous organizations not one of which has complete sovereignty. Furthermore, they do not have direct face-to-face relations with more than a small minority of their fellows and these relations are not universally amicable. Nevertheless, the French are a social group and not merely in a political, economic or geographical sense but also a social psychological one; they tend to define themselves and be defined by others as a distinct social entity and, under certain conditions, they tend to act in a collective or unitary manner towards their social environment.

Thus, in intergroup relations there seems to be only the perceptual or 'identity' (see Turner, 1982; chapter 3) theory to fall back on. It looks as if a number of individuals constitute and act as a group to the extent that they define themselves as such. This suggests that we can define intergroup behaviour not merely as interaction between members of different groups but as action determined by the perception or identification of interactors as members of different groups. This definition distinguishes between intergroup and other forms of behaviour in terms of psychological determinants and also seems consistent with our naive interpretations of social encounters. It makes clear that although intergroup behaviour characteristically implies collective action, this is not a *sine qua non*. Indeed, no particular kind or form of action is intrinsically intergroup. Interactions between large numbers of members of different groups may not constitute intergroup behaviour, whereas an encounter between just two people may be (but is not the same as dyadic interaction). What matters is whether the individual's recognition of his or her own and the other's membership in different groups plays a causal role in determining the special features of the interaction. Some of these issues are discussed in more detail in chapter 2.

To sum up this brief discussion and define intergroup behaviour as a psychological phenomenon, we can follow Tajfel and Turner (1979, p. 40):

> We can conceptualize a group, in this sense, as a collection of individuals who perceive themselves to be members of the same social category, share some emotional involvement in this common definition of themselves, and achieve some degree of social consensus about the evaluation of their group and their membership of it. Following from this our definition of intergroup behaviour is basically identical to that of Sherif [see above] . . . any behaviour displayed by one or more actors toward one or more others that is based on the actors' identification of themselves and the others as belonging to different social categories.

3 Intergroup research and social psychology

What role has intergroup research played in the general development of social psychology and what role should it play?

Selecting the first important work relevant to intergroup behaviour is inevitably arbitrary to a degree, but in terms of subject matter, ideas and influence Le Bon's *The Crowd* (1896) would seem to be a natural choice. Le Bon studied and sought to explain collective or crowd behaviour as an expression of the 'popular mind' (as he put it in the subtitle of the book). He was very much a theorist of intergroup behaviour, since his main source of ideas were the activities of French revolutionary crowds (for example, in the French Revolution and the Paris Commune). Such crowds did not exist in isolation but came into being as part of a political struggle between different classes of society.

Le Bon described the distinctive characteristics of crowds as the similarity or homogeneity of their members in terms of action and mentality, intellectual inferiority, irrationality and primitivism, and the antisocial gratification by members of their destructive and violent animal instincts. To explain them he postulated social psychological mechanisms to do with the anonymity of the person in the crowd, the contagion of psychological states, and the increased suggestibility of crowd members to extremes of emotion and ideas. His basic proposition was that people were

psychologically transformed in the crowd; their conscious individual personalities were submerged in a collective or 'group
mind' ('the law of the mental unity of crowds', p. 26). Thus,
decent peaceful citizens become primitive, irrational and savage
in a crowd, completely unlike their normal selves (it is evident
that Le Bon was a political enemy of the populace – see
Reicher, 1982). This theory has been extremely influential: on
Freud, practising politicians (Billig, 1976, 1978), and modern
experimental social psychology (Milgram and Toch, 1969).

Le Bon's analysis of the crowd raised the general problem of
the relationship of the individual to the group. On the one hand
he recognized the apparently unitary and coordinated character
of much collective action and postulated a single, directing consciousness or 'group mind' to explain it. On the other, he saw
such action as primitive, irrational and instinctual, definitely
inferior to that of the conscious individual personality. We shall
return below to these issues and the general problem they reflect.

Social psychology began to assume its modern form in the
1920s and 1930s. Two noteworthy books were F. H. Allport's
Social Psychology (1924) and Sherif's *The Psychology of Social
Norms* (1936). Both discussed and attempted to answer the
problem of the relationship of the individual to the group. Both
rejected the concept of the 'group mind', but from different
points of view. Allport was a thoroughgoing advocate of
individualism; he argued that the individual was the sole
psychological reality and the group merely a nominal fallacy.
Sherif replied that individuals were changed in group
contexts because the group had a phenomenological reality
for its members which could not be reduced to the sum of its
parts. He demonstrated empirically how the emergent product
of a social process, a social norm, could come to regulate
individual behaviour. This work on the development of
social norms was a scientific milestone in the progress of
social psychology: a complex social process revealed its secrets
to psychological analysis and experiment. Allport, too, reported
seminal studies of social facilitation and social influence. Both
these books were directly relevant to intergroup behaviour
because of their general views about the individual–group relation, and their empirical research into social influence. The latter
topic is fundamental to explaining the spontaneously unitary
character of collective action.

Cartwright (1979) declares that these decades saw the pioneering research on significant, substantive problems: Allport and Sherif on social influence; Newcomb and Hyman on reference groups; Murray on motivation; the Yale group on frustration and aggression and on social learning and imitation; Lewin, Lippitt and White on leadership styles and group atmospheres, etc. They also saw the beginning of empirical research explicitly directed at intergroup behaviour. The main object of enquiry was race relations and racial prejudice (in the United States).

There were several highlights in the early work and only a few can be mentioned. As part of the developing interest in the concept and measurement of 'attitudes', Bogardus (1925, 1928) initiated the systematic study of racial attitudes and produced his measure of 'social distance' between ethnic and national groups. Katz and Braly (1933, 1935) likewise introduced an empirical technique for the elicitation of 'stereotypes'. They concluded from their results that 'racial prejudice is thus a generalized set of stereotypes of a high degree of consistency which includes emotional responses to race names, a belief in typical characteristics associated with race names and an evaluation of such typical traits' (1935, pp. 191–2). The Yale group published their theory of frustration and aggression (Dollard et al., 1939), which contributed to the explanation of racial prejudice. Prejudice against minority groups was seen as a form of scapegoating in which frustration-induced aggression was displaced from its instigators onto more vulnerable targets. Finally, Clark and Clark (1947), in their work on racial identification in black children, explored the effects of prejudice on its victims and found evidence that a significant number of black children tended to misidentify with whites and prefer them to blacks. These data and their implications inspired a whole tradition of research which still excites controversy (see chapter 4).

The Second World War and the political events which preceded it had a big impact on social psychology. Cartwright (1979) notes two main developments: the expansion and consolidation of the field in terms of personnel, activity and public support as war-related research was undertaken, and the migration to the United States of many European scholars such as Lewin, Heider and others who subsequently exerted an important personal influence on numerous leading researchers. After the war social psychology had become established as a thriving discipline; large quantities of research began and have continued to be published on a wide variety of topics.

One important consequence of the European migration was to strengthen the influence of 'Gestalt' thinking in social psychology over the behaviourist outlook. By and large, this emphasis and its derivations have remained dominant ever since. Its contributions to social psychology have been basic, for instance, Lewin and his associates on group dynamics, Sherif on social norms and social conflict, Asch on person perception and conformity, Heider on cognitive balance and attribution processes, Festinger on social comparison and cognitive dissonance, and others too numerous to mention. This influence was perhaps most visible and striking in the impact of Lewin's 'field-theoretical' approach on research into group behaviour. Lewin attempted to conceptualize the determinants of behaviour as structures and forces in the individual's 'life-space'. The life-space was not the objective but the phenomenological or psychological environment. Thus, whether social groups were 'real' in some objective sense became largely irrelevant: there was no doubt that they were psychologically real as entities or regions in the life-space and were thus able to influence behaviour. Furthermore, the influence of the group could be analysed as a 'Gestalt' or 'dynamic field' of social and psychological forces, so it became permissible and natural to describe such forces in terms of group properties and group concepts without reference to the characteristics of individual members. This approach helped to liberate group research and was soon backed up by data to substantiate its insights.

During the 1940s and 1950s group dynamics became a central area of social psychological enquiry. Intergroup research also continued to develop. The war added fascism and social conflict in general to racism as issues for study. In consequence, some major advances took place and were reported around the early 1950s. G. W. Allport's classic book *The Nature of Prejudice* (1954) appeared, surveying and summarizing the whole area; Adorno *et al.* (1950) published *The Authoritarian Personality*, an enquiry into the psychological roots of fascism and antisemitism; and Sherif and Sherif (1953) conducted their field experiments on intergroup conflict. The theoretical interest was now in the conditions under which prejudiced (or intergroup) attitudes could or could not be changed. There could not have been more different answers.

Adorno *et al.* (1950) explained prejudice in terms of a pathological personality syndrome. It represented the externalization of
unconscious hostilities and fears. G. W. Allport was theoretically
eclectic; he accepted the role of historical, sociocultural, situational and psychological factors in determining prejudice. However, he and others also argued that it could be dispelled by
interracial contact under the right conditions. Sherif and Sherif
attacked all attempts to 'individualize' prejudice. To them it was
the product of a rational social process, as was social conflict itself.
They considered it a negative outgroup attitude, and argued that
intergroup attitudes followed intergroup relations. Outgroup
hostility developed from intergroup competition which was a
rational social strategy to achieve conflicting group interests.
Thus, prejudice was not a matter of sick or deviant individuals; it
derived from an individual's membership in a social group and
intergroup relations.

Since 1950 developments have become much more complex. In
social psychology at large the dyad has gradually replaced the
group as the unit of analysis. The contemporary emphasis is on
interpersonal relationships and individual processes: group cohesiveness is now interpersonal attraction; social justice is about
equitable interactions between individuals; aggression refers
more to personality than intergroup conflict, etc. Even topics such
as cooperation, altruism and social influence have been studied as
if they had little to do with social groups. For example, it has
taken nearly two decades for the 'risky-shift' to be accepted as an
instance of the more general group process of 'polarization', and
even now the most widely cited theories pay little attention to
specifically group factors. Thus, Steiner (1974) was able to ask as
a rhetorical question: 'What ever happened to the group in social
psychology?'

A related trend has been the tendency to investigate less the
social influences on perception and more the cognitive processes
determining social behaviour. There seems to be an unbroken
continuity in this respect stretching from Festinger's theory of
informal social communication (1950) to social comparison processes (1954) to cognitive dissonance (1957) and other cognitive
consistency theories to causal attribution processes to the modern
field of 'social cognition'. The latter topic refers to the role of
relatively asocial individual cognitive mechanisms in the perception of social objects. In part these changes have represented a

healthy move towards more exact and intensive empirical analyses; they have certainly provided a wealth of new insights and
data. At the same time, however, the state has now been reached
where social psychology seems in danger of losing its momentum
in relation to its central problem of the interaction between
psychological and social processes.

Research on intergroup behaviour has partly reflected and
partly compounded this drift towards an implicit individualism.
Indeed, in some respects specifically intergroup problems had at
least until recently disappeared from mainstream thinking. The
current state of the field can be summarized as follows.

The frustration–aggression hypothesis still inspires work but
more in the area of personality than intergroup conflict or prejudice. Aggression is now primarily studied as an individual
behaviour. Extrapolations to intergroup relations are sometimes
attempted, but these tend to be afflicted with the same difficulties
that beset the original hypothesis (see chapters 2 and 4). The
same could be said about research on authoritarianism except
that work developing the basic theoretical ideas seems to have
ceased. In the years immediately following the publication of
Adorno *et al.*'s book (1950) there was justifiably great interest and
activity in the topic. This has long since receded. Researchers
looked at the family determinants of the personality syndrome,
the relationship between personality variables and political
ideologies and considered the status of authoritarianism
methodologically and as a 'personality' or 'subcultural' syndrome
of attitudes. However, today, they tend to employ the concept
merely as a convenient personality variable of secondary interest
to some other preoccupation.

The consensus in social psychology seems to be not to doubt
personality determinants of prejudice but to question their importance. Following the Sherifs, Pettigrew (see chapter 4) and general social psychological studies of reference groups and social
conformity, it seems to have become accepted that prejudice is to
be understood as a social or cultural norm, and that, furthermore,
where this is not the case, it is unlikely to be of social significance.
Thus, the problem with personality theories is that they are only
likely to be predictive in settings where social factors tend to
minimize prejudice (Billig, 1976, 1978). From this perspective the
explanation of prejudice has to do with the determinants of group

identifications, the development and maintenance of social norms and theories of intergroup relations.

Prejudice researchers themselves have devoted their main efforts to describing the development of social attitudes in the child, the cultural transmission of prejudice and the effects of racial discrimination on the mental wellbeing and identity of the victims (see chapter 4). They have also looked at specific theoretical issues such as the effects of interracial contact and desegregation, race versus belief differences as causes of outgroup rejection and colour-bias in antiblack attitudes. They have been little concerned with developing general theories of intergroup behaviour. The reasons are not fully clear. It may be that they accepted the analysis of Sherif and Sherif, that they defined their task as the description of how prejudice as a cultural given was maintained, or that they believed (and believe) that the locus of causality is to be found at the level of individual attitudes and personality (see Ehrlich, 1973).

In any case, the reluctance to look at intergroup behaviour as such has been until recently general to social psychology. The reception that greeted the Sherifs' studies of intergroup conflict was the opposite of that accorded to Adorno *et al*. With only one or two exceptions researchers ignored or at least did not pursue the line of enquiry pioneered by the Sherifs. Instead, cooperation, competition and conflict–resolution have been studied as dyadic interactions in experimental games such as the Prisoner's Dilemma. Gaming research has now declined dramatically in popularity; there remain much data and some hypotheses potentially applicable to intergroup relations, but also grave doubts about the extent to which interpersonal bargaining provides real insight into intergroup behaviour. During the late 1960s and early 1970s a change took place; innovative experiments on intergroup behaviour directly in the tradition of the Sherifs began to be published (see chapter 3). This trend has continued and promises to flourish. Perhaps more importantly it seems to indicate the return of theoretical vitality to intergroup research and a greater readiness on the part of mainstream experimental social psychology to look at the specific problems of intergroup behaviour.

The same positive conclusion can be drawn from a contemporary resurgence of interest in stereotyping. To a large extent

research on stereotyping has been descriptive or an adjunct to the
study of prejudice. An important departure was Tajfel's work in
the 1950s and early 1960s in which, under the influence of the
problems espoused by the 'New Look' in perception, stereotyping began to be analysed as a form of normal cognitive processing
applied to the perception of social groups. This emphasis is again
being actively pursued in the wake of the current cognitive orientation in social psychology represented by the rapidly growing
field of social cognition. Fascinating data are already being produced, and sharp but constructive theoretical controversies are
waiting to emerge (see chapter 5).

Other aspects of the current scene that deserve mention are the
developing recognition of collective bargaining and negotiation as
forms of intergroup behaviour (chapter 6), the emergence of a
new topic on the social psychological relationship between language and intergroup relations (part of a social psychology of
language in which Canadian research in the 1950s and 1960s
played a pioneering role), and the explosion of interest in
male–female relations and sex-role stereotyping. All these are
positive signs, although the potential contribution of the last topic
to intergroup research and vice versa has not yet been realized.

Thus, since the 1950s the social psychology of intergroup
behaviour has been through a period of relative quiescence.
There has been solid empirical progress in some areas but few
dramatic conceptual advances. Moreover, individualistic theories
and paradigms seem to have lost their vitality. This picture began
to change in the 1970s when it became evident that new problems, data and ideas had emerged. The field now looks more
promising than it has done for some time. One aim of the present
book is to survey the field in the light of this new work and try to
indicate the implications for future research.

What conclusions can be drawn about the role of intergroup
research in social psychology? There are at least three. Firstly,
intergroup behaviour is a core theoretical topic. It represents a
major class of social behaviour which raises just the kinds of
issues that define social psychology as a distinctive science (for
example, cooperation and competition, attraction and aggression,
social influence, the self-concept and identity, the attitude concept, the individual–group relation, etc.). For this reason research
into its different aspects has made a seminal and formative contribution to the discipline, even where the theories have failed in

their original intentions. It follows, too, that advances in inter-group research often have theoretical implications for the basic problems of social psychology.

Secondly, intergroup research has provided an important input of 'social problems' into social psychology. The area is in fact often defined as an applied field, but this is not strictly true; even in areas such as prejudice or bargaining much of the work has been primarily theoretical and only indirectly applied. However, whether or not research has been conducted for applied or theoretical reasons, there is no doubt that the field has focused on 'social problems' as its subject matter. The theoretical traditions and concepts have developed out of attempts to make sense out of and if possible prevent social conflict, ethnocentrism, racial discrimination and prejudice, fascism, and so on. Thus, the field demonstrates that social and applied problems can provide a fruitful basis for social psychological research; it also suggests that such problems *are* fruitful because they tend to raise large theoretical issues which then need to be pursued to some extent for their own sake if real progress is to be made.

Thirdly, intergroup behaviour is at perhaps the most social extreme of the subject matter of social psychology. This is so in two senses. On the one hand, it takes place in, and is usually largely determined by, the macrosocial context: it represents the functioning of historical, cultural, political, economic and other societal processes as well as psychological factors. On the other, it includes some of those instances in which human sociality seems to be demonstrated in an extreme form. Thus the altruism, heroism, self-sacrifice, solidarity or dehumanization and cruelty found in intergroup conflict provide striking examples of the psychological subordination of the individual to the group.

This social extremity tends to ensure that the field brings out or at least makes explicit some basic tensions between the social and the psychological aspects of the discipline. These tensions are expressed, for example, in the problems of the relationship of social psychology to other social sciences (what are the bound-aries of our phenomena and at what level do they operate? What is the political role of the subject as an applied science?, etc.), the integration of the abstract, universalistic laws produced by experimental research with concrete historical settings to make specific predictions, and the relationship of the individual to the group or the validity of the individualistic thesis which dominates contemporary social psychology. All these issues are difficult to avoid in intergroup research. Thus, the field has perhaps a unique role to play in reminding social psychologists that the interaction between psychological and social processes in social behaviour is their special object of study.

4   *An outline of the chapters*

The following chapters discuss six different but interrelated aspects of intergroup behaviour.

In chapter 2 Rupert Brown and John Turner consider how intergroup differs from interpersonal behaviour. They assume (following Tajfel, 1978a) that social interaction can be conceptualized as varying along a continuum from pure interpersonal to pure intragroup and intergroup behaviour and seek to clarify the psychological processes which shift interactions towards the latter pole. Their solution is in terms of the concept of 'social identification' and associated processes of stereotyping in self- and other-perception. It is argued that these processes produce 'psychological depersonalization', which is believed to describe the special empirical features of group behaviour. This analysis suggests that there is an important psychological difference between the actions of individuals as individual personalities and as group members, and that theories of interpersonal relationships cannot be extrapolated to the social relations of individuals as members of different groups.

To illustrate this conclusion two still popular attempts to extrapolate from interpersonal to intergroup relations are considered. These are the hypotheses that interethnic discrimination and prejudice and their elimination can be understood in terms of belief congruence or similarity and interpersonal contact. These theoretical positions and the related empirical research are discussed in some detail. It emerges that the hypotheses cannot be regarded as adequate theories of intergroup behaviour and that much of their supportive data is not demonstrably relevant to the issue. Brown and Turner's critique follows directly from their analysis earlier in the chapter of social identification, stereotyping and depersonalization. These concepts prove able to specify often in precise terms why interpersonal similarity, attraction and contact do not predict intergroup relations.

Thus, chapter 2 not only contributes to the description and explanation of the general characteristics of intergroup behaviour, but also highlights the dangers of generalizing from social relations where personal identities are dominant to those where social identities are salient.

In chapter 3 John Turner then moves on to consider intergroup relations as determinants of intergroup behaviour. The relevant research consists primarily of experimental studies on intergroup cooperation and competition as causes of social conflict and harmony. The starting point is Sherif and Sherif's field experiments on intergroup conflict and the functional or more specifically 'realistic conflict' theory which they represent. In its most general form, the theory states that the formation of a group depends upon mutual cooperation and attraction between people interdependent for need-satisfaction, and that intergroup hostility and discrimination reflect competitive interaction between two such collectivities for conflicting interests. The resolution of intergroup conflict requires cooperation between groups for 'superordinate' goals. The chapter acknowledges the importance of the Sherifs' ideas for later research and the validity of their main empirical insights, but after a detailed review of the relevant studies takes issue with the functional perspective as a psychological theory.

The review demonstrates, for example, that intergroup discrimination can be obtained as an effect of social categorization *per se* (the mere perception of belonging to one of two groups) or even between cooperating groups, and that group formation and cohesiveness are not necessarily dependent upon cooperation, interpersonal attraction or cooperative success. Turner advances an alternative theory in terms of the concept of 'social identification' (in line with chapter 2) and also the 'social identity principle' as an hypothesis about intergroup behaviour. The former makes shared self-definitions in terms of some social categorization the basis for group behaviour and thus explains group-formation as concerning the formation and acceptance of socially significant, self-inclusive social categorizations (for example, not cooperative success but simply acting as group members may be sufficient for individuals to define themselves as such). The latter states that stereotyping and social comparison processes linked to ingroup–outgroup identifications can cause competitive intergroup differentiation even in the absence of real conflicts of interests.

This analysis of psychological group membership, its implications for conflict resolution and related empirical evidence are discussed in depth. Perhaps the most important conclusion is that cooperative and competitive interaction and cohesiveness and hostility may not be so much determinants as effects of ingroup–outgroup formation. Thus, conflict resolution may depend less upon cooperative intergroup relations and more upon the elimination of the ingroup–outgroup divisions. The chapter illustrates that adequate theories of intergroup behaviour require adequate conceptualizations of the psychological significance and character of group membership.

Much of the research reviewed in chapter 3 is concerned to explain how intergroup relations and ingroup–outgroup membership produce negative intergroup attitudes. Derogatory and hostile outgroup attitudes are studied as symptoms of intergroup conflict. In chapter 4 David Milner summarizes the research into racial prejudice, the most extensively studied instance of such attitudes. The emphasis in this area is not merely to explain prejudice in terms of general theories of intergroup relations, but also more concretely to describe the development of racial attitudes, the socialization of the child into cultural or reference group norms of prejudice, and the effects of racism in specific societies on the victims. Thus, this chapter complements the earlier ones by examining the cultural and psychological mechanisms whereby a particular negative intergroup attitude is maintained against the background of specific societal contexts.

Milner begins with a look at the history of social psychological attempts to explain prejudice towards racial minority groups. The different theories, in terms of personality syndromes, emotional states, sociocultural norms and intergroup relations are evaluated and Milner argues for the advantages of 'social identity theory' (see the next section), which focuses firmly upon processes of discrimination operating at the intergroup level and also elucidates the social strategies available to minority group members to protect and enhance their self-esteem or positive social identity. Theoretically, therefore, Milner accepts the relevance of the ideas reviewed in chapter 3 for the analysis of prejudice. The chapter proceeds to consider the nature of prejudice, underlines the importance of its more covert manifestations in the form of 'tokenism', symbolic and institutional racism, and discusses the development of racial awareness in young children with particu-

lar emphasis on studies documenting prowhite and antiblack preferences at a very early age. Socialization factors contributing to
and reinforcing these intergroup attitudes are described and one
currently controversial developmental theory, of a universally
learned bias against the colour 'black' and all objects, physical or
social, which are so 'tainted', is examined in some detail.

Attention then moves to the studies of racial misidentification
and preference which have been traditionally interpreted as
demonstrating that black children internalize their culturally
imposed 'inferiorities' and so suffer problems of identity, self-
esteem and mental health. Currently some researchers argue that
these data are or were spurious and that blacks never had low
self-esteem in any case. In a careful analysis Milner provides a
resolution of this controversy. Thus, he points out that social
changes in black–white relations have taken place and that present findings do not necessarily invalidate earlier data; that the
link between racial misidentification and low self-esteem has
been more assumed than demonstrated, but that some evidence
does favour it, and that a distinction between the racial and the
global self-concept must be made: the latter does not necessarily
reflect the negativity of the former. He goes on to stress that
negative racial self-concepts need not be accepted nor coped with
through purely individualistic means; they can and have motivated group strategies to achieve and create positive black identity, as predicted by social identity theory. Such transformations
in the interracial climate are feeding back into the the research
paradigm to produce the new result that, for example, black or
Maori misidentification is now more difficult to find than
hitherto.

This chapter stresses the primacy of sociocultural and group
processes in racial discrimination, underlines the need for social
psychological theories of intergroup behaviour and also puts
intergroup relations into a developmental and societal context.
Chapter 5 discusses social stereotyping. Stereotyping has been
traditionally studied as an adjunct to prejudice and so has been
regarded as an intellectually inferior, bigoted, invalid and irrational cognitive process. On the other hand, as is apparent from
chapters 2 and 3, stereotyping can also be regarded as simply the
categorization process operating in social perception. The latter
tradition was initiated to a large extent by Henri Tajfel and is
becoming more influential. In fact, the whole issue of stereotyp-

ing is becoming of the utmost interest to social psychology. This
is so not merely because it is coming to be considered as causally
fundamental to intergroup behaviour and group processes,
but also because it provides a testing ground for the conflict
between the individualistic and the more social theories of
social cognition' that is emerging in the discipline. In microcosm, stereotyping poses the general problem of the interaction
between cognitive and social processes in social behaviour. In
chapter 5 Henri Tajfel moves towards a solution by trying to
reconcile the cognitive (that stereotyping is a relatively rational
asocial cognitive process) and prejudice (that it is an irrational
judgement serving social and motivational ends) traditions.

Tajfel's approach is to identify the functions of stereotyping in
intergroup relations. He acknowledges that there are individual
functions such as those assumed by researchers into underlying
cognitive mechanisms inherent in the individual. In fact, he
proposes two such functions with reference to principles of, and
research on, categorization and physical judgements. The first of
these is to make a complex social environment orderly and predictable and it is here that individual cognitive processes such as
those implicated in the perceptual accentuation of intracategory
similarities and intercategory differences and the 'illusory correlation' of infrequent events, play their explanatory role. The second, less highlighted in recent work, is to preserve and defend
people's value systems. Thus, there are distinct differences and
consequences arising from judgements of 'neutral' categories and
judgements of categories associated with social value differentials.

' However, these two functions, although necessary, are insufficient to explain stereotyping. They ignore the fact that
stereotypes are social products, that they represent *shared* or *consensual* beliefs held by ingroup members about the characteristics
of outgroup members, the contents of which are likely to be
mediated by the particular social relationships that obtain between the groups in contact. Thus, a complete theory must
include but go beyond individual functions to the collective purposes stereotypes serve for group members as a whole in intergroup contexts. There are at least three of these, but the first two
can be classed together as the creation and maintenance of
group ideologies which *justify* and *explain* existing intergroup
relations and in particular reactions to and treatment of outgroup

members. The last collective function concerns the role of stereotypes in preserving, creating or enhancing positively valued differentiations between the ingroups and relevant outgroups. These collective functions can be considered social analogues of justificatory dissonance-reduction, the causal attribution of intergroup relations, and the need for positive self-esteem. It is argued that the contents of stereotypes (the particular traits attributed to groups), which vary from one intergroup relationship to another, will depend on which group function(s) they serve and the concrete social context.

It is further argued that the most fruitful theoretical approach to social stereotypes is to move from an analysis of their collective to individual functions and not vice versa. The former provide the context of social reality and social influences within which the individual group member acquires information and social values. Thus, in looking at the cognitive component of intergroup attitudes, or intergroup perceptions, this chapter reminds us that 'social cognition' is not merely to do with the perception of social objects; it must also be accepted that individual subjectivity is in large part constructed by social processes. The implications of Tajfel's analysis for the adaptiveness or rationality of stereotyping will be discussed in the next section.

In chapter 6 Geoffrey Stephenson discusses the negotiation of intergroup relationships. Despite conflicting interests and negative intergroup attitudes and stereotypes, social groups must needs often coexist and find means to regulate their social contact. The relationships between groups are often negotiated through bargaining by representatives rather than overt conflicts between the members. Stephenson points out that much research on bargaining has been interpersonal in perspective. It has involved two-person, short-term exchanges where the aim has been to identify the conditions under which both parties have achieved satisfactory personal outcomes. In consequence, the emphasis has been on interpersonal variables such as the negotiators' relative concern for agreement, perceived trustworthiness and strategy choices as determinants of success. Collective or intergroup bargaining has been conceptualized and studied as no more than a particular form of interpersonal negotiation. Thus, variables to do with the intergroup relationship such as the salience of the representatives' role obligations as group members have been simply 'grafted' onto interpersonal models

as just another set of factors affecting, usually deleteriously, successful outcomes. The argument (based on Sherif and Sherif's
theory of conflict resolution) has been that effective bargaining
requires representatives to become less responsive to their different group affiliations and to join together as a problem-solving
group pursuing the negotiation as a superordinate goal.

Stephenson criticizes this viewpoint. Collective bargaining is a
consequence of intergroup relations and cannot be considered
independent of the latter. For example, his own and other work
on phases of negotiation shows that satisfactory outcomes for
both parties are produced by the airing of differences and conflicts between the groups and not by the pretence that they are
engaged in a superordinate problem-solving exercise. Also,
negotiation issues may not represent 'real' problems at all; they
may become important only because they reflect the tendencies
towards competitive differentiations in intergroup relations predicted by social identity theory. He argues that the negotiating
process involves the pursuit and reconciliation of both interpersonal and intergroup objectives by representatives. Moreover,
interpersonal and intergroup relationships may vary independently of each other. Thus, intense intergroup conflicts may bring
interpersonal dynamics into play that act as an ameliatory bridge
across otherwise fraught encounters between committed representatives. Both the conflicts between representatives' interpersonal and intergroup relations and those between the groups
per se need to be resolved in the negotiation process.

Chapter 6 again argues for and illustrates the distinction between interpersonal and intergroup behaviour, but considers it in
the context of face-to-face interaction and negotiation. In so doing
it draws attention to the fact that intergroup behaviour may occur
in settings with strong interpersonal overtones and indeed that
interpersonal and intergroup relations often coexist between
people. It thus indicates some of the subtleties and complexities
in the interrelations between interpersonal and intergroup orientations in social interaction that still await study.

Chapter 7, by Howard Giles and Patricia Johnson, also focuses
upon face-to-face interactions in intergroup settings. The authors
discuss the role of language in ethnic group relations and in particular the conditions under which members of ethnic groups
attenuate or accentuate their distinctive languages, dialects and
speech styles in the presence of ethnic outgroup members. They

explain that language behaviours are important in ethnic relations because they are often a criterial attribute of ethnic group membership, a basic cue to interethnic categorizations, a salient dimension of ethnic identity and a means of fostering intragroup cohesion.

The chapter then proceeds to outline current perspectives on and data from the crosscultural and multidisciplinary study of language and ethnicity. The different approaches are termed 'sociological', 'sociolinguistic' and 'communication breakdown'. These are evaluated and criticized to the degree that they are unable to specify who in an ethnic group uses which language strategy, when and why. To answer these questions a theoretical system is constructed in terms of social identity theory and the concepts of ethnolinguistic vitality, group boundaries and multiple-group membership. In this social psychological approach social identity theory provides the basic framework for the other concepts. It permits an analysis of social strategies for 'positive distinctiveness' (to which linguistic differentiations are related) and suggests hypotheses about when these will be adopted. Thus, in this vein, the authors propose, for example, that individuals will emphasize their distinctive ethnic language varieties when they identify strongly with their ingroup (which values language as a dimension of its ethnic identity) and are aware of 'cognitive alternatives' to their intergroup status position. The other concepts are introduced and discussed to specify more precisely some of the personal and situational factors enhancing the salience of ethnic identification for individuals and so to allow more concrete predictions about the accentuation or attenuation of ethnolinguistic behaviours. This analysis of the field concludes with eight theoretical propositions which summarize the conditions under which individuals are likely to maintain, accentuate, attenuate or create a positively valued ethnolinguistic distinctiveness.

This chapter does more than indicate the importance of language as both a dependent and independent variable in ethnic relations. It also represents a sustained attempt to contextualize social psychological theory, to apply general ideas about intergroup behaviour to a specific social activity in varying political and social settings. In so doing it demonstrates how such ideas can be elaborated in terms of hypotheses about group boundaries and the effects of multiple-group membership in concrete situations and the value of analysing individuals' cognitive representations of sociostructural forces in order to take into account the impact of societal reality.

There are several themes common to these chapters which we shall now consider.

5 General themes

5.1 Social identity

The concept of social identity occurs throughout the book. The present usage was introduced by Henri Tajfel (1972b) who defined it as an individual's knowledge of his or her membership in various social groups together with the emotional significance of that knowledge. The term served to link the self-concept with group membership and intergroup behaviour. Latterly, Turner (1982) has defined social identity as the sum total of a person's social identifications where the latter represent specific social categorizations internalized to become a cognitive component of the self-concept. There are several hypotheses associated with the concept and it will be useful to clarify how they differ.

Social identity began as a theory of intergroup behaviour. Tajfel (1972b) argued that individuals define themselves to a large extent in terms of their social group memberships and seek positive social identity, or self-definition in terms of positive group memberships. Furthermore, he considered that social groups acquire evaluative significance in the context of their relations with other groups and therefore that social comparisons between groups are basic to the appraisal of social identity. It was concluded that to achieve positive social identity intergroup comparisons are focused on the establishment of positive distinctiveness between one's own and other groups (unlike intragroup comparisons which lead to 'uniformity pressures'; see Festinger, 1954).

Turner (1975a) applied these ideas to the explanation of social categorization effects. Studies by Tajfel, Billig and others (see chapter 3) had shown that the classification of subjects by the experimenter into two distinct but minimal social categories (social categorization *per se*) could cause intergroup discrimination favouring ingroup over outgroup members in the distribution of monetary rewards. Turner argued that the experimenter-imposed social categorization was internalized by subjects to form an ingroup–outgroup identification and that they discriminated to achieve positive distinctiveness on the salient and value-laden dimension of monetary comparison. He also pointed out that self-evaluative intergroup comparison led directly to intergroup competition that was socially motivated and not based on conflicts of interest.

At this stage Tajfel (1974, 1978a) employed the developing theory to analyse intergroup conflict and social change in stratified societies. These 'contextualized' extensions of the theory are systematized most recently in Tajfel and Turner (1979). It is assumed that social stratification is associated with status (evaluative or prestige) differences between groups and that low status implies negative social identity. Thus status differences create social psychological pressures for social change. There are three main strategies for subordinate groups to restore and dominant groups to protect their positive distinctiveness:

1 *Individual mobility*: members may leave or aspire to leave the ingroup and seek to join the higher status or threatening outgroup.
2 *Social creativity*: they may seek to redefine or reinterpret the elements of the status comparison (i.e. the comparative dimension, the associated social values or the salient outgroup) so as to change subjectively negative into positive distinctiveness.
3 *Social competition*: they may compete directly to change the relative positions of the ingroup and outgroup on the relevant status dimension; this strategy may develop into intergroup conflict where the status dimension is related to an unequal division of scarce resources.

These strategies are considered to represent analogues of macrosocial phenomena. Thus, social creativity and competition are assumed to indicate competitive ethnocentrism between different status groups. Tajfel and Turner hypothesize that the development of competitive ethnocentrism (and intergroup conflict) depends upon the maintenance of ingroup identification and cohesion amongst subordinate group members, their perception of the status relationship as unstable and illegitimate, and the perception by dominant group members that their superiority is either legitimate but threatened or illegitimate but stable (Turner and Brown, 1978). This is a very bare outline and the reader is referred to Tajfel (1978a) and Tajfel and Turner (1979) for a more detailed statement.

In this book the term 'social identity theory' is restricted to these ideas about the role of positive distinctiveness in intergroup behaviour. Thus, it embraces both an interpretation of social categorization effects and an analysis of basic processes in intergroup competition, and also a theory of societal conflict and change. This duality needs to be kept in mind since some chapters (chapter 3, for instance) emphasize the former aspect and others (such as chapters 4 and 7) the latter. The usefulness of the theory is that it identifies general determinants of intergroup competition, makes predictions which differ from Sherif and Sherif and lends itself to macrosocial contextualization.

However, the social identity concept also has other derivations. In his initial analysis of social categorization effects, Turner (1975a) stressed the role of self-evaluative social comparisons; others, notably Doise and Sinclair (1973), emphasized categorization processes. In chapter 3 Turner modifies his original position and argues that categorization and social comparison processes are complementary determinants of intergroup discrimination; to distinguish this hypothesis from social identity theory (the earlier view) it is termed the 'social identity principle' (the self-concept is still afforded a central role). The final derivation which we discuss next comprises a general theme on its own.

5.2 *The social group*

Another application of the social identity concept has been to develop a psychological theory of the social group. This 'social identification model' (chapters 2 and 3) extends some of the ideas about group behaviour already briefly presented.

Just as Tajfel (chapter 5) points out with reference to stereotyping, the theory states that the group is both a psychological process and a social product. On the one hand, it is a cognitive construct. It is assumed that individuals in the social environment are perceptually represented as social categories and that the latter are defined as 'wholes' on the basis of the correlated (representative, prototypical, distinctive, etc.) characteristics of their members. These social categorizations can be internalized as cognitive structures in self-conception, and as such function to process stimuli and regulate the individual's behaviour. Where social categorizations (or social identifications) influence self-perception, their effect is to change the content of the self-concept from individual differences and unique personality traits to shared stereotypes of the attitudes, values, goals, norms, etc. associated with social category membership. The basic consequence is the stereotypical minimization of individual differences and the enhancement of perceptual interchangeability between the self and other ingroup members. It is argued that this consequence produces the distinctive features of intragroup relations such as mutual cohesiveness, cooperation and relative uniformity. Thus the psychological hypothesis is that group behaviour and relationships are mediated by a cognitive redefinition of the self in terms of shared social category memberships and associated stereotypes.

On the other hand, however, the group is a social reality. It refers to real interrelated people engaged in concrete social activities as a function of their social relationships and goals. The psychological group becomes a social reality to the extent that a number of individuals share and, in relevant circumstances, act in terms of the same social identification. The cognitive processes instigate collective interaction and thus the emergence of social processes. The latter produce social structures, roles, norms, values, purposes, etc. which in turn become determinants of individual psychological functioning. The same also applies to the development of social identity itself. There is a sense in which the social group constructs itself and its picture of itself over time through the intermediary of members' psychological processes. This is apparent in that the theory takes for granted that real intergroup relations presuppose *shared* social categorizations and stereotypes, with a specific *sociocultural* content, related to members' *collective purposes* and the explanation, justification and evaluation of *concrete political and historical contexts*. All these features testify that the group is a product of social influences as well as cognitive and motivational processes. Thus, the general implication of the identity model is that we need to assume a continual causal loop between psychological and social processes in the determination of group members' attitudes and actions.

In chapter 3 Turner argues that the identity model is more consistent with available evidence than Sherif and Sherif's functional theory. It is important to stress that the argument is directed at the hypothesis that cooperative interdependence is a direct psychological determinant of cooperative interaction and group formation and not at the idea that group behaviour serves adaptive functions. On the contrary, the model postulates group identity as the immediate basis for, and not the effect of, social cooperation and supposes that this is precisely its adaptive role, since social cooperation is often the most effective means of achieving members' goals. It needs to be remembered that much research on mixed-motive games (such as the Prisoner's Dilemma) demonstrates that individual rationality and interpersonal orientations make social cooperation between players surprisingly difficult to achieve even where it is plainly the sensible strategy. Thus the group should perhaps be conceptualized, the model suggests, as not so much the product of cohesive and effective social relationships as the psychological mechanism that creates them in appropriate self-relevant circumstances. The distinction needs to be borne in mind between the functions served by social processes and the causal psychological theories of how the latter emerge.

5.3 *Social cognition*

The identity model of the group, social identity theory, Tajfel's analysis of stereotyping, and indeed the theoretical orientation found throughout the book, could be referred to as a social cognitive perspective. The problem is that in current usage 'social cognition' has an almost opposite meaning to that intended. To distinguish these two senses, it is useful to put them in an historical context.

In some sense the development of intergroup research and social psychology can be seen as a progression through theories and metatheories which represent different answers to the fundamental problems posed by Le Bon. He argued that the group had a psychological reality but was maladaptive; group processes were a regression to the primitive, instinctual and irrational. The dominant tradition in early intergroup research rejected the first propostion but not the second. Since researchers confronted the 'pathological' aspects of intergroup behaviour and since too they were individualistic in orientation, the tendency was to deny group processes but label them as irrational in so far as they intruded. This tradition is embodied in the frustration–aggression hypothesis, the authoritarian personality, the conceptualization and investigation of intergroup attitudes as individual 'prejudices', the rejection of stereotyping as an immoral, inferior and prejudiced form of cognition, and the pervasive assumption that the applied objective is the 'resolution' of intergroup conflict (which implies that it is inherently dysfunctional).

Stereotyping provides an excellent example of how the individualistic thesis – that there is nothing in the group which was not previously in the individual, and that social psychology is merely the application of the principles of individual behaviour to more complex stimulus conditions – tends to deny the independent validity of intergroup behaviour and so label it as individual deviance. Stereotyping is no more and no less than the perception of people as group members and not individual personalities. In consequence it is condemned in textbooks and elsewhere on the grounds that we should treat people as individuals: the justification is that there are only individuals and therefore it is irrational not to do so!

At the same time that this tradition could be said to have reached its height with the authoritarian personality (although it is far from dead), the alternative perspective had also been developed. During the 1940s and early 1950s the Lewinian school and others popularized at least in practice the conception that the group was (a) a stimulus in the psychological environment, and (b) could be analysed as a structural whole, as more than the sum of its parts. The research of Sherif and Sherif made this conception fully explicit as an argument for both the reality and adaptiveness of group processes. They hypothesized that group interaction emerged as a rational and purposive strategy for the achievement of collective goals. Furthermore, individuals were changed in group contexts because they internalized products of social interaction such as stereotypes and social norms. Similarly, Asch (1952) pointed out the fundamental implausibility of individualism: that it denies the presence of a socially structured field within the individual.

However, this line of thought was not followed up in intergroup research. Social psychology at large studied group processes for a while at the level of intragroup relations, but the emphasis then moved to interpersonal relations and so back to the individual. The result was with some exceptions a period in which theoretical advances focused on individual and interpersonal processes.

Those advances explored the idea of the individual as a relatively rational information-processing hedonist. Thus, social interaction was conceptualized as an interpersonal exchange in which the participants sought to maximize rewards and minimize costs. Social justice became associated with the principle of equity in the exchange of rewards and costs and was supposedly an outcome of individual self-interest. Cooperation and competition were studied as strategic interpersonal choices in mixed-motive settings to maximize individual benefit. Theories of attitude change assumed a need for cognitive consistency, attribution theory made use of a rational ANOVA model to explain the inference of cause and effect in person perception, and so on. In general, the attempt to explain social behaviour in terms of the functioning of individual cognitive processes now seems to have been the central trend in the 1970s and also bids fair to flourish in the 1980s.

This work has been very productive, especially the last trend, which in its current form can be referred to as the field of social cognition. However, the trend has been characterized by a tendency to study cognitive mechanisms in social perception solely at the level of the individual or at best interpersonal relationships. The result from the very beginning has been that unwanted social and motivational influences are assumed to distort the veridicality of individual perception. Thus, these effects are described and explained in derogatory terms in social psychology as errors, biases, prejudices, justifications, dissonance reduction, compliance, conformity or 'group pressure', diffusion of responsibility, 'deindividuation' or loss of identity, the 'risky-shift' and so on. The implication once more is that somehow the cognitively complex human being has still managed to remain a social primitive. This view is untenable: human social processes are complex, subtle and sophisticated. Furthermore research into human evolution and history suggests that social cooperation, the formation of groups and development of culture are foremost adaptive traits that developed in harmony with our cognitive capacities.

Within the field of social cognition the perspectives embodied in the present book regard individuals as group members and assume a functional interaction between cognitive and social processes in social perception. Social cognition is not merely the perception of social objects but also the social determination of the perceptual process. We have seen that group factors enter directly into individual subjectivity even with respect to that core area of psychological determination, the system of self-reference. Moreover, as Tajfel (chapter 5) states with respect to stereotyping and as Sherif and Sherif argued in relation to intergroup relations, group influences serve collective functions and so can be regarded as in some sense adaptive. The implication is that just as cognitive strategies and mechanisms should be described as 'heuristics' rather than 'errors' or 'biases', so too should the impact of social stereotypes, values and norms on perceptions. They represent a reservoir of cultural wisdom upon which the individual naturally draws.

There is no contradiction here with the fact that in intergroup relations we spend much of our time investigating 'pathological' attitudes and ideologies such as racism and fascism. These are scientifically irrational and politically objectionable, but not necessarily the expression of a maladaptive psychological process. The cultural norm may be prejudiced because of specific societal and historical conditions, but this does not demonstrate the inherent irrationality of social influence. On the contrary those that condemn racism, for example, do so from the standpoint of social values which are themselves products of social influence. 'Pathological' attitudes may be produced by group processes that are in principle adaptive, but operating in a sick or conflicted society. This idea is implied most strongly in chapter 5, where Tajfel explains derogatory stereotypes in terms of the social realities within which intergroup relations take place.

The present social-cognitive perspective is a return to the tradition of Sherif and Sherif and others, but is also a development in empirical ideas about the problems of intergroup behaviour. We believe that it can contribute to much other work in social psychology.

5.4 *Individualism*

Individualism is the thesis that the individual is the sole psychological reality and that that reality does not include a distinct component corresponding to group behaviour. It is our final general theme because it is criticized throughout the book in different ways and for different reasons. The theoretical objections to the thesis can be summarized as: (1) it denies the psychological reality of the group; (2) it misconstrues group processes as in opposition to individual rationality; and (3) it disconnects the individual from social reality and produces theories difficult to contextualize in society. The alternative hypotheses employ concepts of the distinction between interpersonal and intergroup behaviour, social identity, the functional interaction between psychological and social processes in group behaviour and cognitive representations of sociostructural forces. There are some disagreements between chapters but these often proceed from shared assumptions about the inadequacy of individualism. Thus Stephenson (chapter 6) suggests that interpersonal and intergroup behaviour vary along independent dimensions as opposed to inversely, but nevertheless argues that the theoretical distinction between the two must be maintained. Individualism has been so much as background for our introduction that we need not repeat nor anticipate further. It will suffice to stress that the chapters do not set out to criticize the thesis but do so primarily as a byproduct of reporting recent thinking about the substantive empirical problems of intergroup behaviour.

To conclude this introduction we should note that the chapters do not pretend to offer final answers to these problems. Their alternative hypotheses are provisional attempts to summarize data and indicate new research directions, and must be judged by future results. In the meantime, they provide an orientation and introduction to the field of intergroup relations.

CHAPTER 2

Interpersonal and Intergroup Behaviour

RUPERT J. BROWN and JOHN C. TURNER

1 Introduction

The relationship of the individual to the group is surely one of the oldest and most fundamental problems faced by students of human behaviour. Floyd Allport, one of the founders of social psychology, went so far as to describe it as the 'master problem' of the discipline (F. H. Allport, 1962). The question as it has traditionally been posed is as follows: Is there more to groups and group behaviour than the simple aggregate of the individual group members and their behaviour? Or, to put it in a way which provides us with a focus for this chapter: *Is there any psychological difference between people's behaviour in interpersonal settings – that is, those which do not raise either explicitly or implicitly the notion of group – and people's behaviour in collective settings – that is, those in which group membership is made salient?* In this chapter we shall argue that there are good conceptual and empirical reasons for believing that there is such a discontinuity and that explanations of intergroup behaviour which fail to recognize this difference are likely to prove inadequate.

Allport himself, in an earlier analysis of the problem (1924, p. 6), was in no doubt as to the answer to these questions:

> There is no psychology of groups which is not essentially and entirely a psychology of individuals. Social psychology must not be placed in contradistinction to the psychology of the individual; *it is a part of the psychology of the individual*, whose behaviour it studies in relation to that sector of his environment comprised by his fellows.

In writing this, Allport was attacking the ideas of people like Le Bon (1896) and McDougall (1920) who had proposed that crowds and groups were possessed of superordinate mental and emotional attributes over and above the consciousness and feelings of the individuals who comprised them. Quite correctly Allport pointed out that such notions were essentially metaphysical and

had no place in a scientific study of behaviour. But in his rejection
of these 'group fallacies' he appeared to be abandoning altogether
the 'group' concept as a theoretical construct. One consequence
has been that many social psychologists since Allport have
tended to reduce all group processes to interpersonal or individual dynamics. Thus, both theory and research in social
psychology, and especially in North American social psychology,
have been dominated by attempts to conceptualize such
phenomena as group prejudice and social conflict as interpersonal or intrapersonal processes simply writ large. (In fact, group
processes in general have been recently neglected by social
psychology, as Steiner, 1974, has pointed out.) Examples of this
tendency have been the frustration–aggression theory of Dollard
et al. (1939), later elaborated by Berkowitz (1962, 1972), the
belief congruence theory of prejudice (Rokeach, 1960), some contact theories of interethnic relations (see for example, Cook, 1962;
Pettigrew, 1971), and the concept of the authoritarian personality (Adorno *et al*., 1950).

     F. H. Allport's (1924) intransigent individualism did not go
completely unchallenged. Two important critics were Sherif
(1936, 1967) and Asch (1952). While never departing from their
commitment as social psychologists to study the individual, nor
ever doubting that psychological processes reside only in individuals, they insisted on the reality and distinctiveness of social
groups. They believed that groups had properties and dynamics
related to and based upon individual functioning but not wholly
determined by or reducible to that functioning. Their assumption
was that the whole is more than the sum of its parts: that groups
have emergent properties unlike those of their individual members in isolation. Thus Sherif (1936) pointed out that there was a
determinism of chemistry acceptable at its own level, although
chemical reactions all depend upon realities at the subatomic
level. Asch offered another chemical analogy. A substance like
water, he argued, is composed of hydrogen and oxygen and yet,
physically and chemically, has very different properties from
either of its constituent elements.

     Both Sherif and Asch saw the important task as understanding
how individuals create group facts and how the latter control
their further actions. Asch (1952, p. 251) expressed it as follows:

For an adequate formulation of the individual–group relation, we need a way of describing group action that neither reduces the individual to a mere target of group forces of mystical origin, nor obliterates the organized character of group forces in the welter of individual activities. We need a way of understanding group processes that retains the prime reality of individual *and* group, the two permanent poles of all social processes. We need to see group forces arising out of the actions of individuals and individuals whose actions are a function of the group forces that they themselves (or others) have brought into existence. We must see group phenomena as both the *product and condition* of actions of individuals.

Their solutions were very similar and stressed the role of perceptual or cognitive processes in the production of group realities. Sherif (1936, pp. 75–88) argued that individuals in group interaction constitute a perceptual field for each other. This field is subject to the Gestalt Law of *interdependence of parts*: that is, parts or members are perceptually structured in relation to each other to form an organized whole or system so that each part influences the other parts, and the characteristics of any part are determined by its membership in the total system. Thus group members do not perceive themselves as isolated individuals but as members of a social entity whose properties are thereby modified. This perceptual reaction modifies subsequent experience and action accordingly and so brings the group into existence as a psychological fact and objective reality. In particular individuals internalize group products such as slogans, norms, values and stereotypes (which initially confront them as external stimuli) and so achieve shared frames of reference which regulate and coordinate their actions and attitudes. There is no doubt that Sherif saw his classic (1936) work on social norms as a demonstration of the development of shared frames of reference between persons and so, to a degree, an empirical refutation of Allport's individualism.

Asch (1952, pp. 240–72) also contended that group behaviour is made possible at the human level through our capacity to engage in *mutual reference* in the context of a *shared psychological field*. The field in question is again ourselves as a perceived whole. Thus he states that coordinated group action, the subordination of the individual to the requirements of joint action, and the very idea of collective goals, are all made possible only because each individual has a structurally similar, cognitive representation that includes the actions of others and their relations as group facts. It is false to suggest that groups are 'merely' individuals since this denies the presence of a *socially structured field within the individual* such that group realities may be perceived and responded to. The relationship of the individual to the group represents a part–whole relation unprecedented in nature, since it depends upon the recapitulation of the structure of the whole in the part. Group facts, in other words, achieve objective expression because we are capable subjectively as individuals of cognizing group relations and possibilities.

The above hardly does justice to the power and subtlety of Sherif's and Asch's ideas (nor in particular to the latter's critique of both the individualistic and 'group mind' theses), but it should make clear that both are adamant that there are important psychological differences between the actions of individuals as individuals and their actions as group members. This is also the position to be espoused below. Our view, in the words of Sherif (1967, p. 9), is that:

> We cannot do justice to events by extrapolating uncritically from man's feelings, attitudes, and behaviour when he is in a state of isolation to his behaviour when acting as a member of a group. Being a member of a group and behaving as a member of a group have psychological consequences. There are consequences even when the other members are not immediately present.

Our purpose in this chapter is to argue for a definite distinction between interpersonal and intergroup behaviour. One aspect of this will be to seek to clarify the precise nature of the 'psychological consequences' to which Sherif refers. To this end we shall suggest a possible psychological mechanism for the transformation of interpersonal into intergroup behaviour. It is also our intention to demonstrate that this distinction is fully compatible with the scientific analysis of social behaviour. Another aspect will be to discuss the inherent difficulties in applying theories of interpersonal relations to intergroup behaviour.

2 Social identification and the interpersonal—intergroup continuum

2.1 The behavioural continuum

Echoing the views of Sherif and Asch, some European social psychologists (for example, Billig, 1976; Moscovici, 1972; Tajfel,

1972a) have recently argued against what they see as the influence in the discipline of a pervasive North American ideology of individualism. Tajfel (1978a, 1979) in particular, stresses the need to distinguish between interpersonal and intergroup behaviour, and his ideas form our starting point. He defines intergroup behaviour in the same way as Sherif (1967, p. 12), 'Whenever individuals belonging to one group interact collectively or individually, with another group or its members *in terms of their group identification*, we have an instance of intergroup behaviour'. This type of interaction is contrasted with interpersonal behaviour and, in their pure forms, Tajfel (1978a) considers that the two kinds of behaviour represent the extremes of a bipolar continuum upon which all instances of social behaviour can be placed:

> At one extreme . . . is the interaction between two or more individuals which is *fully* determined by their interpersonal relationships and individual characteristics and not all affected by various social groups or categories to which they respectively belong. The other extreme consists of interactions between two or more individuals (or groups of individuals) which are *fully* determined by their respective memberships of various social groups or categories, and not at all affected by the interindividual personal relationships between the people involved. (Tajfel and Turner, 1979, p. 34)

It is acknowledged that these theoretical extremes are probably seldom achieved in reality, but examples which come close to them are, on the one hand, the intimate conversations of two lovers and, on the other, the conflicts between police and strikers at a picket line. In the first case the lovers are unlikely to interact with each other as representatives of different groups; in the second, however, the social categories to which the individuals belong are likely to be overwhelmingly important in determining their relations.

There are three empirical characteristics of a social encounter which, Tajfel proposes, tend to define it as lying towards the intergroup pole of his continuum (and by implication, therefore, their absence or opposite define the interpersonal pole). The first and most basic is the presence of at least a dichotomous social categorization so that individuals are identifiable as members of distinct social categories, for example, black and white, male and female, worker and employer. The second is that intergroup

behaviour typically shows low intersubject variability within
each group, despite a normal range of individual differences on
organismic and other variables. That is, group members tend to
behave in a homogeneous or uniform fashion. The behaviour of a
football crowd chanting its songs and slogans is an example of
such intragroup uniformity. And the third characteristic is that
there is usually low intrasubject variability in the treatment and
perception of different outgroup members, again despite an
actual diversity in their personal and physical attributes. That is,
the same person tends to act uniformly towards a wide range of
different others.

These characteristics are perhaps best exemplified at the level
of social perception in the process of stereotyping – the agreement
among members of a group that a particular cluster of attributes
or adjectives describes all or most members of a human classification (Sherif, 1967, p. 33) – and in this form are well documented
in the areas of ethnic, class and sex relations (see Ehrlich, 1973).
This fact has been seized upon by Turner (1982) in an attempt to
identify the psychological processes which produce intergroup
behaviour.

2.2   *The self-stereotyping hypothesis*

Turner (1982) has advanced a 'cognitive' hypothesis in the tradition of Asch and Sherif (and Tajfel himself: see 1978a, pp. 28–38)
to explain variation along Tajfel's continuum. He argues as follows. The self-concept can be conceptualized as a cognitive structure which functions to regulate behaviour under relevant conditions. It comprises two major subsystems: personal identity and
social identity. The former refers to self-descriptions in terms of
personal or idiosyncratic attributes such as personality, physical
and intellectual traits. The latter denotes self-definitions in terms
of social category memberships such as race, class, nationality,
sex and so on. A person's total social identity, then, is comprised
of specific social identifications. Different situations 'switch on' or
make salient different self-conceptions which are used to construe
social stimuli and regulate behaviour in an adaptive manner.
According to this idea, the transition in self-concept functioning from personal to social identity corresponds to and is responsible for a shift from interpersonal to intergroup behaviour.

The basic feature of the latter is that it is controlled by a person's perception of self and others in terms of their social category memberships. Once some specific social identification is salient, a person assigns to self and others the common, typical or representative characteristics that define their group as a whole. (These criterial or stereotypical attributes are inferred from the properties of individuals which are perceived to correlate with their group membership.) In consequence there is a perceptual accentuation of similarities between individuals in the same group and differences between those belonging to different groups (see Tajfel, 1969a; Tajfel and Wilkes, 1963; and chapters 3 and 5).

Thus the special cognitive output of a social identification is stereotypic perception. It is important to emphasize that individuals stereotype *themselves* as well as others in terms of their common attributes as group members and that the latter may include not only personality traits but also social attitudes, prestige, needs, motives or goals, social norms and perhaps even emotional states. Not only do individuals see outgroup members as homogeneous and undifferentiated, but in the same way they perceive themselves as relatively interchangeable with other ingroup members. Turner refers to this process as 'depersonalization'. Depersonalization on appropriate dimensions, he argues, can explain some common features of intragroup relations such as perceived similarity between members, mutual attraction and esteem, emotional empathy, cooperative altruism, and behavioural and attitudinal uniformities. In each case the crucial process is that individuals react to themselves and others not as differentiated, individual persons but as exemplars of the common characteristics of their group. It is through this process that salient or functioning social identifications help to regulate social behaviour; they do so directly by causing group members to act in terms of the shared needs, goals and norms which they assign to themselves, and indirectly through the perceptual homogenization of others which elicits uniform reactions from the perceivers.

This theory suggests that the distinctive property of both intragroup and intergroup relations is psychological depersonalization. This term should not be confused with 'deindividuation' (Festinger, Pepitone, and Newcomb, 1952; Zimbardo, 1969). One key difference between the two concepts is that deindividuation implies a loss or shedding of identity in group situations, while depersonalization implies only a *change* – from personal to social. Under conditions where a shared social identification becomes salient, social behaviour tends to become more uniform both within the ingroup and towards the outgroup (in line with Tajfel's empirical criteria for intergroup behaviour). This is because, under such conditions, individuals define themselves and others in terms of their common attributes as group members and not in terms of their idiosyncratic features as unique persons. Thus it states clearly why interpersonal processes cannot be directly extrapolated to explain intergroup behaviour. The latter is, in fact, 'depersonalized': based on the formation of shared self-attitudes and the shared attributions of characteristics to self and others in the context of common or different category memberships and not on the differentiated aspects of individual persons. Interindividual interaction, therefore, reflects intergroup and not interpersonal relations when category memberships become sufficiently salient psychologically.

⁺ It needs to be stressed that Turner's theory is as yet tentative. Future research will undoubtedly require it to be modified in some respects. Nevertheless, it is already consistent with a certain amount of evidence (see Turner, 1982, and chapter 3), and can be considered a useful working hypothesis. Making use of these ideas of Tajfel and Turner, several points can be made. Firstly, Tajfel's continuum might perhaps be more properly renamed the interpersonal–group continuum since the same processes may tend to distinguish both intragroup and intergroup behaviour from interpersonal relations. Secondly and most importantly, the distinction we are drawing is not between individuals on the one hand and 'something else' on the other. Both interpersonal and group behaviour are the actions of individuals as F. H. Allport (1924) correctly pointed out. But in one case the actions are of individuals *qua* individuals, while in the other they are of individuals *qua* group members (see also Taylor and Brown, 1979; and Tajfel, 1979 for a related discussion). Whether or not Turner's theory proves to be valid, it does demonstrate that the scientific postulate of individual psychological processes is at least in principle fully compatible with the idea that group behaviour is more than some socially structured aggregate of interpersonal relationships.

Thirdly, it should now be clear why in this chapter the terms 'social group' and 'social category' tend to be used almost interchangeably. In the context of intergroup relations, our preferred definition of a social group is two or more people who perceive themselves to be members of the same social category or share a common social identification of themselves (see Tajfel, 1978a, pp. 28–38; Turner, 1982, and chapters 1 and 3). In terms of the above discussion, this definition can be restated simply as two or more people who stereotype themselves in terms of the same social category.

Fourthly, the distinction between interpersonal and intergroup behaviour is based partly on descriptive and partly on theoretical grounds. That is, we consider not only that they have special empirical characteristics but also that they are controlled by differing psychological processes. Thus the three characteristics described by Tajfel provide empirical criteria for the tentative evaluation of specific social encounters as intergroup or not, but the fundamental criterion is whether the encounter is actually being determined by the interactors' different category memberships. In the example we gave above, the interaction between strikers and police does not represent intergroup behaviour simply because there are many people involved, or they act in certain ways, or just because they belong to different social categories. Empirically, the issue is whether the participants seem to be interacting in terms of their distinctive personal characteristics or their shared group attributes. If the encounter seems to indicate shared uniformities in attitudes and behaviour extending beyond the specific persons and related to their group memberships, then it is probably intergroup. The theoretical issue is whether their social identification of themselves as strikers and police are psychologically salient and are thereby helping to make possible and determine the nature of the encounter.

This is an important point because whether encounters are interpersonal or intergroup is frequently ambiguous. Some instances, such as political demonstrators chanting slogans or soldiers shooting at anonymous enemy targets, are easy to characterize on both empirical and intuitive grounds. But what, for example, of interactions between just two people belonging to different categories (for example, a man and a woman or a black and a white person)? Are such encounters interpersonal because just two individuals are involved, or intergroup because of the category difference? It should now be apparent that, in the abstract, no answer can be given to this question. The same two people may interact at times on an interpersonal and at other times on an intergroup basis, depending upon the salience of their social identifications, which in turn is highly situation-specific.

Some experiments by Turner (1978a) and R. J. Brown and Deschamps (1980/81) illustrate that social behaviour varies with the salience of group membership. In a 'minimal group' situation (Turner, 1978a), subjects distributed sums of money or points between themselves and others when half the others were ingroup and half outgroup members. When the salience of group membership was varied (in different ways in the two experiments) the subjects' behaviour changed accordingly. When conditions de-emphasized group membership, high levels of self-favouritism were observed, irrespective of the affiliation of the other recipients. But when the group memberships were made more salient, the self-favouritism discriminated between ingroup and outgroup members, decreasing for the former and increasing against the latter. In fact, in Brown and Deschamps' experiment practically no self-ingroup differentiation occurred at all under conditions of maximum group salience, clearly supporting Turner's self-stereotyping hypothesis.

Thus far, unfortunately, research does not permit a systematic theoretical delineation of the conditions under which social identity becomes salient. Nevertheless, some of the important factors have been identified. For example, group membership seems to become more salient in a conflict, confrontation, or encounter with an outgroup (Dion, Earn, and Yee, 1978; Doise, 1978; Sherif, 1967). Salience is also affected by the distinctiveness of the group in a given environment (Bruner and Perlmutter, 1957; McGuire and Padawer-Singer, 1976), by the number of group members present (Doise, 1978), by factors which emphasize intragroup uniformities (R. J. Brown and Deschamps, 1980/81; Wilder, 1978), and by variables which can act as criteria for common category membership, or perceived 'social entitativity' (Campbell, 1958), such as similarity, proximity, or common fate. Additional factors which may be important are whether or not an individual is acting as a group representative (White, 1977), and the relevance of the setting or behaviour to important group norms (Boyanowsky and Allen, 1973; Minard, 1952). Furthermore, it seems very likely that the same characteristics which symptomatize intergroup behaviour (such as, social categoriza-

tions, intragroup uniformities, and the perceived homogeneity ᴄ
outgroup members) also function as cues to others to define and
react to the setting in intergroup terms. They may sometimes
function as criteria for the participants themselves so as to play a
circular cause as well as effect role in shifting social behaviour
along the interpersonal–intergroup continuum. There is still a
long way to go before we understand precisely when the factors
described above are operative and how they might interact with
one another. Nevertheless, they do provide some means of anti-
cipating the salience of group membership independently of the
behaviour it is meant to explain.

To conclude this section we can note that there is already evidence that the interpersonal–intergroup distinction does have
empirical reality. For example, it has been consistently observed
that groups are more competitive than individuals under the
same conditions (Wilson and Kayatani, 1968; Dustin and Davis,
1970; Doise and Sinclair, 1973; Doise and Weinberger, 1973; see
chapter 3). In research on negotiation and bargaining it is becoming clear that there are important differences between interpersonal and interparty exchanges (Stephenson, 1978; see also chapter 6). In a recent study comparing individual and group aggression, marked differences between the individual and collective
situations were reported (Yaffe and Yinon, 1979). Finally, in a
series of three experiments which bear directly on our third
empirical criterion, it was found that if an outgroup was seen as a
single unity there was always more discrimination against it than
if some lack of uniformity within it could be perceived (Wilder,
1978). In Tajfel's terms, the conditions which 'individuated' the
outgroup members shifted the situation towards the interpersonal pole, with corresponding behavioural changes.

2.3 Some implications of the interpersonal–group continuum

If the above distinction is accepted, then important implications
follow for the kinds of theories that will be necessary to understand intergroup phenomena. In particular, it means that theories
of interpersonal relations are unlikely to prove of much predictive
value, except by way of providing very loose analogies upon
which new explanations can be built. The explication of this latter
statement will follow later in the chapter, but for the moment let

us consider the reasons why interpersonal theories are essentially inadequate for the study of group behaviour.

Theories about interpersonal behaviour typically invoke either or both of two kinds of explanatory process. One is the operation of some organismic or intraindividual factor so that variation in social behaviour is explained by differences in constitutional or motivational states in individuals – for example, personality type or emotional frustration. The other is the nature of the interpersonal relationship. Here social behaviour is inferred from differences in relations between the particular individuals involved in the interaction – for example, similarities or differences of attitude, personality, status or power. But neither of these two models is sufficient to account for intergroup behaviour. In the first case the theoretical model is clearly insufficient since, as we noted above, the group pole of the behavioural continuum is usually marked by *uniformities* of interindividual response across a wide spectrum of individually differing people. When the British coal miners called a strike in the winter of 1974, literally thousands·of men behaved in a relatively similar fashion despite the fact that any individual difference variables in a population as large as this must surely have been normally distributed (see Billig, 1976; Sherif, 1967; and Tajfel, 1978b, for a more detailed critique of 'personality' explanations of intergroup behaviour). The postulation of some individual motivational state is equally implausible and this can be shown by examining the most important example of this type of explanation, the frustration–aggression hypothesis (Dollard *et al.*, 1939).

In its original form, the hypothesis proposed that frustration was a necessary and sufficient condition for the occurrence of aggression. Its implications for intergroup behaviour stemmed from the Freudian notion of displacement. It was suggested that individual frustrations were inevitable in any organized society or group and hence, to preserve the stability of that group, it was functional for the resulting aggression to be displaced onto people who were not seen as part of it (minority groups or foreigners, for example). However, in the 40 years since its formulation the hypothesis has met with a number of difficulties, perhaps the most important of which being whether frustration really is both a necessary and sufficient condition for aggression, and also the question of predicting the choice of target for the displaced aggression (see Billig, 1976). In the light of these problems the theory has undergone substantial revision and more emphasis is now placed on situational cues as releasers of aggression (see Berkowitz, 1962, 1974). However, even in its revised form an emotional state (anger arousal) is still seen as a central causal variable and, as Billig (1976) and Tajfel (1978b) have pointed out, this renders the theory rather implausible as an explanation of intergroup behaviour. It makes it implausible because it implies that collective aggression against some outgroup represents the simultaneous aggregation and convergence of individual motivational states and the apparently coincidental selection of the same target for the resulting aggression. This is a bit like saying that several hundred people eating their lunch at the same time in the same cafeteria do so because, and only because, they are all hungry – an explanation which ignores such important socially determined factors as the prevailing norms about appropriate mealtimes, the time people are allowed off from work, and the availability of alternative hostelries. As both Billig and Tajfel argue, the origins of collective frustration and the selection of appropriate targets are more probably related to shared goals and norms which are based in turn on common group memberships and intergroup relations. Thus, while frustration may well be involved in acts of intergroup aggression, to postulate a direct causal link between the two inside the individual is at once too simple and too general an account to permit any genuinely social analysis of group behaviour.

The second alternative – the argument from interpersonal relations – is not very useful either since there are several reasons why it, too, is unable to account for the uniformity so typical of intergroup situations. First, people may simply be quite unaware of the various interpersonal relations between themselves and outgroup members and yet their behaviour is still ordered and predictable. One football fan will taunt another, particularly if they are wearing different coloured scarves, quite oblivious of the many personal attributes that they may or may not have in common. And even if, objectively speaking, relations of attitude similarity, personal status, and so on between a given ingroup member and a variety of outgroup members could be ascertained, these relations would be likely to vary widely and yet typically in the relevant settings that ingroup member will not discriminate between those outgroup members in attitude or behaviour. To that same football fan, one opponent is as good a target for abuse (or worse) as a thousand others, despite many differences of attitude, socioeconomic status, physical appearance and personality. And finally, in genuinely collective situations, that is, where many individuals are interacting with many others, the multiplicity and complexity of interpersonal relations between the protagonists becomes enormous and yet the behaviour is often strikingly uniform.

We can conclude, then, that the direct extrapolation of theories about interpersonal behaviour to group contexts is inherently fraught with difficulties and thus that alternative theories, relating specifically to group behaviour, are necessary. This is not the place to review those theories – that task has been undertaken elsewhere in this volume (chapter 3) – but it will be useful perhaps to indicate in general terms what form these theories are likely to take. As a starting point, consider once again Turner's proposed demarcation between personal and social identity. A key feature of the latter, he argues, is its self-stereotypic nature – the individual's depersonalization of him or herself in the group. Once this has occurred, or once identification has moved in this direction, it follows that what affects the group as a whole has implications for the individual and his or her behaviour. Thus, what elements are likely to affect social identity, and hence a person's intergroup behaviour, are not intraindividual and interpersonal relations, but intergroup relations of status, power, material interdependence and so on. Therefore, theories of intergroup behaviour, if they are to do their job, must give highest causal precedence to independent variables relating to people's social relations as group members and not as individual persons. In proposing this, we are only reaffirming, in a more general and inclusive fashion, what Sherif wrote some years ago (1967, p. 12):

> The appropriate frame of reference for studying intergroup behaviour is the functional relations between two or more groups, which may be positive or negative. The functional relationship between groups whose members perceive them as ingroups has properties of its own . . . (and) cannot be deduced or extrapolated solely from the properties of relations that prevail among members within the group itself.

3   *Two theories of ethnic group relations*

We now move from the general perspective outlined above to consider its specific implications for two current theories of intergroup relations: belief congruence theory (Rokeach, 1960) and the contact hypothesis (G. W. Allport, 1954; Cook, 1962; Pettigrew, 1971). These are selected partly because they are not discussed in detail elsewhere in the book but are too influential to be overlooked, and partly because they represent good examples of the attempt to extrapolate directly from interpersonal to intergroup behaviour.

3.1   *Belief congruence theory*

Rokeach (1960, 1968) like others (Byrne, 1971; Festinger, 1954) proposes that the similarity or 'congruence' between individuals' belief systems is an important determinant of their attitudes towards each other. He argues that we are attracted to persons with similar beliefs since they tend to validate our own. He also suggests that in many situations similarities and differences between people's beliefs are more important for their mutual acceptance or rejection than their social group memberships.

Thus Rokeach explains race prejudice as an outcome of perceived or assumed belief incongruence. He hypothesizes that blacks are discriminated against not because they are 'black', that is, members of a specific social group, but because they are perceived or assumed to hold different beliefs from and by the discriminators. (He accepts that there are 'exceptions' in which racism is 'institutionalized' or results from 'extreme social pressure' – Rokeach, 1968).

To test this theory of prejudice Rokeach, Smith, and Evans (1960) devised what has become known as the race–belief experimental paradigm. In this paradigm, the subjects indicate their attitudes towards a number of individuals who may be physically present but are more usually portrayed by written descriptions. The stimulus persons are arranged to differ in terms of two independent dimensions, race and belief; they may belong either to the same or a different racial group as the subject, and at the same time hold either similar or different beliefs to the subject. Thus the subject's responses to these stimulus persons can be analysed to determine whether their attitudes are influenced more by race or belief. It has been established in several studies that belief seems to be more important than race (although it should be noted that race occasionally does have some effect). White subjects are usually more attracted to a black person with *similar* beliefs than to a white person with *different* beliefs (see Byrne and Wong, 1968; Hendrick, Bixenstine and Hawkins, 1971; Rokeach and Mezei, 1965; Rokeach, Smith, and Evans, 1960).

3.1.1 *Belief congruence as a theory of intergroup behaviour*

Applied to racism, belief congruence seems to be an interpersonal theory of intergroup relations. The paradigm described above operationalizes individuals' beliefs as their personal attributes, not as shared effects of their common group memberships. Belief congruence is therefore seen as a property of interpersonal relations. Moreover the principal hypothesis seems to be that racism arises because individuals like or dislike each other on the basis of their personal beliefs rather than on the basis of their group memberships. The other side of the coin, that racism represents intergroup behaviour, needs little justification. There is wide agreement in social psychology that prejudice describes negative attitudes directed at *all* the members of a specific social group (see Aronson, 1976; Baron and Byrne, 1977; Sherif and Sherif, 1969; Wrightsman, 1977), that it implicitly assumes identification with some ingroup, and that it is typically a *social* problem and so is manifested not merely in isolated individuals but in whole collectivities. Our three criteria for group behaviour are therefore met.

The theory, therefore, suggests that intergroup relations depend upon the aggregated attitudes between individual persons (who just happen to be members of different groups). We have already stated some general objections to this position, but now let us specify more concretely the difficulties in extrapolating from interpersonal attraction on the basis of belief congruence to intergroup behaviour. We can postulate a hypothetical social interaction between two individuals belonging to different groups but with similar beliefs and ask what is likely to be the outcome. To simplify matters, we shall assume that similarity does lead to interpersonal attraction and that the interaction may take place on an interpersonal or intergroup basis (that is, the individuals' group memberships may be either salient for them or not). There are at least four points.

Firstly, if the individuals interact on an interpersonal basis, then, although mutual attraction should develop, this has no implications for intergroup attitudes. Since they did not interact psychologically as group representatives, there is no basis for generalizing their positive attitudes to other outgroup members. As the outgroup member was not perceived as such but as an individuated, unique person, his or her opinions may not be regarded as informative about the beliefs of the outgroup as a whole. In consequence, the other person may be liked without any corresponding change in feelings about other outgroup members. (The phrase 'some of my best friends are Jews/blacks etc.' has become a cliché for prejudice partly because it illustrates this discrepancy between interpersonal and intergroup attitudes.)

Secondly, as soon as the individuals' group memberships become salient for whatever reason then their normative beliefs as group members should become important for them and these may differ from their personal beliefs (see Boyanowsky and Allen, 1973; Charters and Newcomb, 1952; Doise, 1969a; Shomer and Centers, 1970; White, 1977). Thus, despite interpersonal similarity, the individuals may nevertheless come to dislike each other when their group memberships are salient because the latter may elicit normative attitudinal differences between them. (Again it is a cliché that close friends and families, for example, can be turned against each other by ideological divisions rooted in wider group loyalties.) Moreover, there is evidence that salient ingroup–outgroup divisions lead to the perceptual accentuation of intergroup differences in beliefs and attitudes (that is, to assumed belief dissimilarity between groups) independently of interpersonal similarities and differences (see Allen and Wilder, 1979; Byrne and Wong, 1968; Stein, 1966; Stein, Hardyck, and Smith, 1965). This follows from the stereotyping process discussed earlier. The clear implication, then, is that one cannot extrapolate from interpersonal similarity and attraction between individuals to their social relations when their group memberships are salient, since the latter tend to produce perceived or stereotypical differences in beliefs between them.

Thirdly, if the individuals interact as group members and still have similar beliefs, whether the latter are perceived as such or maintained is likely to depend upon the nature of intergroup relations. For example, if the latter are positive, then presumably belief similarity should tend to be accepted as congruent with this state of affairs. But if intergroup relations are negative, it seems more likely that the interactors will misperceive, reinterpret or simply change or polarize their beliefs (Doise, 1969a) than that they will redefine their intergroup relationship. Intergroup attitudes are often very difficult to change because they are not simply based on the sum of individual experiences but are rooted in a normative consensus amongst ingroup members. Thus perceived belief similarity between ingroup and outgroup members may well tend to reflect rather than determine positive intergroup relations.

᾿Fourthly, if the individuals interact as group members and perceive similarity in group beliefs, it still cannot be assumed that the effects of belief similarity on interpersonal and intergroup relations are identical. Again, at the very least, its effects on intergroup relations are probably mediated by the characteristics of the latter. For example, there is some evidence that belief similarity interacts with the nature of the goal relationship between the groups.

Turner (1978c) found that in a *competitive* situation groups with similar values demonstrated more ingroup–outgroup bias than groups with different values. Similarly, in a field study of engineering workers, it was found that three groups of very similar status and with similar sociopolitical attitudes showed marked evidence of intergroup discrimination and mutual distrust (R. J. Brown, 1978a). On the other hand, another experiment (R. J. Brown, 1978b) established that, in a *cooperative* context, attitudinal similarity between groups of schoolchildren did decrease differentiation and increase friendliness and cooperation between them. A fourth study (R. J. Brown, 1978c) demonstrated both relationships depending on the type of subject; highly competitive subjects liked similar less than dissimilar outgroups, whereas less competitive subjects preferred the former to the latter. These results imply that the effects of similarity at the intergroup level depend on the dominant goal orientation between the groups; where intergroup relations are cooperative, it seems to enhance attraction, but when they are competitive, it contributes to discrimination. This is an important finding if we remember the evidence that, *ceteris paribus*, intergroup relations tend to be more competitive than interpersonal relations (see also chapter 3). This again argues that the effects of interpersonal similarities cannot be directly extrapolated to intergroup behaviour, and that interpersonal relations may indeed be irrelevant to their interaction when participants are acting on the basis of group memberships.

There is another issue that needs to be discussed at this point. Similarity can be a criterion for assigning a person to the same group as oneself. Furthermore, as we have seen, it also tends to be an effect of group membership; one tends to perceive or assume that ingroup members have similar and outgroup members dissimilar beliefs to oneself. Thus it has been argued that race or group effects can be reduced to belief effects; even where intergroup discrimination seems to obtain, this may merely reflect the fact that members of different groups are assumed to hold different beliefs. This argument seems somewhat paradoxical. As we shall see presently in this chapter and chapter 3, interpersonal similarities seem to be neither necessary nor sufficient for group-formation and subsequent intergroup discrimination. Social categorization *per se*, however (simply being assigned to different categories) seems to be both (Billig and Tajfel, 1973). Thus belief incongruence may in fact only be important in so far as it functions as a cue to group membership and not otherwise. Similarly, the fact that assumed belief incongruence is a direct product of ingroup–outgroup membership does not make the former an alternative explanation to the latter; on the contrary, it becomes merely a mechanism whereby group membership influences social relations – it has itself to be explained in terms of the race variable.

It would be an alternative explanation only in the sense that it might be hypothesized that intergroup discrimination would automatically disappear where members of different groups discovered that their assumptions of belief incongruence were false. As we have argued, there seems no reason to suppose that there is any such automatic link. At the least, the outcome would depend upon the relevance and importance of the disconfirmed assumptions to the norms and processes prescribing the discriminatory intergroup behaviour. In some instances it is reasonable to suppose that unexpected similarity with an outgroup could intensify discriminatory reactions. Novak and Lerner (1968), for example, find that subjects prefer interaction with an attitudinally different 'normal' person to a similar 'emotionally disturbed' person. Thus, in general, when individuals' group memberships are salient, the effects of both disconfirmed and untested assumptions about outgroup members are likely to vary with intergroup relations.

3.1.2 *Reinterpreting the race –belief literature*

If belief congruence is inadequate *as a theory of intergroup behaviour*, what of the empirical evidence that appears to support it? Does the basic finding that subjects prefer similar blacks to dissimilar whites contradict our analysis? We would argue not. One would only expect subjects to act more in terms of race than belief if the former were made psychologically more salient, significant or relevant to them in the experimental situation. Since the researchers took no special pains to ensure that this was the case, there is no reason to expect subjects to act more on an intergroup basis. In fact the conditions of the paradigm seem to be such as to decrease the salience of group membership and encourage an interpersonal orientation.

This can be seen if we examine the race–belief paradigm more closely. The subject is presented with a stimulus person who happens to be white or black and who also just happens to be more or less similar in beliefs. There is no information about how other ingroup or outgroup subjects react to the stimulus person nor about how typical or representative is the latter of his or her group. Indeed, the typically 'within-subjects' design of these studies where subjects rate more than one member of the ingroup and outgroup provides explicit information that there is personal heterogeneity within both groups, since the members disagree with each other. Such a lack of intragroup uniformity should make it difficult to treat the stimulus persons as stereotypical examples of their groups, which we have argued is a basic feature of intergroup behaviour, and so it is not surprising that responses should be controlled by the stimulus persons' personal attributes rather than by their group memberships. The only cue to the subjects that this might be an intergroup situation is the dichotomous social categorization (the race manipulation), the other two cues – low variability within groups and in relation to outgroup members – being noticeably absent. Since the subjects are not provided with relevant norms and stereotypes in terms of the categorization, there may be little situational incentive to make use of it.

Thus the importance of belief in these experiments suggest to us not that Rokeach has an adequate theory of ethnic prejudice, but simply that it is an effective determinant of *interpersonal* attraction.

As some support for this interpretation, we may note that there are a few studies in which race has been more influential than belief. These contrary data obtain under conditions consistent with our prediction that race effects should be found to the degree that group membership is made more important to subjects and/or perceived as more relevant to their responses. Thus prejudiced subjects are more likely to demonstrate race effects. Byrne and McGraw (1964) found some support for Rokeach on a liking measure, but also reported that, in terms of choosing a work partner, prejudiced subjects 'tended to indicate dislike or indifference towards negro strangers irrespective of their similarity to themselves' (p. 206). These subjects preferred dissimilar whites slightly more than similar blacks. Unprejudiced subjects, however, chose on the basis of similarity. Triandis and Davis (1965) confirmed that prejudiced subjects were more likely to show race than belief effects, but Byrne and Wong (1968) and Rokeach, Smith, and Evans (1960) did not.

In addition, it seems that we need to distinguish between different levels of discriminatory attitudes. For relatively formal, or, at least, non-ego-involving responses such as expressing mild friendliness or making evaluations, it appears that belief similarity is the operative variable. Race seems to be more important for more intimate or more obviously rejecting attitudes such as getting married or wishing to exclude from one's neighbourhood (Triandis and Davis, 1965; Stein, Hardyck, and Smith, 1965).

Both these results are relatively easy to explain from the present perspective. Prejudiced persons are presumably people for whom the race categorization is permanently more important and salient across a range of settings where others would see it as irrelevant. They are simply more likely than other subjects to perceive the experimental setting in intergroup terms. Very intimate or strongly hostile attitudes represent responses for which there are more explicit or entrenched group norms. As Triandis and Davis (1965) themselves point out, the responses showing race effects tend to be those for which social norms are clearly specified, whereas responses showing belief effects are those for which there is often less social prescription. Obviously, subjects can only be expected to act as group members where their responses are relevant to group norms; irrelevant responses allow them to behave as free-floating individuals. These ideas are related in that prejudiced subjects are more likely than others to perceive the experimental situation as relevant to the expression of their specific norm of intergroup discrimination.

3.1.3   *Race–belief effects in situations of varying group salience*

If the race–belief paradigm has minimized 'groupness' cues by personalizing the experimental situation, then it follows that situations which are personalized still further should produce even weaker race effects, and conversely that situations which are relatively depersonalized should elicit more evidence of the power of group membership to influence responses. An illustration of the first conclusion is provided by the effects of attaching photographs to the written stimulus protocols in the race–belief paradigm. When this was examined systematically by Byrne and McGraw (1964) they found, contrary to their hypothesis, that the addition of the photograph of a black stranger actually *increased* the interpersonal attraction towards him or her. From our point of view, this was to be expected since the presence of the photographs would be likely to personalize the otherwise anonymous, and hence potentially stereotypic, outgroup member. To illustrate the second conclusion we turn to studies which have examined the effects of belief similarity where the salience of group membership has been deliberately increased and the importance of individual characteristics correspondingly reduced.

Boyanowsky and Allen (1973) replicated and extended an experiment by Malof and Lott (1962) using the Asch (1952) conformity paradigm. They faced white subjects with a choice between accepting the support of a lone ally (who might be white or black) or going along with the incorrect judgements of the (white) majority. The lone ally responded correctly on the task and hence demonstrated similar beliefs to the subject (unlike the incorrect and hence dissimilar majority). The researchers reasoned that if Rokeach was correct, subjects should accept the support of the agreeing confederate whatever his or her colour. A race effect would be revealed by subjects refusing to accept support from the black ally and hence showing less than the usual decrement in conformity as a function of social support. Boyanowsky and Allen required subjects to make judgements about personal and general social reality as well as physical reality (visual perception tasks) and also provided conditions of ingroup surveillance.

Like Malof and Lott, Boyanowsky and Allen found that on visual perception tasks, social support decreased conformity whether the ally was black or white and the subjects prejudiced or not. They also found the same on tasks relating to opinions referring to society in general. However, on tasks dealing with personal reality (self-referent opinions), high prejudiced subjects conformed less with a white than with a black ally, whereas no such discrimination against the black confederate occurred with low prejudiced subjects. In other words prejudiced subjects preferred to remain with the incorrect but white majority rather than openly express agreement with the correct but black confederate; this effect was magnified where the subjects were under surveillance by the ingroup majority.

These results can be interpreted as follows. The black–white distinction is not relevant as a basis for judgements about physical or general social reality. The appropriate reference group, even for prejudiced subjects, includes all the people present, black and white. Thus, since on these responses both black and white supporters are ingroup members, they both decrease conformity. However, the race categorization is normatively relevant for prejudiced (but not unprejudiced) subjects in judgements about self-referring opinions, since for these individuals it is important to be 'white'. Thus, on these items, lack supporters are outgroup members for prejudiced subjects and consequently have less impact than white ingroup supporters in decreasing conformity. When the ethnic categorization is salient and relevant to their opinions, the subjects are less likely to accept support from an outgroup member even though the ingroup is dissimilar and the outgroup member similar.

Two other experiments illustrate the power of social categorizations (awareness of ingroup–outgroup membership) when interpersonal cues for action are virtually absent. Billig and Tajfel (1973) investigated the effects of social categorization *per se* and opinion similarity on social discrimination using the 'minimal group' paradigm of Tajfel *et al.* (1971, see chapter 3). They examined how subjects distributed sums of money under four different conditions. The first was the standard situation in which subjects were assigned to one of two groups on the apparent basis of a trivial criterion of aesthetic preference (for one painter over another). The groups remained anonymous, however, and subjects were then asked to allocate money between people identified only by code number and group affiliation. In this condition the similarity and categorization variables are confounded since the categorization is made on the basis of a presumed similarity in artistic taste, and hence subjects could infer greater similarity between themselves and ingroupers than between themselves and outgroupers. In the second condition this similarity was removed by assigning subjects to groups on an explicitly arbitrary basis – simply the toss of a coin. In the third condition the categorization variable was removed by informing subjects that they, along with a number of others, preferred one painter to another but, importantly, no mention was made of the word 'group' in the instructions. Finally, there was a control condition in which subjects were neither categorized nor informed of their aesthetic preferences.

It is the second and third conditions which are of particular interest here. If belief similarity provides the basis for people's behaviour then one should expect more social discrimination in the third condition, where there were similar and dissimilar others to choose between, than in the second, where there was no basis for assuming any greater similarity to the ingroup than to the outgroup. In fact, the levels of discrimination observed were the complete opposite of this. Few significant departures from a fairness strategy were observed in the third condition whilst definite evidence of ingroup favouritism was found in the second. Social categorization *per se*, then, even on a purely random basis like this, can be sufficient to cause people to discriminate between other individuals. The similarity variable was not completely unimportant, however. The highest levels of ingroup favouritism were observed in the first condition where it was confounded with, and probably reinforced, group membership, and in the analysis of the overall favouritism scores a significant statistical effect was observed for similarity, even if it was dwarfed by the size of the categorization effect.

Allen and Wilder (1975), using a similar methodology, sought to test belief congruence theory even more directly by independently manipulating how far the majority of the ingroup and the majority of the outgroup agreed with the subject's own attitudes. Belief congruence theory predicts in this situation that there should be less discrimination against outgroup members with similar attitudes than against those with different attitudes. Once again, this prediction was not upheld. On all measures, subjects showed high levels of ingroup favouritism, regardless of the similarity of the outgroup. In fact, in certain conditions – namely, those in which there was attitudinal consensus in the ingroup – the levels of discrimination actually appeared to *increase* slightly against the similar outgroup.

Here, then, are two experiments finding marked effects due to group membership and much smaller or negligible effects due to interpersonal similarity. It is worth noting how group-like these experimental situations really were. First, there was a well-defined categorization, albeit a flimsy one. Second, there was no possibility of distinguishing, recognizing, or interacting with particular individuals from either group since the groups remained anonymous throughout. Subjects were forced, in other words, to view both groups in a completely stereotypic fashion. Thus, with two of the three defining criteria of 'groupness' being clearly present, these situations were clearly well towards the 'group' pole of Tajfel's continuum. So the fact that a variable like interpersonal similarity was found to be of minor predictive value in them provides some support for our original contention that different psychological processes operate at the two extremes of the continuum.

Also relevant in this context are three field studies of helping behaviour conducted by Sole, Marton, and Hornstein (1975). These investigators unobtrusively measured the likelihood of help being given to an anonymous stranger who appeared to hold opinions of varying degrees of similarity to the subject's own. Their consistent finding was that when these opinions were important to the subjects, frequency of helping was not linearly related to opinion similarity. Rather, the data revealed a sharp discontinuity between helping for a stranger who expressed 100 per cent agreement with the subject and those strangers who disagreed on one or more items. The authors suggested that this stepwise pattern indicated that the opinion similarity was being used by subjects as a basis for categorization of the strangers into 'we' and 'they' groups. Total similarity of opinion appeared to allow the unambiguous classification of the stranger into the ingroup and hence increased the probability of help being given; partial or complete dissimilarity seemed to prevent this inclusion and decreased the level of helping. What was also interesting was that this helping behaviour was quite unrelated to interpersonal attraction for the stranger. In one experiment, for instance, the attraction increased smoothly and monotonically with opinion similarity while the helping data showed the discontinuous pattern already described.

Finally, the one study inconsistent with our second conclusion should be mentioned. D. M. Taylor and Guimond (1978) extended the race–belief paradigm by adding a number of experimental conditions which might have been expected to increase the salience of group membership (for example, having subjects seated amongst other members of the ingroup, and across the room for some apparent members of the outgroup, while answering their questionnaires; telling them to regard themselves as group representatives; allowing prior discussion of the stimulus persons). However, these manipulations made little difference to the outcome. The results showed that belief similarity accounted for most of the variance on all dependent measures regardless of experimental condition, and that the group affiliation of the stimulus persons had only a very minor impact.

These findings seem to support belief congruence theory. However, it may be that the methodology still retained some interpersonal characteristics, despite the experimenters' attempts to remove them. In particular, manipulating similarity on the basis of the individual subject's beliefs and having the subjects make judgements about five individual stimulus persons in the standard manner may have been enough to lead the subjects to interpret the situation in interpersonal terms. As D. M. Taylor and Guimond (1978, p. 24) concluded: 'For future research it will be important to manipulate important beliefs *shared* by members of a group and require Ss to make judgements about ingroups and outgroups on a collective basis'.

In conclusion our analysis suggests that in attempting to apply an interpersonal theory of belief congruence to intergroup behaviour, Rokeach meets the following difficulties. Firstly, interpersonal similarity between individuals may be irrelevant to their attitudes and actions once their respective group memberships become salient. Secondly, intergroup similarity may not have the same effects as interpersonal similarity since it will tend

to be perceived in terms of and interact with the nature of intergroup relations. Thirdly, the *shared* perception of similarities and
differences between people which influence intergroup relations
are themselves products of group formation and do not reflect
interpersonal relationships.

3.2   *The contact hypothesis*

The idea that contact between members of different groups will
improve relations between them has a long history, and has provided some of the rationale for such social policy decisions as the
racial integration of housing and education and the promotion of
international sporting and cultural exchanges (Amir, 1969).
Within social psychology the most prominent contact theorists
have been G. W. Allport (1954), Cook (1962), and Pettigrew
(1971). Allport, the earliest and most influential of the three,
concluded that whether or not contact led to intergroup harmony
depended on its precise form. Specifically, he proposed that the
conditions which provided the most favourable climate were
those where the contact was between equal status participants
pursuing common goals in an atmosphere of social and institutional support (G. W. Allport, 1954, p. 281). Although he never
made the rationale for this conclusion entirely clear, shared group
identifications and the pursuit of jointly valued objectives
appeared to be the main causal factors in his analysis:

> The nub of the matter seems to be that contact must reach below the
> surface in order to be effective in altering prejudice. Only the type of
> contact that leads people to *do* things together is likely to result in
> changed attitudes. The principle is clearly illustrated in the multi-
> ethnic athletic team. Here the goal is all important; the ethnic com-
> position of the team is irrelevant. It is the cooperative striving for the
> goal that engenders solidarity. So too, in factories, neighbourhoods,
> housing units, schools, common participation and interests are more
> effective than the bare fact of equal-status contact. (1954, p. 276)

In marked contrast, other theorists, although endorsing Allport's criteria for successful contact, have developed a rationale
for these from a theory of interpersonal attraction. Cook (1962)
for instance, lays some stress on the need for the contact to
involve intimate rather than merely casual personal relationships.
Only in this way, he argues, would the positive affect generalize
to other situations and to the outgroup as a whole. Pettigrew

(1971) makes the interpersonal basis for his contact hypothesis even clearer. Drawing on the ideas of Newcomb (1961) and Rokeach (1960), he comments on Allport's criteria as follows (1971, p. 311): 'These criteria are actually an application of the broader theory of interpersonal attraction. All four conditions maximize the likelihood that shared values and beliefs will be evinced and mutually perceived'. (And, hence, according to the similarity–attraction thesis, increase the probability that members of the two groups will be attracted to one another.)

Empirical evidence bearing on the contact hypothesis has been fully reviewed elsewhere (G. W. Allport, 1954; Amir, 1969; Harding et al., 1968; McClendon, 1974) and there is no need to recapitulate it here. What we shall do instead is to evaluate some of the major conclusions that have been drawn from that evidence in the light of the theoretical perspective outlined earlier in the chapter. From the previous discussion, and especially the analysis of belief congruence theory in section 3.1.1 above, our general position should be clear; to the extent that the contact takes places on an 'interpersonal' basis it is unlikely to modify intergroup attitudes and behaviour since the two domains are controlled, we suggest, by different psychological processes. What is more probable, if contact is confined to social interaction between individuals *qua* individuals, is that a few interpersonal relationships will change but that the intergroup situation will remain substantially unaltered. If, on the other hand, the contact can be characterized in 'group' terms, that is as interaction between individuals *qua* group members, or in ways that alter the structure of group relations, then genuine changes at the intergroup level may be expected. Even here, however, we suspect that the nature of the social contact is often more likely to be symptomatic of pre-existing group affiliations and intergroup relations, rather than a decisive determining factor.

With this in mind, let us now briefly examine some of the conclusions that have been drawn from research on the contact hypothesis. The first, almost unanimous, one is that contact *per se* will not necessarily improve intergroup attitudes and, indeed, may even worsen them (G. W. Allport, 1954; Cook, 1962). Probably the single best illustration of this conclusion is provided by the experiments of Sherif and his colleagues in which it was found that simply bringing groups of children into contact with one another served to heighten rather than reduce the conflict between them in spite of the fact that the groups were of roughly equal status and had originally been comprised so as to maximize the friendship links across the groups (Sherif, 1967). Why should this be so? It is hard to account for from an interpersonal perspective since interaction between individuals normally leads to greater attraction (Festinger, Schachter, and Back, 1950; Newcomb, 1961). A more plausible explanation is that contact situations which involve no positive interdependence between the groups, or which provides no new common locus of identification for group members, may simply provide an opportunity to engage in social comparisons and hence exacerbate an already conflictual intergroup relationship. The implication is that interindividual encounters in such settings are primarily determined by intergroup rather than interpersonal relations.

A second conclusion concerns the degree of intimacy of encounters between members of different groups. Some observers (such as G. W. Allport, 1954; Cook, 1962) have suggested that to be effective in reducing prejudice contacts should be of a relatively enduring and intimate nature rather than transitory and casual. As evidence for this contention, studies of racial integration in housing are often cited (see Deutsch and Collins, 1951; Wilner, Walkley, and Cook, 1952). These typically show that there are more frequent and intimate cross-race contacts in integrated housing schemes than in segregated ones, and, in addition, that residents in integrated housing have more favourable racial attitudes. Although this is *prima facie* evidence for the importance of intimacy (and hence for the interpersonal theory on which it is based), precise interpretation of studies like this is always rather difficult. For one thing, it is not always clear how generalized the reported reduction in prejudice actually is. In other words, did the respondents' improved attitudes relate merely to particular black neighbours or to blacks in general? A second, and more serious, point is that the intimacy variable in these studies is often confounded with other factors, any one of which might account for the reduction in prejudice or, indeed, for the variation in intimacy itself. For instance, the lack of social sanction against associating with outgroup members is consistently reported as being correlated with the frequency of intimate contacts. Similarly, in integrated housing schemes there are often opportunities for common membership of various neighbourhood groups, many of which involve cooperative activities. As will be seen below, any of these factors might be expected, on grounds other than interpersonal attraction, to reduce the degree of group differentiation and increase the likelihood of black–white friendships developing. In other words, increased intimacy may be an indicator or an *effect* of improved intergroup relations, rather than a cause of them.

The third conclusion, drawn by numerous commentators (such as Deutsch and Collins, 1951; Pettigrew, 1971), concerns the importance of social or institutional support for non-discriminatory practices. With this conclusion we would not disagree since the presence of such a normative factor may help to redefine the situation in ways which reduce the salience of the original category division, and increases the probability that minority group members will be seen as part of a larger ingroup. In addition, such support often takes the form of institutions such as tenant associations, community councils, trade unions, and so on which, by providing a basis for social identification and joint action along non-racial lines, will also reduce the prevalence of prejudiced attitudes. But it is important to note that these effects may still be quite situation-specific. This is clearly illustrated by studies such as Minard (1952) and Harding and Hogrefe (1952) which found marked reductions in prejudice at the workplace, where integration was explicitly sanctioned by unions or employers, but *not* in the wider community where segregation was still officially practised.

A fourth condition for contact to be successful has been found to be the presence of some positive interdependence between the groups, leading to cooperative activity (G. W. Allport, 1954; Sherif, 1967). The rationale for this is most simply derived from an instrumental theory such as realistic group conflict theory (Campbell, 1965) which places prime causal emphasis on the way groups' objective interests clash or coincide. Once again, we would concur with this position and add only, as McClendon (1974) and Worchel (1979) have suggested, that it may be necessary for the cooperative activity to be successful for it to achieve the desired increase in friendliness (Worchel, Andreoli, and Folger, 1977).

The fifth and final conclusion, attested to by nearly all observers from G. W. Allport (1954) on, is that the contact must take place between equal status participants, by which is usually meant that they should come from groups of similar socioeconomic standing or consensual prestige. However, on closer inspection, this assertion turns out to be somewhat more complex than most people have assumed. We can begin by noting that the criterion of 'equal status' has at least three distinguishable connotations. One is that the members of the two groups in question, because they come from an equivalent stratum of society, also belong to a number of other superordinate categories. These common category memberships, as we have already suggested, might indeed be sufficient to subsume the initial dichotomy and help to reduce discrimination in terms of it. A second interpretation is that equality of status implies a similarity of values (by virtue of the common socioeconomic background) and hence a greater potential for interpersonal attraction (Pettigrew, 1971; McClendon, 1974). But, as we have already seen in section 3.1.1, whether this kind of similarity has beneficial effects on subsequent intergroup relations depends both on the nature of the encounter (that is, whether it is interpersonal or intergroup) and on the type of relationship that already exists (that is, cooperative or competitive). A third interpretation of 'equal status' is its more literal meaning of prestige similarity. Here again, when this refers to an intergroup relation, similarity does not lead uniformly to decreased differentiation. In the research cited earlier, the effects of status equivalence were also examined and it was found that they were again context-dependent – in appropriate conditions, both increased (Turner, 1978c) and decreased (R. J. Brown, 1978b) ingroup favouritism may be observed as groups become more similar to one another.

In conclusion, then, there is some theoretical and empirical justification for the idea that intergroup contact under the right conditions will reduce prejudice. But we suggest that it does so not because, as Cook (1962) and Pettigrew (1971) suggest, it permits and encourages interpersonal friendships between members of different groups, but rather because it changes the nature and structure of the intergroup relationship. The changes at the interpersonal level which undoubtedly do occur in contact situations are thus more appropriately viewed, we believe, as an *effect* rather than a *cause* of a more general alteration of intergroup relations – in other words, as mere epiphenomena with little or no consequence for wider social change. As stated earlier, prejudice and discrimination between groups are likely to be reduced more effectively by policies addressed directly to changing people's social identifications and intergroup relations. Such policies require an analysis of the basic processes responsible for group formation and cooperative or competitive intergroup relationships. An attempt at such an analysis is made in the next chapter.

4   Conclusion

We have tried in this chapter to establish two things. First, that group and intergroup behaviour can be distinguished conceptually and empirically from individual and interpersonal behaviour. Second, that this distinction has important consequences for the kinds of theoretical analyses that are appropriate for the explanation of intergroup phenomena. In doing so we may have given the misleading impression that studies of interpersonal and intergroup behaviour are rigidly separated from each other. In this final section we would make three last comments to help dispel that impression.

The first is that research in the interpersonal domain has proved useful in the study of intergroup behaviour in the limited sense of providing suggestive empirical hypotheses. Our argument in the last section was not that belief congruence or social contact did not improve intergroup relations; on the contrary, we saw that these hypotheses established at the interpersonal level do have analogies in some intergroup situations. Our objection was to the thesis that they would do so because they had been validated at the interpersonal level, because in other words intergroup relations consist of nothing but interpersonal relationships. The point is that unless theories recognize the depersonalized character of intergroup behaviour, they will ultimately be able to provide only analogies and not the explanatory concepts that are really needed.

The second point is to stress once again that the interpersonal–group dimension of social behaviour is continuous and not dichotomous. We have stressed the discontinuity between interpersonal and group behaviour and thus implied a dichotomy in two ways. For the purposes of exposition, it has been easier to ignore the more complex intermediate instances on the continuum and focus on the pure extremes. Also, much of our discussion has been concerned with processes rather than the description of concrete behaviours. The fact that there is a discontinuity of social psychological *processes* between interpersonal and group behaviour does not mean that *empirically* the forms of behaviour do not coexist to a greater or lesser degree. Very probably social situations always contain elements of both and the different processes can operate at the same time. A central theoretical task for the future is to understand not only the nature and functioning of these processes in isolation, but also how they combine or interact with one another.

Finally, returning to F. H. Allport's (1962) 'master problem', let us recall that the theoretical framework advanced here is only an approximate and tentative step towards its solution. But it does suggest that the scientific study of individual psychological processes is quite compatible with a theoretical distinction between interpersonal and group behaviour and does not, as Allport thought, necessitate a lapse into metaphysics. To this degree it should hopefully stimulate other and perhaps better attempts to conceptualize that distinction. In this way and also by indicating the dangers in uncritical extrapolations from one sphere to the other, we believe it should open up new lines of research in both realms.

CHAPTER 3

The Experimental Social Psychology of Intergroup Behaviour

JOHN C. TURNER

1 Introduction

This chapter reviews the experimental social psychology of intergroup behaviour. The central objective of this research field is to
discover the social psychological causes of conflict and harmony
between social groups, and its main preoccupation is to investigate basic processes in intergroup cooperation and competition.
The chapter summarizes the important research findings and
ideas and discusses their implications for the aetiology of
intergroup conflict.

The following two sections describe work relevant to the two
dominant themes in contemporary studies: the effects of cooperative and competitive social interaction on intragroup and intergroup relations, and the role of social categorization in intergroup
discrimination. The next section brings these themes together in a
more speculative discussion of theoretical issues related to the
resolution of intergroup conflict. The final section summarizes
the main conclusion and identifies some directions for future
research.

Some terms need to be defined at the outset. *Ingroup favouritism*
describes any tendency to favour ingroup over outgroup members on perceptual, attitudinal or behavioural dimensions. It
includes partisan intergroup attitudes, sociometric preferences
for the ingroup, discriminatory intergroup behaviour and more
favourable evaluations of the products and performances of the
ingroup than the outgroup. *Ingroup bias* describes instances of
ingroup favouritism which seem to be unreasonable or unjustifi-
able in that they go beyond the objective evidence or requirements of the situation such as derogatory outgroup attitudes
which have no veridical basis or discriminatory intergroup
behaviour which does not directly benefit ingroup members.

Thus its use always implies some interpretative judgement on the part of the researcher. *Intergroup discrimination* and *differentiation* indicate mutual favouritism between groups. Where these terms are distinguished, the former specifies behavioural or quasi-behavioural, and the latter perceptual and attitudinal, responses. Later in the chapter differentiation is used in a theoretical sense to describe any form of favouritism motivated by a desire for positively valued distinctiveness for one's own group, and thus can include discrimination.

2   Cooperative and competitive interaction between groups

The pioneering research on this issue was conducted by Sherif and Sherif and their colleagues. Their work was important because it demonstrated experimentally the role of intergroup relations in social conflict, identified social and psychological consequences of intergroup competition, and also presented a specific theory of intergroup behaviour.

Three field studies were carried out in 1949, 1953 and 1954 in the United States with young male subjects at summer camps (Sherif, 1951; Sherif and Sherif, 1953; Sherif, White and Harvey, 1955; Sherif et al., 1961). They were similar in basic design and comprised four stages in the development and reduction of intergroup conflict. In the first stage, the subjects engaged in sports and outdoor activities on a camp-wide basis, and normal friendships developed. In the second, they were divided into two groups through the separation of their living arrangements and camp activities; close friends were assigned to different groups. The groups gradually evolved status and role differentiations between their members and shared social norms. In the third stage, the camp authorities (the researchers) instituted an organized competition between the groups embracing sports contests and other camp activities. In consequence, overt hostility developed between them both within and outside the organized contests. The last study included a final stage which provided the warring groups with *superordinate goals*: compelling objectives desired by them both but which neither could achieve without the help of the other. They were placed in settings where collaborative action was necessary such as a lakeside outing where they had to join forces to rescue a truck which was to bring them food. A series of such encounters reduced mutual antipathy and led to favourable intergroup attitudes.

The researchers interpreted their observations as support for the following hypotheses (Sherif, 1967):

1   Where individuals interact under conditions that embody common goals requiring cooperatively interdependent activities for their attainment, a definite group structure will emerge, consisting of differentiated status and role positions and shared social norms.

2   Where two groups come into contact under conditions that embody a series of incompatible goals – where both groups urgently desire some objective which can be attained only at the expense of the other – competitive activity towards the goal changes over time into hostility between the groups; also:

(a)   unfavourable attitudes and images (stereotypes) of the outgroup come into use and become standardized, placing the outgroup at a definite social distance from the ingroup;

(b)   intergroup conflict produces an increase in solidarity within the groups and other changes in intragroup relations;

(c)   increased solidarity and pride in one's own group lead to ingroup biases which overevaluate the characteristics and performances of ingroup members and underevaluate those of outgroup members.

3   Where conflicting groups come into contact under conditions that embody a series of superordinate goals, cooperative activity towards the goal has a cumulative impact in improving intergroup relations: in reducing social distance, dissipating hostile outgroup attitudes and stereotypes, and making future intergroup conflicts less likely.

These hypotheses constitute a functional theory of intergroup behaviour. They imply that functional interdependence (positive or negative) between individuals or groups for the achievement of their goals leads directly to cooperative or competitive social interaction and also that cooperative or competitive interaction directly produce cohesive (solidarity, friendly, etc.) or antagonistic social attitudes between the participants. Thus the social relations between individuals or groups are primarily determined by their functional or goal relations.

The important predictions are that objective conflicts of interests (incompatible goals) cause intergroup conflict, and superordinate or collaborative goals induce social harmony. The theory explains the formation of social groups as an outcome of the same processes which reduce social distance between conflicting groups; cohesive social relations and group structure emerge from cooperative social interaction for interdependent goals. Thus it implies that conflict resolution is partly a process of weakening group boundaries and that competitive interaction should tend to consolidate ingroup–outgroup divisions.

The next major research programme on intergroup behaviour helped to corroborate some of Sherif and Sherif's ideas. Blake and Mouton (1961a, 1962) conducted a series of quasi-experimental laboratory studies in which discussion groups of nine to 12 adult members met over 10 to 14 day periods. Pairs of groups created solutions to human relations problems and compared their products on a win–lose basis to assess their problem-solving effectiveness.

 * The introduction of a competitive intergroup orientation had several consequences. Ingroup biases in the perception of the groups and their products (and even third parties) were enhanced and consolidated. Intergroup attitudes became extremely partisan and led to deadlocks in negotiations between the groups. Where the groups were provided with opportunities to discuss their respective solutions, they tended not to exchange objective information but to attack and attempt to discredit each others' views. Moreover, their communications were marred by perceptual distortions whereby agreements in the solutions were minimized and disagreements enhanced. Intragroup relations became more cohesive and organized and conformity pressures upon group members increased. Finally, competitive victory tended to increase the power of group leaders and enhance cohesiveness, cooperativeness and work-motivation, whereas defeat had the opposite effects.

These results support the hypothesis that intergroup competition produces a syndrome of interrelated effects tending to strengthen social relationships *within* groups and disrupt them *between* groups. It is not so evident that they confirm the theory that competition is determined by extrinsic group interests. Blake and Mouton report that the provision of a win–lose orientation (and not incompatible goals) was sufficient to elicit the dynamics of competitive behaviour. In other words, their subjects were competitive because they wanted to win, and they wanted to win, not to achieve some extrinsic objective, but simply because they were in a competition. The implication is that intergroup competition may often be intrinsically and not extrinsically motivated. In this case, the most obvious explanation is that self-evaluative social comparisons between the groups to assess their problem-solving abilities led directly to a mutual desire to win.

The research of Wilson and his colleagues (Wilson, Chun, and Kayatani, 1965; Wilson and Kayatani, 1968; Wilson and Robinson, 1968; Wilson and Wong, 1968) also suggests that social processes can contribute directly to competitive intergroup behaviour. In these studies pairs of dyads made cooperative or competitive choices to divide monetary rewards in an experimental game; the members made both intergroup and intragroup choices. The important point is that the reward structure or payoff matrix and hence the functional relations between players were identical on both kinds of trials. Nevertheless, intergroup choices were approximately twice as competitive as intragroup choices. Team partners were also rated more favourably than members of the other team, especially on sociometric and motive traits relevant to the game-playing situation. Thus intergroup behaviour seems to be inherently more competitive or discriminatory than intragroup behaviour.

There is, however, an alternative interpretation of these results. The experimental game employed by Wilson normally leads to predominantly competitive responses even between individual players. In the above studies, intergroup relations may have reflected whereas intragroup relations may have counteracted this baseline tendency. Members of the same dyad had to cooperate to make joint decisions about interteam choices. Hence, there were differences in both degree and kind between social interaction within and between groups. These differences could and should have led to more attraction and understanding within than between dyads (as the subjects reported) and so encouraged cooperativeness (Billig, 1976, pp. 208–10).

This alternative explanation is interesting in its own right because it makes the simple but easily forgotten point that differential interpersonal relations can account for some forms of ingroup favouritism. We need not assume competitive or hostile intergroup relations to recognize that there are many variables such as social interaction, proximity, familiarity and attitudinal similarity which tend to ensure more interpersonal attraction within than between groups. We can also suppose that individuals naturally tend to have different information about ingroup and outgroup members and appraise their actions from different perspectives. Any individual tends to be more aware of the intragroup than intergroup actions of ingroup members and the intergroup than intragroup actions of outgroup members. These constant discrepancies between intragroup and intergroup relations should cause ingroup favouritism under the most minimal conditions of group-formation and need not imply prejudiced outgroup attitudes. Thus where there is more face-to-face interaction with ingroup than outgroup members we should not assume that favouritism represents bias; it may reflect a sociometric preference for ingroup members based on real differences in contact and information.

Other research during the two decades following Sherif and Sherif's studies tended to corroborate the functional theory (Avigdor, 1953; Bass and Dunteman, 1963; Diab, 1970; Fiedler, 1967; Harvey, 1956; Johnson, 1967; Sussman and Weil, 1960). But more recent experiments have created difficulties. Sherif and Sherif, and Blake and Mouton confound functional interdependence with cooperative and competitive social interaction. Later studies compare the effects on intergroup attitudes of cooperation, competition and coaction (functional independence with face-to-face contact) under conditions where intragroup and intergroup interaction are controlled or manipulated. They find that the early work is probably correct about the different effects of cooperative and competitive interaction but may be incorrect in its implicit stress on the importance of functional interdependence *per se*.

Doise *et al*. (1971, 1972) and Brewer and Silver (1978) exclude both anticipated and actual social interaction within and between groups, and measure intergroup attitudes before and after subjects make cooperative or competitive, or cooperative, competitive or independent decisions about rewards for ingroup and outgroup members. There are no significant differences between the effects of the different forms of intergroup behaviour. Before and after intergroup behaviour subjects evaluate ingroup more favourably than outgroup members.

Doise also finds ingroup bias in a control condition where intergroup behaviour was not even anticipated, but to a lesser degree than in the experimental conditions. It appears then that a simple ingroup–outgroup division with neither face-to-face contact nor social interaction between group members can create ingroup bias, and that the mere expectation of intergroup behaviour increases this bias to the same level as that obtained after intergroup behaviour.

In contrast to these two studies which manipulate intergroup behaviour unconfounded with intergroup interaction, Kahn and Ryen (1972) and Doise and Weinberger (1973) explore the effects of expected intergroup interaction. Under conditions without face-to-face contact between subjects, the former find ingroup bias with expected cooperation but less than with expected competition. Under conditions of face-to-face contact between ingroup and outgroup dyads, the latter find bias with expected coaction and competition but not cooperation.

Three studies manipulate cooperative interaction within groups. Rabbie and de Brey (1971) measure intergroup attitudes before and after intragroup task-interaction under conditions of some face-to-face contact between cooperating or competing groups. The subjects prefer the ingroup to the outgroup on cohesiveness measures and more so after interaction. Performance ratings are more complex. There is little or no bias before interaction and, in fact, competing groups favour the outgroup over the ingroup. Interaction increases ingroup bias for both cooperating and competing groups, but more so for the latter subjects. Under similar conditions, Rabbie and Wilkens (1971) find no significant differences between intergroup coaction and competition. Both conditions produce bias in ratings of the groups as collective entities before and after task-interaction, but interaction does increase ingroup bias in evaluations of individual group members. Janssens and Nuttin (1976, experiment 2) find that verbal interaction increases ingroup bias in performance ratings for both competing and isolated, independent groups. Intergroup competition is associated with more bias than independence only under conditions of intragroup interaction.

Finally, four studies hold constant some degree of intragroup interaction and face-to-face contact between groups. Rabbie *et al*.

(1974) find that ingroups are preferred to outgroups on cohesiveness measures and that this preference is greater with anticipated intergroup competition than cooperation especially where the groups have strong bargaining positions. Intergroup competition also produces more negative outgroup attitudes than cooperation on other measures, especially where the groups have weak bargaining positions. Ryen and Kahn (1975) report that ingroup bias increases from intergroup coaction to cooperation to competition. Worchel, Andreoli, and Folger (1977) find that attraction to the ingroup increases, and attraction to the outgroup decreases, from intergroup cooperation to coaction to competition. Janssens and Nuttin (1976, experiment 1) also observe that coacting groups are less biased than competing ones.

These experiments make several important points. Firstly, intragroup interaction increases ingroup favouritism. Secondly, ingroup favouritism or bias seems to be the rule rather than the exception under conditions of intergroup competition, coaction or independence, or cooperation. Even the anticipation of intergroup behaviour, with or without intragroup interaction, seems sufficient for ingroup bias. Only one study (Doise and Weinberger, 1973) finds that anticipated cooperation actually eliminates ingroup bias. There is also evidence that simply being divided into groups, without social interaction, face-to-face contact or anticipated intergroup behaviour, can create ingroup bias (Doise et al., 1971, 1972; see also the next section).

Thirdly, not only does intergroup cooperation tend to produce biases, but it sometimes does so to the same extent as competition. To explain this we need to remember that any intergroup orientation implies both an ingroup–outgroup division and cooperative intragroup interaction and thus should tend to encourage ingroup favouritism. Intergroup competition should tend to accentuate this effect because: (a) it should enhance the salience of the ingroup–outgroup division; (b) it should motivate or lead to the expectation of more cooperative intragroup interaction; and (c) actual or expected competitive intergroup interaction should increase hostility towards outgroup members. Likewise intergroup cooperation should normally attentuate the effect by reducing the salience of the ingroup–outgroup division and/or promoting as much or more cooperative interaction with outgroup as ingroup members. Thus the differences between intergroup cooperation and competition might tend to disappear where intergroup behaviour takes place under experimental or real-world conditions which maximize the salience of the ingroup–outgroup distinction and minimize social interaction.

This analysis is consistent with the conditions of those studies which do not find the expected difference between cooperation and competition (Brewer and Silver, Doise *et al.*, and Rabbie and de Brey's pretest results). It also explains why cooperation eliminated bias in Doise and Weinberger's study, since these researchers provided much face-to-face contact and anticipated interaction between as within groups.

Thus cooperative and competitive relations *per se* do not necessarily produce different intergroup attitudes. Their different effects are probably mediated by their implications for the perceptual or cognitive salience of ingroup–outgroup membership and social interaction.

Fourthly, coaction or independence does not seem to represent a unitary psychological orientation. It sometimes produces as much bias as competition and sometimes less than cooperation. There seems little doubt that coaction can sometimes develop spontaneously into competition through intergroup comparisons to evaluate task-performance or some other characteristic (see Rabbie and Wilkens, 1971; Turner, 1975a). It may also be the case at the other extreme that coacting subjects sometimes have a minimal awareness of themselves as members of a distinctive social unit. Thus the experiments may produce different results depending on whether their specific conditions encourage or impede group-formation and intergroup comparisons.

The main conclusions to be drawn from this section (see Dion, 1979; Hinkle and Schopler, 1979; Rabbie, 1974) are that:

1 Cooperative intragroup interaction tends to increase ingroup favouritism.
2 Competitive intergroup interaction tends to increase intragroup cohesiveness, morale, cooperativeness, work-motivation, conformity pressures, status and leadership differentiations and develop into mutual hostility accompanied by ingroup–outgroup biases.
3 Cooperative intergroup interaction tends to decrease social distance and ingroup–outgroup biases.
4 The different effects of cooperative and competitive intergroup behaviour tend to disappear when social interaction

is minimized and the salience of the ingroup–outgroup division maximized; under these conditions all forms of anticipated and actual intergroup behaviour seem sufficient for ingroup–outgroup biases.

The functional theory seems partly correct in its prediction about the effects of cooperative and competitive interaction, but partly incorrect in that social interaction seems to matter more for intergroup attitudes than functional interdependence. Under some circumstances, for example, cooperative relations do not improve intergroup attitudes even when there has not been a history of previous conflict. Its major difficulty is that ingroup–outgroup membership sometimes seems to cause intergroup differentiation when there is neither cooperative interaction within, nor competitive relations between, groups. The next section considers this issue directly.

3   Social categorization and intergroup discrimination

During the 1960s and early 1970s several studies reported results which openly challenged the functional theory. They found that incompatible group goals were not necessary and that ingroup–outgroup membership *per se* seemed sufficient for intergroup competition (Doise, 1969b; Ferguson and Kelley, 1964; Kahn and Ryen, 1972; Rabbie and Horwitz, 1969; Tajfel *et al.*, 1971).

The results were most clear in the research of Tajfel *et al.* (1971). These investigators explored whether *social categorization per se* was sufficient for intergroup discrimination. A social categorization is a discontinuous cognitive division or classification of individuals into distinct groups. They divided subjects into two groups on the basis of a trivial, *ad hoc* criterion and had them make decisions about monetary rewards for anonymous members of the ingroup and the outgroup. There was no conflict of interests nor history of hostility between the groups, no utilitarian link between intergroup discrimination and subjects' self-interest, no face-to-face interaction within or between groups, and group membership was anonymous. Thus social categorization or the ingroup–outgroup division was isolated from all other variables which normally determine cohesiveness within groups or antagonism between them. It was even explained that the recipients of the monetary sums were identified by their group affiliation solely for administrative convenience.

Nevertheless, the basic result was that subjects discriminated in their decisions in favour of ingroup and against outgroup members. Moreover they were competitive; not only did they give more money to ingroup than outgroup members but they were willing to give them less than was possible in absolute terms in order to give them relatively more than outgroup members. These findings have been extensively replicated (see Turner, 1980).

It is also worth noting there is no evidence that the data are artifactual. Post-experimental enquiries do not reveal the subjects to believe that they are expected to discriminate, to share any notion of how they should behave, or to be trying to please the experimenter (Billig, 1972; Turner, 1975b). There are three relevant experiments. Tajfel and Billig (1974) suspected that subject's responses might be due to their unfamiliarity with and hence anxiety about the experimental setting. Contrary to hypothesis, familiarizing subjects with the setting increased intergroup discrimination. Billig (1973) hypothesized that subjects were behaving in terms of what they perceived to be the appropriate social norms. He allowed subjects who were about to make their decisions to discuss the study with those who had already discriminated, assuming that the latter would communicate their normative expectations and so increase the former's discrimination. Again contrary to hypothesis, the second set of subjects discriminated less than the first. Thus if normative expectations were communicated, they seem to work against rather than explain the usual data. Both these experiments illustrate that subjects in the minimal group paradigm (as the experimental setting is described) do not always conform to researchers' expectations. Nevertheless, it has been argued that their actions reflect 'demand characteristics'. St Claire and Turner (in preparation) reasoned that if this were true, then observer-subjects exposed to the same experimental cues as categorized subjects should be able to predict the latter's responses. In fact they overestimated their fairness. There was also evidence, in line with Billig's study, that fairness was perceived as the socially desirable strategy.

Thus subjects' responses do not seem to be based on the subjective strangeness of the setting, cultural norms or demand characteristics, but seem to be a genuine psychological effect of the ingroup–outgroup division.

This discriminatory effect seems to generalize across independent and dependent variables and methodological paradigms. Billig and Tajfel (1973) demonstrated that it does not depend upon criterial classification, but is obtained even when division into groups is explicitly random. Other studies illustrate that social categorization *per se* also causes perceptual and attitudinal biases and differential attraction to ingroup and outgroup members (Brewer and Silver, 1978; Brown and Turner, 1979; Doise *et al.*, 1972; Turner, 1978a). The experiments cited at the beginning of this section report findings similar to those of Tajfel *et al.* in different settings. Since they were published there has been continual flow of research results all tending to confirm their initial implications (for example, Brewer, 1979; Doise, 1978; Tajfel, 1978a; Turner, 1975a, 1980). Thus far, the more carefully researchers have examined whether social categorization *per se* or ingroup–outgroup membership is sufficient for intergroup discrimination, the more the answer has been clearly in the affirmative. The conclusion must needs be that there are social psychological processes intrinsic to or stimulated merely by ingroup–outgroup divisions which tend to create discriminatory social relations.

One process which has been proposed, the cognitive balance principle, will not be discussed here. Firstly, because there are both consistent and inconsistent data (Hinkle and Schopler, 1979; Rabbie and Horwitz, 1969; Worchel, Lind and Kaufman, 1975). Secondly, because what seems to be its central proposition, that discriminatory intergroup behaviour simply reflects differential ingroup–outgroup attraction, seems to be untrue. There is no direct relationship between differential attraction and discriminatory biases in terms of either independent or dependent variables (see Dion, 1973; Kennedy and Stephan, 1977; Turner, Brown, and Tajfel, 1979; compare Rabbie and Huygen, 1974). Intragroup attraction does have effects, but in ways that can be accounted for by other theories. Thirdly, the principle seems somewhat *ad hoc* and partly vacuous: its derivations in this field tend to be non-distinctive and leave explanatory gaps; thus it may be cognitively consistent to favour members of an arbitrary

ingroup over members of an arbitrary outgroup, but it is not
obvious why this should be true. Fourthly, there seems to be no
direct evidence that ingroup favouritism is mediated by a need for
cognitive consistency.

Two processes, however, do seem plausible: the categorization
process, and the social comparison process.

3.1 *The categorization process*

Tajfel (1969a, 1972b; Tajfel and Wilkes, 1963) proposes a
categorization process such that the systematic superimposition
of a classification upon a stimulus dimension leads to the perceptual accentuation of intraclass similarities and interclass differences on that dimension. He assumes that the criterial or defining
attributes of a class are inferred from the correlated characteristics
of its members and that these criterial attributes tend to be
assigned to all members of the class as common properties. In
consequence, imposing classifications upon stimuli tends to
transform continuous but correlated similarities and differences
into perceptual discontinuities between classes. He also assumes
that the process operates in social perception to produce
stereotyping: the assignment of characteristics to individuals on
the basis of their group membership (see chapter 5).

Doise (1978) considers that the process causes intergroup discrimination: social categorization *per se* induces individuals to
perceive themselves and others in terms of their group memberships; therefore, they perceive themselves as similar to ingroup
members (or ingroup members as similar to themselves) and different from outgroup members; these cognitive distinctions produce differential intergroup behaviour and attitudes.

There are several data consistent with Doise's analysis. Firstly,
social categorization (the independent variable) seems to be the
effective cause of intergroup discrimination. Some studies have
unconfounded it from similarities and differences between the
subjects (as antecedent conditions not consequent effects). Billig
and Tajfel (1973; see Billig, 1973) assigned similar or different code numbers to subjects on the basis of a criterion or
explicitly randomly under conditions where they were either
divided into groups or not consistent with their code numbers.
Both the criterial and the arbitrary social categorization, but
neither criterial nor arbitrary similarities and differences *per se*,

were sufficient for intergroup discrimination. Brewer and Silver (1978) also found that both criterial and arbitrary social classifications cause attitudinal biases. Allen and Wilder (1975) divided subjects into groups on the basis of a trivial criterion and manipulated explicit similarity in beliefs to both ingroup and outgroup members. There was discrimination in all conditions, which increased with similarity to ingroup members. Thus the ingroup–outgroup division was sufficiently powerful that subjects favoured dissimilar ingroup members over similar outgroup members. These experiments suggest that it is not just similarities and differences but the discontinuous similarities and differences produced by the categorization processes which are crucial to favouritism.

Two studies indicate that intergroup discrimination depends upon subjects perceiving each other as representatives of their group. Wilder (1978) provided information which 'individuated' outgroup members so that they could be perceived as differentiated persons instead of as anonymous group members. In consequence, intergroup discrimination decreased. Brown and Turner (1979) asked subjects to estimate the performances of ingroup and outgroup members with whom they had some degree of face-to-face contact as individual persons and found no discrimination. Under similar conditions where two ingroup–outgroup divisions were criss-crossed, subjects seemed to resort to intergroup as opposed to interpersonal evaluations because the former were more informative; intergroup discrimination reappeared and was most pronounced where members of two ingroups were judged in relation to members of two outgroups.

Secondly, there is direct evidence that social categorization *per se* induces the perception of intragroup similarities and intergroup differences (Allen and Wilder, 1979; Doise, Deschamps, and Meyer, 1978; Hensley and Duval, 1976, as discussed in Brewer, 1979). Research on stereotyping also produces supportive data (see chapter 5, and Tajfel, 1969a, 1972b; Tajfel and Wilkes, 1963).

Thirdly, manipulating the salience of social categorization increases ingroup bias. Doise (1978) reports that 'symbolic' encounter between ingroup and outgroup members (making subjects aware that they must rate outgroup as well as ingroup members) tends to enhance differentiation, as does 'collective' encounter (interaction between more than one representative of the ingroup and outgroup). Turner (1978a) investigated self-favouritism where group membership was either salient or not. Under the latter conditions, subjects favoured themselves over both ingroup and outgroup members, but less against ingroup and more against outgroup members in the former conditions.

Finally, intergroup differentiation is sometimes enhanced by common fate, proximity and social interaction, and similarities and differences (Allen and Wilder, 1975; Hensley and Duval, 1976; Rabbie and Horwitz, 1969; Rabbie and Huygen, 1974). These variables can be conceptualized as cognitive criteria for social categorization which help to define individuals as members of a distinct social unit.

Thus the categorization process may be one reason for the effects of social categorization *per se*: subjects may discriminate because they tend to stereotype themselves as similar or different on the basis of their group memberships. Even under conditions of arbitrary social categorization, there is a distinctive subjective correlation between the salient aspects of the self-concept and ingroup–outgroup membership and hence a basis for attributing similarities and differences.

3.2 *The social comparison process*

Tajfel and Turner (1979) propose that social categorization *per se* stimulates a self-evaluative social comparison process. They assume that social categorizations tend to be internalized to define the self in the social situation and hence contribute to self-evaluation. They further assume that one's self-esteem as a group member depends upon the evaluative outcomes of social comparisons between the ingroup and the outgroup. Since it can be supposed that individuals desire positive self-esteem, they conclude that there is a tendency to seek positive distinctiveness for the ingroup in comparison with the outgroup. Thus their hypothesis is that self-evaluative social comparisons directly produce competitive intergroup processes which motivate attitudinal biases and discriminatory actions.

The most direct evidence for this analysis is that intergroup discrimination seems to contain a competitive component even under conditions of functional independence. The tendency to maximize the differences in relative outcomes for ingroup and outgroup members seems the most important single motive in the minimal group paradigm (Turner, 1980). Brewer and Silver (1978) find that both independent and competitive groups adopt this 'winning' strategy. Turner, Brown, and Tajfel (1979) demonstrate that it is maintained even where it conflicts directly with subjects' self-interest. Studies in other paradigms also report a spontaneously competitive element in intergroup differentiation and implicate social comparison as the cause (Doise and Weinberger, 1973; Ferguson and Kelley, 1964; Rabbie and Wilkens, 1971).

Three experiments have attempted to manipulate the social comparison process. Turner (1978b) finds that stable status similarities between groups produce more ingroup bias than stable status dissimilarities. Turner and Brown (1978) report some complex results generally consistent with the idea that secure (stable and legitimate) status differences between groups tend to minimize and insecure differences to enhance competitive biases. Turner, Brown, and Tajfel (1979) find that subjects are less fair and more discriminatory towards relevant than irrelevant comparison outgroups, especially where they distribute high monetary rewards. Thus at least under some conditions both spontaneous and manipulated social comparisons seem to increase ingroup bias.

More evidence is that there seems to be a definite motivational bias for positive self-esteem in intergroup behaviour. Oakes and Turner (1980) confirmed the prediction that minimal intergroup discrimination would increase self-esteem compared to a control condition in which categorized subjects were not able to discriminate. Alternative explanations of the result are possible, but it is consistent with the positive distinctiveness principle. There is also the fact, of course, that ingroups are usually favoured over outgroups. Even where there are prior evaluative differences between groups it is not the case, as the categorization process predicts that these correlated differences tend to be directly accentuated; evaluative superiorities tend to be enhanced and evaluative inferiorities minimized (Brewer, 1979; Van Knippenberg and Wilke, 1979).

The role of the self-evaluative motive is also supported by the effects of status differences on intergroup behaviour. Status differences represent the outcomes of intergroup comparisons conferring positive or negative distinctiveness and also the antecedent conditions for different social strategies (individual mobility, social creativity, social competition, etc.) directed at the maintenance or protection of self-esteem (Tajfel, 1978c, Tajfel and Turner, 1979). Their effects can be complex but there seems little doubt as the social comparison process expects that they are important determinants of competitive intergroup biases (Tajfel, 1978a).

Turner and Brown (1978) manipulated whether status differences were perceived as secure or insecure. High status groups tended to discriminate when either a legitimate superiority was threatened or an illegitimate superiority was perceived as stable; when an illegitimate superiority was also unstable, they tended to stress alternative status dimensions. Low-status groups tended to discriminate when their inferiority was illegitimate and especially when it was also unstable. Thus, as one might expect, there are different reactions to status differences according to whether the groups are seeking to preserve or restore positive distinctiveness.

These data make it difficult to explain discrimination on the basis of ingroup–outgroup divisions solely in terms of cognitive processes; motivational factors need to be superimposed (see Brewer, 1979; Turner, 1975a). The simplest solution is to assume that the categorization and the social comparison process are complementary. There are many possible complexities in such complementarity, but we shall do no more than suggest that the former is the necessary and the latter the sufficient condition for competitive intergroup differentiation (see figure 3.1). The categorization process produces the perceptual accentuation of intragroup similarities and intergroup differences and thus makes salient or perceptually prominent the criterial or relevant aspects of ingroup–outgroup membership. In this way it selects the specific dimensions for self-evaluation and social comparison in the given setting. It also ensures that intergroup comparisons focus on perceptual discontinuities between ingroup and outgroup members so that positive differences (distinctiveness) and not similarities contribute to self-esteem. The social comparison process transforms simple perceptual or cognitive discriminations into differential attitudes and actions favouring the ingroup over the outgroup. It motivates the competitive enhancement of criterial differences between the groups and other strategies apart from direct discrimination to achieve positive distinctiveness.

This hypothesis can be described as the *social identity principle* since it stresses that social categorization *per se* causes intergroup discrimination through its impact on self-perception. Both Doise

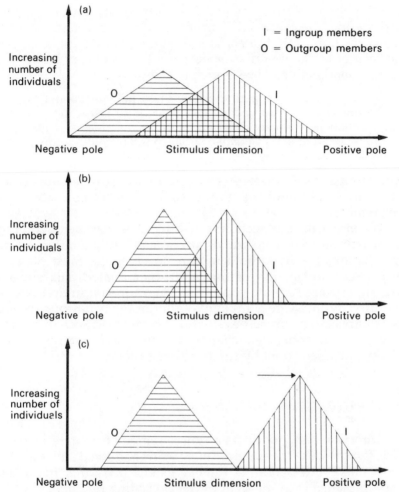

Figure 3.1   The complementary effects of the categorization and the social comparison process on intergroup differentiation.
(a)   The baseline distribution of stimulus values displaying the modal (average, representative, typical, dominant, etc.) characteristics of ingroup and outgroup members.
(b)   The effect of the categorization process: the groups are perceptually differentiated in that fewer individuals occupy the overlapping area but their modal characteristics have not changed.
(c)   The effect of the social comparison process: the ingroup differentiates itself from the outgroup on a perceptually salient dimension in such a way as to increase the distance between their modal characteristics.

and Tajfel and Turner assume that individuals tend to perceive and define themselves in terms of the superimposed social categorization. Tajfel (1972b; see Turner, 1982) uses the term 'social identity' to describe aspects of the self-concept based upon group memberships. The principle states:

> that the systematic superimposition upon individuals of a cognitive division into ingroup and outgroup tends to cause the perceptual accentuation of stereotypical intragroup similarities and intergroup differences and self-evaluative social comparisons in terms of these similarities and differences.

It can be assumed that these effects depend upon the salience and normative relevance of the social categorization for social behaviour.

To summarize this section: much recent experimentation indicates that social categorization *per se* can cause intergroup discrimination; the hypothesis which provides the most plausible theoretical explanation of this and other related data suggests that, under appropriate conditions, ingroup–outgroup divisions can directly motivate competitive intergroup behaviour through their implications for self-evaluation. In the next section we consider how this conclusion changes the analysis of intergroup conflict bequeathed to us by the functional theory.

4   *The resolution of social conflict*

The functional theory offers a simple remedy for intergroup conflict: the provision of superordinate goals and the development of cooperative interaction. To what extent does this hypothesis remain plausible in the light of the preceding research?

The first basic point is that cooperative interdependence (superordinate goals) conflicts whereas competitive interdependence (conflicts of interest) correlates with ingroup–outgroup divisions. If we assume that the latter create competitive tendencies, then it seems likely that there is an asymmetry in the functional determination of intergroup behaviour. Intergroup competition should be much easier to obtain than cooperation.

This does not mean that cooperative interdependence is incompatible with positive distinctiveness. On the contrary, a superordinate goal often demands a division of labour between cooperating groups, the differentiation and coordination of their activities into separate but complementary work-roles. The enactment of such distinctive work-roles should provide each group with favourable intergroup comparisons at the same time as the common objective engenders consensual social values. In consequence, a social consensus could develop that the groups share a series of complementary superiorities and inferiorities across relevant status dimensions. Since each group should be able to admire the distinctive superiorities of the outgroup and derive positive self-esteem from its own, these complementary status differences should help to reconcile positive distinctiveness with positive intergroup attitudes. Such social arrangements should tend to eliminate or reduce the negative consequences of ingroup–outgroup divisions.

The problem is that cooperative interdependence may not be sufficient for cooperative interaction. Since it tends to conflict with the ingroup–outgroup division, the latter may counteract its effects and prevent cooperative interaction. In this case, complementary status differences may not emerge to neutralize the negative effects of group boundaries. It is not evident as yet that cooperative interdependence automatically lowers the salience of ingroup–outgroup divisions. As we saw in the first section cooperative interdependence and even cooperative behaviour unconfounded with social interaction did not reduce biased intergroup attitudes compared to competitive interdependence.

The picture seems to be the reverse for competitive interdependence. Since it tends to be congruent with group boundaries, it seems likely to be sufficient for competitive interaction and may also tend to increase the salience of the social division. Given a salient division into groups, competitive relations may be the natural state of affairs. This does not bode well if conflict-resolution is to depend upon the effects of superordinate goals.

The obvious objection to this analysis is that the functional theory is also a theory of group-formation. It states that a group structure tends to emerge where mutually cooperative interaction between a number of individuals has become sufficiently stabilized. The determinants of social cooperation are functional relationships. Thus group-formation is basically an effect or symptom of cooperative interaction. Its special characteristics are merely the development of social roles and norms and shared values which coordinate and regulate goal-related activities. It

follows that cooperative interaction between groups, once initiated, must inevitably tend to reduce and ultimately eliminate
ingroup–outgroup divisions. The implication is that cooperative
interaction, even if not cooperative interdependence *per se*, does
this automatically and is the basic means of decreasing the salience of group boundaries.

Sherif and Sherif's research demonstrates that this can be true
under certain conditions. There is evidence that their superordinate goals fused the conflicting groups into one (see Doise, 1971).
However, these data may represent a special case, since these
groups came into existence and were defined solely in terms of
their activities in the summer camp. There was no external criterion by which they could maintain their differences during
cooperative interaction. The general validity of the hypothesis
that social cooperation causes group-formation needs to be considered.

To do so, it is useful to bring out the tacit assumptions which
the functional theory shares with the mainstream conceptualization of the social group in experimental social psychology. Turner
(1982) describes these assumptions, or perhaps emphases is
better, as the *social cohesion* model. It is important to point out that
specific theorists such as the Sherifs might not endorse some of
these emphases and indeed would almost certainly reject a few.
However, our discussion is concerned with the functional theory
in its most simple and, we would argue, most general form, not
as the property of any specific individual.

The model can be summarized as follows. Motivational (or
functional) interdependence for the satisfaction of needs,
achievement of goals, or consensual validation of attitudes and
values between persons leads to their social and psychological
interdependence. The main expressions of the latter are mutual
interpersonal influence and attraction and affiliative social
interaction. Over time, social relations tend to become stabilized,
organized and prescribed through the development of a system
of status and role relationships, social norms and shared values
(social structure). Individuals become psychologically attached to
the group through the development of cohesive social relationships. 'Cohesiveness' stands for the degree to which members
are attracted to each other as individual persons, to the characteristics of a group as a whole, and to group activities. In practice,
it indicates interpersonal attraction since, implicitly or explicitly, it

is denied that attraction to the group can be more than attraction to its members and assumed that the latter reflects the extent to which they satisfy one's needs, directly (such as through attitudinal similarity) or indirectly (such as through cooperative goal locomotion). Lott and Lott (1965) define cohesiveness as that group property which is inferred from the number and strength of mutual positive attitudes between group members. The fundamental criterion for group-formation, therefore, is not group structure (which, although important, is derivative) but the development of affective or emotional bonds between persons based on their motivational interdependence.

There is little argument that group behaviour tends to be characterized by mutual cooperation, attraction and influence between members. However, it is not so evident that group-belongingness is based upon motivational interdependence and interpersonal attraction. This theory is difficult to square with the effects of social categorization *per se* and other data to be discussed below. To discuss these data, it is useful to formulate an alternative set of assumptions, the *social identification* model (Turner, 1982).

This theory makes the cognitive component of self-attitudes, not the affective component of interpersonal attitudes, the basis for group behaviour. What matters for group-belongingness is not individuals' social relationships and attitudes to others but how they perceive and define themselves. A social group is defined as two or more individuals who perceive themselves to be members of the same social category or share a common social identification of themselves. The latter is some social categorization which has been internalized as a part of their self-concept. Others are reacted to as group members in so far as they are included within and exemplify some self-defining social category. The theory explains group-formation in terms of the formation and internalization of social categorizations into self-conception.

It is worth noting that this model does not deny group cohesiveness but sees it as a symptom and not a determinant of social identification. It distinguishes between interpersonal and inter-member attraction: liking for others as differentiated, individual persons and as representatives of the common characteristics of the group. The latter is assumed to be a product of the mutual stereotypical similarities perceived between group members due to the operation of the categorization process.

There are at least three stands of evidence for the analysis of group-formation as a process of social identification.

4.1 *Interpersonal attraction and group-formation*

Does group-formation depend upon interpersonal attraction? The main evidence is that variables which determine positive interpersonal attitudes (attitudinal similarity, common fate, shared threat, social interaction, proximity, cooperation and competition, etc.) are known to increase intragroup cohesiveness.

Sole, Marton, and Hornstein (1975) conducted three field experiments on altruism. They manipulated degrees of opinion similarity between subjects and a stranger who needed help. The basic result was that attraction to the stranger tended to increase directly with similarity, but that helping depended on total similarity which allowed the stranger to be categorized unambiguously as a member of the 'we-group'. Thus if altruism indicates group-formation, this depended upon the cognitive and not the affective consequences of similarity. As similarity increased, it passed some critical threshold whereby the subjects perceived not merely similarity to but identity with the stranger, and a discontinuous social categorization was formed. The implication is that similarity may contribute to group-formation as a cognitive criterion for social categorization.

The same may be true of the other variables mentioned above. They all seem to have in common the capacity to generate cognitive boundaries between people, to create social discontinuities, which may define them as members of distinct 'perceptual units' (Dion, 1979). They may increase cohesiveness because they directly promote interpersonal attraction or because, as determinants of social identification, they enhance intermember attraction. It cannot be assumed that their effects in this respect necessarily support the social cohesion model.

This is especially so since there is direct evidence that interpersonal attraction is not necessary for group-formation. The experiments in the last section demonstrate that social categorization *per se*, even on an explicitly random basis, is sufficient for group behaviour in that the subjects display similar or collective reactions to others consistently related to their own and the others' group affiliations. This would have been just as true if they had favoured outgroup members over ingroup members. Thus group-formation takes place in the complete absence of interpersonal relationships or any variables which might predict interpersonal attraction. These studies also show that social categorization *per se* causes intragroup attraction, despite the fact that subjects have no idea of the specific persons in their group. They seem to like individuals as and because they are group members, not because of their personal characteristics. In other words this seems to represent intermember attraction produced by the perception of assumed stereotypical similarities.

Other experiments in different paradigms make the same point more dramatically. They point to group-formation and resultant cohesiveness under conditions where there are or should be negative interpersonal relations and attitudes between group members. It seems that shared threat engenders favourable attitudes to group members despite racial prejudice against them (Burnstein and McRae, 1962; Feshbach and Singer, 1957). Proximity and social interaction create intragroup cohesiveness despite strong and relevant attitudinal disagreements between members (Rabbie and Huygen, 1974). Prejudiced whites include black supporters within their reference groups for some normative judgements but not others (Boyanowsky and Allen, 1973; Malof and Lott, 1962). Intergroup competition and intragroup cooperation induce positive attitudes towards group members who are, in fact, frustrating and detrimental to the collaborative effort (Kalin and Marlowe, 1968; Myers, 1962). And low-cohesive dyad members, who dislike and compete with each other as individuals, rate their group as favourably as a collective entity as high-cohesive dyad members (Dion, 1973). In these studies individuals seem to be defined as group members despite their negative personal attributes and, once so defined, they are liked. These data suggest that one can like people as group members at the same time that one dislikes them as individual persons.

It is noticeable that the same experiments which create problems for the social cohesion model indicate the central role of social categorization. In the studies immediately above the relevant variables, shared threat, proximity, common fate, etc., can easily be construed as determining perceptual unit-formation. Other researchers have come to the same conclusion that cognitive factors play an important role in group-formation (Brewer, 1979; Dion, 1973, 1979; Rabbie and Huygen, 1974; Sole,

Marton, and Hornstein, 1975; Worchel, 1979). Thus social categorization and not interpersonal attraction may be necessary and sufficient for group behaviour. Individuals may become a group simply because they perceive themselves to share some form of discontinuous homogeneity.

This conclusion, we should remind ourselves, does not imply that social groups do not tend to be cohesive. They should be so for several reasons consistent with the social identification model: social categorization directly produces intermember attraction; social categorization and interpersonal attraction may sometimes be correlated effects of the same variables, and because of the need for positive self-esteem, individuals should tend to define their group attributes positively, and be more likely to perceive inclusive similarities between themselves and attractive than unattractive others.

4.2 The effects of group failure on cohesiveness

If cohesiveness depends upon motivational interdependence or mutual need-satisfaction, then it should be the case that groups which mediate rewards for their members, which succeed in reaching their goals, should be more cohesive than those which do not. Failure, defeat, deprivation, or other negative outcomes related to group membership should reduce intragroup cohesiveness. This is perhaps the central prediction of the social cohesion model; individuals come together for cooperative success not failure. There is much supportive evidence, but also some disconfirmations of the prediction (Lott and Lott, 1965).

One recent example will suffice. Kennedy and Stephan (1977) manipulated the success or failure of dyad members on a task under conditions of intragroup cooperation or competition. They expected cooperative success to increase cohesiveness. One might also have expected competitive success to reduce cohesiveness, since an antagonistic relationship produces positive consequences. The opposite results were obtained; cooperative failure led to more ingroup bias than success, and competitive success more than failure. These data are obviously problematic for a theory which makes cooperative reward-mediation the basis for cohesive social attitudes.

 Lott and Lott (1965), who are reinforcement theorists, accept that instances in which shared threat and failure do not reduce and even increase group cohesiveness pose a serious difficulty for the reward or need-satisfaction perspective. Their solution is two-fold. Firstly, they assume that failure is sometimes attributed to factors external to the group (bad luck, temporary difficulties, etc.) and so reinterpreted as shared, external threat. Secondly, they suggest that where group efforts can defeat the threat, it will motivate increased cooperation (and so cohesiveness). Thus they deny that failure *per se* can increase cohesiveness; shared threat stimulates intragroup cooperation precisely to avoid failure and achieve success.

This is a plausible hypothesis in many circumstances and yet, theoretically, it is not fully satisfactory. It tends to assume what it needs to explain. Why should individuals react to failure as a shared threat to the group, or believe that they can cope with the threat through group action, unless they remain cohesive? The whole issue is to explain why the actual or expected costs of group membership do not make them less cohesive and so less likely to adopt such tactics. A possible solution (which does not necessarily reject Lott and Lott's specific hypothesis) is to assume that shared threat and failure can have a positive impact on social identification and that the latter mediates cohesiveness.

There are two available hypotheses. Firstly, shared threat and failure are forms of common fate which should directly enhance the salience of group boundaries. Whether positive or negative, common fate induces perceived homogeneity between group members and so social identification. The more salient and distinctive the fate, the more there is cohesiveness. Thus the relative impact of success and failure would vary with their relative distinctiveness in specific settings (importance, frequency, novelty, the degree to which they differentiated between groups, etc.).

Rabbie and Horwitz (1969) provide some relevant data. They imposed differential, common fate on pairs of groups by rewarding one and depriving the other. Positive and negative fate increased ingroup bias. Deprivation could have been externally attributed, but it was nevertheless final; so it is difficult to interpret cohesiveness as instrumental to future rewards. The parsimonious explanation is to assume that reward and deprivation worked in the same way as shared experiences which highlighted the ingroup–outgroup division.

Secondly, if social identification represents a self-attitude, then it should tend to change as do other attitudes. There seem to be

two basic inducements to attitude change: as a result of direct
social influence from others, and as a reaction to one's own overt
behaviour. Social identification could change in both ways. In the
former case, individuals may be directly persuaded to define
themselves in terms of certain social categories by attractive or
credible others, as when, perhaps, subjects are categorized by
prestigious experimenters. We shall concentrate on the latter
case.

Research indicates that private attitudes tend to follow public
behaviour (Wicklund and Brehm, 1976). Therefore, it may be
that simply acting as group members is sufficient for individuals
to define themselves as such. Three relevant processes have been
identified, reinforcement or incentive effects, cognitive dissonance, and causal attribution. The important point is that only
the incentive theory expects more attitude change when overt
behaviour produces positive outcomes. The latter two can both
predict the opposite. Cognitive dissonance theory states that
where individuals engage in counterattitudinal behaviour with a
sense of personal responsibility for their actions (high choice,
commitment, awareness of possible negative consequences, etc.),
they need to change their attitudes to justify their actions; the
need for justification, to maintain cognitive consistency, is greater
where there are negative outcomes. Attribution theory states that
individuals may tend to explain their behaviour in terms of internal factors such as attitudes to the degree that they cannot explain
it in terms of external factors such as the situation, role demands
or rewards. Thus some data indicate (see Harvey and Smith,
1977) that where subjects are rewarded for activities which they
would normally perform, their intrinsic motivation decreases
since they now explain their actions in terms of the extrinsic
rewards.

If we apply these ideas to social identification, we can suppose
that under some conditions individuals will tend to justify and
explain their actions more in terms of their self-definition as a
group member the more negative the outcomes, whereas under
other conditions, there will be more self-attitude change with
positive outcomes. Thus both group success and failure could
increase or decrease social identification depending on the circumstances in which they occurred.

Turner *et al*. (in preparation) conducted two experiments to test
the dissonance hypothesis. They predicted that where subjects

engaged in self-discrepant group behaviour with personal responsibility, group failure would create more social identification than success, but that the opposite would be true without personal responsibility (the incentive effect). They assumed that social identification would increase cohesiveness.

In the first study subjects had high or low choice about doing a group task on which they expected to and did succeed or fail. With high choice, there was more cohesiveness after failure than success, but less after failure than success with low choice. In the second study, subjects either committed themselves or not to staying in their group for the duration of an intergroup competition and either won or lost on the first task. Committed groups became more cohesive and biased against the outgroup after defeat than victory. They also developed *higher* self-esteem and attributed their performance more *internally* after defeat than victory. The reverse results were found in the uncommitted groups. The self-esteem and attribution data seem to rule out Lott and Lott's explanation in this instance and provide some evidence that changes in self-attitudes are taking place. It looks as if once subjects identify, they evaluate their group and hence themselves positively, whether or not they were successful. It is also worth noting that both the high choice, success and the committed, winning groups showed remarkably low levels of cohesiveness. There is a strong implication that self-attribution processes were at work: these subjects did not seem to need to feel part of their group, since the extrinsic rewards were a sufficient explanation of their group actions. Thus it may be that cooperative success sometimes provides extrinsic rewards which decrease intrinsic social identification.

In general, the above studies suggest that group cohesiveness is not simply a matter of mutual need-satisfaction. There is a sense in which under appropriate conditions individuals cannot but see themselves as group members for good or ill.

4.3 *The effects of cooperative and competitive interaction*

Is it the case that cooperative and competitive interaction themselves directly produce positive and negative intergroup attitudes? One might think that this could be taken for granted. However, we suggested above that they might determine social attitudes indirectly as cognitive criteria for social categorization. Other researchers have come to very similar conclusions. They argue that cooperation and competition reduce or enhance the salience of we/they distinctions and that the latter are the important determinants of intergroup biases.

Dion (1973, 1979) describes this as the cognitive differentiation hypothesis. He conceptualizes social groups as 'perceptual units' and considers that intergroup competition contributes to unit-formation because it induces perceived homogeneity (common fate and similarity) within the ingroup and perceived heterogeneity (opposed fate and dissimilarity) between ingroup and outgroup members. So, too, Brewer (1979) argues that explicit competition can serve to clarify ingroup–outgroup boundaries where the cognitive distinction might otherwise be ambiguous, and Worchel (1979) states that it draws clear boundaries, accentuates we/they differences and makes these groupings a salient feature of the situation.

It can be presumed that intragroup cooperation has the same effects as intergroup competition, and that intragroup competition and intergroup cooperation tend to blur and even redraw group boundaries. There is in fact a definite implication that ingroup–outgroup formation is more important than intergroup relations in determining intergroup attitudes. Thus intragroup cooperation and competition could be more effective in increasing and decreasing ingroup biases than intergroup competition and cooperation. An experiment which seems to illustrate this, but which can also be explained to some extent by the social cohesion model, is reported by Goldman, Stockbauer, and McAuliffe (1977). They manipulated both intragroup and intergroup co-operation or competition. Both variables produced definite behavioural effects, but the former was much more important for social attitudes. Ingroup ratings were more favourable with intragroup cooperation (5.64) than competition (0.77). but outgroup ratings were only non-significantly more favourable with intergroup cooperation (2.59) than competition (1.56). Thus the consequence is that intragroup cooperation led to ingroup favouritism and intragroup competition to outgroup favouritism, independently of the functional relationship with the outgroup.

Worchel (1979) draws the important inference from the cognitive hypothesis that the best way to reduce intergroup conflict is to remove or reduce salient differences between the groups, and that cooperative interaction mitigates conflict only to the degree that it can and does accomplish this result. In other words, to produce lasting positive attitudes, intergroup cooperation has to eliminate the ingroup–outgroup distinction and tend towards intragroup cooperation. Worchel outlines several variables which may maintain group boundaries despite cooperative encounters: distinctive physical or visible differences between ingroup and outgroup members, cooperative failure, the intensity of previous conflict, the infrequency of and limited duration of cooperative encounters, disparities in power and status between the groups, etc. He reports two experiments to support his analysis that such variables mitigate conflict-reduction despite intergroup cooperation.

Worchel, Andreoli, and Folger (1977) hypothesized that the effects of cooperative intergroup interaction would depend upon whether previous interaction had made the ingroup–outgroup division salient. In the first stage of the study, they manipulated intergroup cooperation, independence or competition; attraction to the outgroup decreased in that order. In the second stage, the same groups now all cooperated and either succeeded or failed. Cooperative success increased attraction to the outgroup, but cooperative failure increased it only where the groups had not previously competed and decreased it where they had. In other words, the groups which had previously cooperated or been independent reacted to the outcomes of later cooperation as if they were one common group: either success or failure increased cohesiveness. The previously competitive groups reacted as if they were still separate entities, willing to distance themselves if cooperation was unsuccessful. This experiment makes two clear points. Firstly, that cooperative interaction can function to redefine cognitive boundaries. It is impossible to explain the qualitatively different effects of previous cooperation and competition on reactions to success and failure if we assume that they merely created more or less attraction to the outgroup. The data imply the elimination or maintenance of a social division. Secondly, that where cooperative interaction does not eliminate the ingroup–outgroup division, it does not necessarily improve intergroup attitudes. In this case, its effects may depend at the least on whether it results in success or failure.

Worchel *et al.* (1978) investigated the effects of distinctive visible differences on the results of intergroup cooperation. The

design of this experiment was similar to that above except that
ingroup and outgroup members also either wore identical or distinctive laboratory coats (both white or white and red). Similarity
of dress produced a strong main effect; cooperation led to more
intergroup attraction when the groups dressed identically than
distinctively. It also interacted with the other variables. Differences in dress retained conflict-reduction when cooperation
ended in failure, regardless of the type of previous interaction.
They also inhibited intergroup attraction for previously competitive groups when cooperation ended in success, but not for previously cooperative groups. These results support the hypothesis
that intergroup attitudes are a function of salient intergroup differences and that cooperation does not reduce conflict where
such differences are maintained. They also help to confirm the
interpretation of the first experiment. So long as a visible difference maintained the ingroup–outgroup division, even previously
cooperative groups reacted to cooperative failure like the competitive groups.

    These two elegant experiments provide evidence that the role
of cooperative and competitive interaction may be to define individuals as members of the same or different social categories or to
minimize or accentuate the salience of existing social categorizations. They may not produce very different effects on intergroup
attitudes unless they have these cognitive consequences.

4.4   *An alternative perspective: group-formation as*
a determinant of social cooperation

If the social identification analysis is valid, then group-formation
is not merely a symptom of cohesive social attitudes developed
through cooperative interaction. There are at least three classes of
determinants: (a) social or physical variables which induce individuals to perceive themselves as defined by distinctive common
attributes and experiences; (b) social action on the basis of such
attributes producing positive or negative outcomes; and (c) other
processes of direct social influence aiming at persuading people to
change their self-attitudes towards self-definition in terms of
some social category. Social cooperation is an important empirical
determinant of group-formation because it can and does operate
through these processes. However, there is no intrinsic theoretical link. The ingroup–outgroup division may not be reduced or

eliminated during intergroup cooperation because there may remain distinctive differences between the groups, joint action may be attributed to or justified by the extrinsic outcomes and not explained in terms of common group membership; and group members may adhere to social norms of ingroup–outgroup identification. The ingroup–outgroup division may then tend to reproduce negative intergroup attitudes as soon as the immediate demands of collaborative action are at an end.

Before drawing conclusions from this section, there is one more important point to be made. Much social cooperation may not reflect objective functional relations at all, but may be a direct effect of group-formation. It seems likely that the social group can be an independent variable in the perception of cooperative and competitive interdependence. This can be understood through the operation of the social identity principle. In many cases individuals should tend to perceive their goals, needs or motives as correlated with their group membership; thus their interests should become stereotypical characteristics of the group as a whole. The categorization process, therefore, predicts that individuals should tend to perceive themselves as having similar or identical goals to members of their own group and different or opposed goals to members of other groups. This should provide a powerful basis for intragroup cooperation since group members should perceive their interests not merely as interdependent but as literally identical. Through common category membership we should assign others' goals to ourselves and assume that our goals are shared by others. Some evidence comes from the research of Hornstein (1972, 1976) and his colleagues on altruism. They find that individuals' motivational systems can become linked to the needs of others through common group membership; that is, individuals act (altruistically) as if the goals of other group members have become motives for their own behaviour.

We can assume too that social groups tend to evaluate and compare themselves in terms of their distinctive stereotypical goals and locomotion towards them. The social comparison process predicts that such locomotion should tend to be perceived as competitively interdependent between different groups. Again there is some consistent evidence that social groups seem to be more competitive and perceive their interests more competitively than individuals under the same functional conditions (R. J. Brown and Deschamps, 1980/81; Doise, 1969b; Doise and

Giraud, cited in Doise, 1978; Doise and Sinclair, 1973; Doise and
Weinberger, 1973; Dustin and Davis, 1970; Janssens and Nuttin,
1976; McKillip, Dimiceli, and Luebke, 1977; Wilson and
Kayatani, 1968, and Wilson's other studies previously cited; see
too Brewer and Silver, 1978).

Thus we can derive from the social identity principle the
hypothesis that, under conditions where objective functional
relations are ambiguous, indirect or mixed cooperative and competitive (as they often are in real life), social categorization *per se*
should cause individuals to perceive their interests as cooperatively linked within groups and competitively linked between
groups. The implication is that the formation of a common or
superordinate group tends to induce and stabilize cooperative
behaviour in the same way that an ingroup–outgroup division
elicits competitive tendencies: not merely through the need for
positive distinctiveness, but more basically, because social
categorization directly influences individuals' perceptions of their
goals.

To conclude this section we can summarize the main difficulties with the functional hypothesis that intergroup conflict is
resolved through superordinate goals and state the alternative
perspective. The difficulties are:

1 Superordinate goals need to be perceived to be acted on;
   yet, the social group may constitute an independent variable determining members' perception of their objective
   interests. The very fact of a salient social division into
   groups may create tendencies to perceive competitive
   instead of cooperative interdependence between them.
2 Even where superordinate goals are recognized and intergroup cooperation takes place, the crucial issue for long-
   term conflict-resolution is whether the latter leads to the
   formation of a common or superordinate social group in the
   ways already discussed. Cooperative interaction has no
   special theoretical status as a determinant of group-
   formation and may be counteracted in this respect by other
   variables that may obtain in specific contexts.
3 Where the ingroup–outgroup division is maintained, intergroup cooperation may nevertheless take place and be continued for purely instrumental reasons. However, there is
   no reason to assume in this case that this will produce last-

ing improvements in intergroup relations. On the contrary the expected rewards may provide external justifications of the intergroup behaviour which make changes in private intergroup attitudes unnecessary. As soon as the immediate goal is achieved, the ingroup–outgroup division may tend to reproduce perceived conflicts of interests and partisan social attitudes between the groups.

The evident alternative strategy for conflict-resolution is to take Worchel's hypothesis to its logical conclusion, in other words to attempt directly to minimize and ultimately eliminate ingroup–outgroup distinctions. The most effective social psychological approach may be not so much to seek to manipulate intergroup relations as the encourage their transformation into intragroup relations through the creation of common or superordinate social identifications perceived as relevant to the given social context. The establishment of more salient common identifications between conflicting groups should tend to produce cohesiveness and the perception of cooperative interests between members of the erstwhile subgroups as a direct consequence. The specific measures necessary to achieve this end could include intergroup cooperation, but this would depend upon an analysis of the social forces maintaining group boundaries in the concrete situation. The fundamental point is that the processes implicated in group-formation *per se* may also tend to dictate the cooperative and competitive orientations characteristic respectively of intragroup and intergroup relations.

5 *Conclusion*

The chapter began with Sherif and Sherif's basic proposition that functional relations determine social relations (the character of social interaction and thus the formation of social groups and the relations between them). We have seen that this proposition has proved extremely fruitful in generating research and ideas and that its chief empirical insights into the effects of cooperative and competitive interaction seem still to be valid. However, what is much less certain is any direct impact of functional relations *per se* on intergroup attitudes (section 2), the hypothesis that conflicting interests are necessary for competitive intergroup behaviour (section 3), and the theoretical construal of group formation and conflict-resolution as simple effects of social cooperation (section 4). Ingroup–outgroup membership seems to be an important independent variable in determining cooperation and competition. Thus the recent research argues that in some respects Sherif and Sherif's proposition needs to be reversed; individuals' social relations understood as their social group memberships seem able to determine their functional relations in the sense of their *perceived* goals and hence the character of their social interaction and attitudes. Not objective interests but social identity may be the most predictive social psychological variable for understanding the development and resolution of intergroup conflict.

This conclusion is almost certain to be misunderstood. At least two *caveats* are in order. Firstly, there is no doubt at all that people's objective interests (economic, political, etc.) play a major role in social conflict. The argument is that, at least at the social psychological level of analysis, their effects are probably mediated by their impact on social identifications. There is also no doubt that individuals' goals or purposes do contribute to group-formation and, perhaps even more important, are likely to be critical determinants of the situational salience of specific identifications. However, our theoretical analysis means that we cannot assume any simple one-to-one correspondence between people's objective interests and their group membership nor make the former a direct psychological theory of the latter.

Secondly, there is no implication that social conflict is an inevitable and universal consequence of ingroup–outgroup divisions. Our discussion suggests that at least some processes associated with social categorization produce a *social psychological tendency* to competitive intergroup behaviour. This tendency may at times be counteracted in the real world by other social psychological or more macrosocial processes. The identification of the systematic conditions under which the tendency holds is a large research task to do both with the improvement of social psychological theory and the ascertainment of the boundaries of such theory in relation to other social sciences.

At the moment the usefulness of the present conclusion depends upon the extent to which it helps to stimulate new directions in basic research and provide a fresh perspective for applied work. It is beyond the scope of the chapter to discuss applied implications, but in general terms, the emphasis upon social group membership as an independent or intervening variable in social behaviour would seem to provide a promising perspective from which to consider policies for conflict-resolution (or conflict-intensification). As regards basic research, there are many issues. Perhaps the three most important areas to which attention needs to be directed are: (a) the determinants of group formation (in particular to consider the adequacy of its analysis as a process of social identification or interpersonal attraction); (b) the role of group membership as an antecedent process for social cooperation (the impact of social categorization on group members' perceptions of their needs, goals and motives); and (c) the personal and situational factors that control which of the many social groups to which any individual belongs becomes psychologically salient or prepotent in a specific social enounter.

In general, our conclusion argues that future work needs to be conducted within the context of a wider theoretical interest in basic group processes, and also that the social psychology of the social group needs to confront the questions raised by intergroup behaviour. There seems every hope that research located at the interface of intergroup behaviour and the general psychology of the social group should make a valuable and timely contribution to both fields.

CHAPTER 4

Racial Prejudice

DAVID MILNER

1 Introduction

Racial prejudice presents social psychology with a number of opportunities and problems. On the one hand, given that the concept of attitude is absolutely central to our discipline we can bring a unique understanding to a crucial social issue, and one that disarms many of the accusations of 'irrelevance' that have been levelled at us. On the other hand, racism in its broadest sense is not solely a social psychological phenomenon; it is also a product of historical, economic, political and social factors which fall outside our natural constituency. We have to concede from the outset, then, that the social-psychological perspective is necessary but insufficient.

We cannot cover the broader canvas within this chapter, nor indeed do justice to the entire literature on the subject within social psychology. Consequently we follow three limited objectives: to survey the principal psychological and social-psychological theories of prejudice within a historical perspective; to provide an account of the development of prejudice in children; and to grasp the nettle of describing the effects of prejudice on minority groups. This is not an arbitrary selection of topics but an attempt to bring together three of the most important and potentially fruitful areas of prejudice-related theory and research. The first creates a context of basic individual and group processes within which negative attitudes towards outgroups may develop; the second illustrates the actual sequence of *racial* attitude development in childhood, involving the interaction of these processes with a specific prevailing attitudinal climate; the third considers the psychological consequences of living, as it were, on the receiving end of prejudiced attitudes.

Inevitably, the greater part of both the empirical and theoretical material cited here is American in origin, as a result of that country's pre-eminence in social-psychological research, and of the central importance of race relations in its social and political life. Nevertheless, it will be clear that the insights derived from these sources have relevance to a variety of cultural settings, and empirical material from other contexts will be presented which supports this contention.

2   Theories of prejudice

Social psychology did not seriously engage with the study of racism until the 1920s. When we look at the earlier textbooks in the discipline we find that the Founding Fathers' cognizance of the issue was, to say the least, partial. In William McDougall's *Social Psychology*, published in 1908, 'prejudice' and 'race' merit no mention; however, the section devoted to the 'deleterious consequences of unrestrained and excessive indulgence of the sexual appetite' is followed by a footnote which allows 'the negro' to take a bow. McDougall notes (p. 359): 'It has often been maintained, and not improbably with justice that the backward condition of so many branches of the Negro race is in the main determined by the prevalence of this state of affairs'. This rather grotesque example is not cited to satirize or berate the alchemists of the science with their ignorance. Rather it illuminates the contamination of theory in social psychology by contemporary social values. The very pejorative nature of this instance also helps to explain why race prejudice did not present itself as an obvious area of study; given the persuasive climate of beliefs about the cultural and intellectual characteristics of 'the Negro' (in themselves 'verified' by existing social arrangements), negative attitudes towards him were seen as entirely legitimate and unremarkable.

Over the following 20 years the emergence of black people to demand full citizenship began to influence this perspective. The growing notion that they aspired to (and might even deserve) social equality threw into relief those attitudes and practices which had consigned them to their inferior status. It was still possible for a social psychologist to 'rate the intelligence of the full-blooded negro as roughly between two-thirds and three-fourths of that of the white race' (F. H. Allport, 1924, p. 386), but this was now tempered by the concession that 'this discrepancy in mental ability is not great enough to account for the problem

which centers around the American Negro or to explain fully the
ostracism to which he is subjected' (F. H. Allport, 1924, p. 386).
This change was accompanied by the first attempts to quantify
this ostracism through the measurement of white people's
attitudes and behaviour towards blacks. The 'social distance'
scales of Emory Bogardus (1925) showed that white people felt
more rejecting towards negroes and mulattoes than any other
racial or national group. The pioneering work on attitude scaling
by Thurstone (1931) also focused on racial attitudes; nevertheless, while these initiatives represented an advance in psychology's
consciousness of the issue, and implied an increasing objectivity,
they remained heavily influenced by ingrained racial beliefs.

These descriptive studies signalled a growing concern with the
'white' terms in the prejudice equation. If these attitudes could
not be accounted for solely in terms of black inferiority, then
there was a need to understand their origins in the psychology of
white people. The 1930s saw the first attempts to frame *explanations* of the phenomenon, but in keeping with the spirit of the
times within the science, these were not truly social-
psychological theories as we now understand them. They were
essentially reductionist theories, locating their explanations at the
level of *individual* psychological functioning rather than people's
participation in more complex social behaviour. The frustration–aggression hypothesis, and the scapegoat theory of prejudice which derives from it (Dollard *et al.*, 1939) is a case in
point. Its central proposition is that 'the occurrence of aggresive
behaviour always presupposes the existence of frustration and,
contrariwise, that the existence of frustration always leads to some
form of aggression' (Dollard *et al.*, p. 1). Intuitively the proposition has an immediate appeal; equally our experience of aggression without apparent prior frustration, and of frustration which
does not seem to result in aggression undermines its credibility.
And so it was when the hypothesis was put to experimental test;
subsequently it was modified to allow for those exceptions,
which correspondingly diluted its explanatory and predictive
value. Nevertheless, it is precisely those situations where frustration cannot be expressed in immediate aggression which are of
the most interest for the insights they give concerning the genesis
of prejudice. Clearly, we are often frustrated by persons in positions of superior power, against whom aggression would be fruit-
less, inappropriate or simply self-defeating.

To explain the resolution of this dilemma, Dollard *et al*. draw on the Freudian concept of *displacement* of aggression, and the notion of the *generalization* of aggression drawn from learning theory. It is argued that aggression which cannot be directed against the source of frustration may be expressed against some-what similar targets *via* stimulus generalization. Alternatively it may be displaced against quite dissimilar targets, like social out-groups, who thus become scapegoats blamed for the individual's frustrations. There are clearly problems (which are not ad-equately resolved within the theory) around these opposing predictions concerning the nature of the target. Billig (1976) and Tajfel (1978b) provide extended discussions of this issue; for our present purpose it is sufficient to consider the usefulness of the displacement hypothesis, and in particular the ways in which it has been employed. The authors themselves cited the example of antisemitism in Nazi Germany, attributing much of the animosity of the accumulated frustration of the German people since the Treaty of Versailles. Similarly, they quote studies which, for example, show a correlation between the decrease in cotton pro-fits in the southern states of America and increases in negro lynchings.

Correlation, however, is not causation and while these rela-tionships may well be beyond coincidence, the case is not proven nor can it be within the theory. The hypothesis is perhaps better regarded as an analogue or metaphor, for it does not provide adequate explanation of the processes by which individual moti-vations come to be translated into collective, coherent social actions. The implication that this kind of social behaviour can be regarded as some kind of aggregate of individual dispositions is wholly insufficient. That individuals displace frustration-induced aggression onto scapegoats has been experimentally demons-trated and is not in dispute. That wider social, economic and political 'frustrations' are vented through mass prejudice against minority groups is an entirely plausible hypothesis, but requires to enlist a variety of social and cognitive factors, like conformity to social norms and ideology, to make the explanatory leap a viable one.

The Second World War fomented an intense concern with the dynamics of prejudice. The systematic extermination of European Jews, the ultimate and most obscene manifestation of racism yet encountered, demanded explanation. The climate surrounding these events inevitably influenced the direction of theory; the very obscenity of the holocaust connoted a kind of mass pathology, a collective madness. Explanations were therefore sought in the disturbed personality, for it was hardly conceivable that these could be the actions of normal men. Adorno and his colleagues (1950) set out to identify the characteristics of the fascist (or potentially fascist) person in their monolithic authoritarian personality study. They reasoned that people who are prejudiced against Jews are likely to be similarly prejudiced against other racial or cultural minorities; that these attitudes tend to hang together because they are outward manifestations of a basic personality type, the authoritarian personality. The authors drew upon the Freudian perspective to account for the aetiology of this personality in childhood experience with parents who were harsh and restrictive, securing emotional dependence and obedience from their children by the manipulation of love and its withdrawal. In adult life the love–hate relationship with authority that this regime engenders is resolved by a rigid obedience to power-figures, while the negative aspect of the ambivalence is displaced onto weaker targets who can be hated without danger.

The theory was empirically tested through the administration of scales measuring antisemitism (A-S scale), ethnocentrism (E-scale) and political and economic conservatism (PEC scale) to a large number of adult subjects. These attitude measures were supplemented by a personality measure (the F-scale) which was designed to tap authoritarian tendencies; originally, 'F' was an abbreviation for 'potentiality for fascism' which speaks volumes about the emotional and ideological atmosphere surrounding the study. Substantial correlations between the attitude constellation and the personality measure did indeed emerge from the data, though the PEC measure resulted in considerably lower correlations with the other scales. Additionally, the childhood antecedents of this personality type were investigated in some depth through interviews with selected groups of subjects and the administration of projective personality tests. Again, these yielded a picture of the child-rearing practices and emotional tenor of the authoritarian's family background which the authors felt was broadly supportive of their theory.

There were, however, substantial methodological criticisms of the study, with the result that a long and rancorous debate as to the validity of their findings ensued; this also stimulated a host of further studies which subjected the theory and its predictions to finer scrutiny; for reviews of this literature, see, for example, Christie and Cook (1958), Kirscht and Dillehay (1967). While this inevitably detracted somewhat from the force of the theory, the authors could justifiably claim to have identified a personality type who was particularly prone to develop hostile and rejecting attitudes towards various racial and cultural minorities. The precise origins of that syndrome in childhood experience are less well established. Beyond these simple statements the theory is less sure of itself; when it is enlisted in the explanation of prejudice as a widespread social phenomenon it is found lacking. It is simply not plausible to attribute, for example, race prejudice in the United States to the mass expression of personality dispositions towards authoritarianism and ethnocentrism, occasioned by a nationwide pattern of harsh child-rearing practices. The very notion that the authoritarian is in some sense abnormal or disturbed logically cuts across such a formulation.

Proceeding from the individual's experience to the explanation of pervasive social phenomena, the authoritarian personality theory is beset by the same problems of translation as the frustration–aggression hypothesis, and is similarly ill-equipped to deal with them. Tajfel (1978b, p. 403) has encapsulated the issue as follows:

> Many of the 'individual' theories start from general descriptions of psychological processes which are assumed to operate in individuals in a way which is independent of the effects of social interaction and social context. The social context and interaction are assumed to affect these processes, but only in the sense that society provides a variety of settings in which 'basic' individual laws of motivation or cognition are uniformly displayed. In contrast, 'social psychological' theories tend to start from individuals in groups rather than individuals *tout court*. They do not necessarily contradict the 'preliminary' individual laws, such as those, for example, applying to frustration and aggression or to cognitive dissonance. But they stress the need to take into account the fact that group behaviour – and even more so inter-group behaviour – is displayed in situations in which we are not dealing with random collections of individuals who somehow come to act in unison because they all happen to be in a similar psychological state.

Thomas Pettigrew (1958) depicted theories of prejudice as lying along a continuum, at one extreme of which lie the 'individual' theories which view prejudice as the *externalization* of inner needs and conflicts within the personality; at the other end are socio-cultural theories which 'view intolerance as a mere reflection of cultural norms and neglect individual differences' (1958, p. 29). The focus of the latter is an area where border skirmishes with sociology tend to deter more psychologically oriented research, exacerbating the polarization of theories within the continuum. Minard's (1952) study of a West Virginian coalmining community well illustrates the ways in which the pressure of sociocultural norms may well prevail over individual dispositions towards or against prejudice. In this community these norms required almost total segregation of the races in social life 'above ground' and consequent inequality. In the mines, however, an equality based on common work-roles, achievement and, not least, common danger, made social integration the norm. Minard estimated that some 60 per cent of the white miners conformed to these social expectations in both situations. Of the remaining 40 per cent, roughly half segregated themselves from blacks in both situations while the other 20 per cent attempted social integration with blacks both above and below ground. Clearly, it would be difficult to explain the behaviour of the 'inconsistent' majority in terms of enduring personality dispositions, while these factors may well have a strong influence on withstanding social pressure in the behaviour of the 'consistent' minorities.

While personality and sociocultural factors have been seen as competing explanations in theory, their collective influence in practice has never been better illustrated than by Pettigrew's own studies in America and South Africa (Pettigrew, 1958, 1964). In a comparison of northern and southern communities in the United States he was able to show that heightened antiblack attitudes in the southern sample were not generally accompanied by the heightened antisemitism and authoritarianism that the authoritarian personality theory would predict. While the gross differences between north and south clearly reflected the influence of contrasting social norms, there was evidence within the southern communities that personality factors had a minor role to play: southern women were found to have somewhat greater antiblack prejudice – and also to be more authoritarian – than were the men. Comparing the results of a sample of South African students with their American counterparts, Pettigrew found a higher level of antiblack prejudice amongst the former, but not correspondingly higher levels of authoritarianism. Once again the influence of social norms encouraging prejudice is apparent; nevertheless, the fact that authoritarianism and antiblack attitudes were correlated *within* the South African sample suggests that personality variables play an intervening role. These students' responses also showed a correlation between antiblack attitudes and conformity, suggesting a further mechanism to account for their greater adherence to social norms. Looking at a variety of subgroups across the sample, it was apparent that specific subcultural norms promoted higher prejudice that was not accompanied by higher authoritarianism. In summarizing his data, Pettigrew inevitably concludes that: 'In areas with historically embedded traditions of racial intolerance, externalising personality factors underlying prejudice remain important, but sociocultural factors are unusually crucial and account for the heightened racial hostility.' (1958, p. 40)

Towards the middle of Pettigrew's continuum of prejudice theories we can insert a body of theory which derives both from the investigation of small group relations in experimental settings and from a consideration of relations between larger scale real-life groups occupying different positions in the socioeconomic structure. These are truly social psychological theories in the sense that they take as their point of departure *intragroup* and *intergroup* behaviour.

One cardinal principle concerning the fundamental influence of social structure and the attitudinal and behavioural consequences of the relations between groups within it can be stated as follows: 'The character of the existing relations between ingroup and outgroup generates attitudes toward the outgroup that are consonant with these relations. In other words, the structure of the relation between two groups in terms of relative status and power produces cognitions and feelings that are appropriate to the existing structure.' (Secord and Backman, 1964, p. 413) Clearly, history is replete with examples of hostile ideologies which have grown up between groups who differ in socioeconomic status, particularly where the inferior position of one group is a direct consequence of the other's domination and exploitation. It is not simply the perception of the gross status differences and power relations which is involved here, it is also the perception or fact of *competition*. The Sherifs' (Sherif and Sherif, 1953; Sherif *et al.*, 1961) work with small groups demonstrated how easily hostile attitudes could be generated between groups placed in competitive relation with each other. Conversely, the creation of superordinate goals requiring cooperation between the groups engendered more positive intergroup attitudes. Billig's (1976) analysis of Sherif and Sherif's experiments suggests that the creation of competitive or cooperative relations is not the only determinant of these attitudes. He points to the development of intergroup comparison and rivalry during a phase of the experiments which preceded the establishment of institutional competition. The suggestion is that the social categorization involved in group-formation, and the development of ingroup consciousness and identity *in relation to* other groups initiates the process of intergroup attitude development: '*overt* intergroup competition is not a necessary condition for intergroup attitudes' (Billig, 1976, p. 320). This analysis has grown out of a body of theory and research developed by Tajfel and his associates (see, for example, Billig, 1976; Tajfel, 1978a; Tajfel and Turner, 1979; Turner, 1975a; see chapter 1 for brief description of the different aspects of this work).

They have been concerned to identify the very minimum conditions under which intergroup attitudes will develop and have conducted a long series of studies with 'minimal' groups, that is, artificially created groups which are shorn of all the features which normally characterize intergroup relations in everyday life (see chapter 3). Thus, the groups were formed according to the most arbitrary and superficial criteria (for example, on the basis of their preference for certain painters, or by the toss of a coin) which might be thought to minimize both the sense of ingroup similarity and solidarity, and the sense of difference from the outgroup and any tendency to behave in a discriminatory way towards them. Neither was there any history of competition between these nascent groups, for they were drawn from a single body of people who were at least acquainted with each other in an undifferentiated way beforehand. Nevertheless, in tasks which presented individual group members with the opportunity of behaving in ways which would benefit other members of their own group to the detriment of the other group, this discriminatory course was frequently taken, despite the fact that in some circumstances a non-discriminatory 'cooperative' strategy would have been more profitable overall. This apparent desire to maximize the 'differentials' between the groups, that is, the rewards accruing to each, in a situation which provides no objective

reasons for competitiveness (and where it may actually be coun-
terproductive) suggests some fundamental group processes
which deserve explanation. As Tajfel and Turner (1979, p. 39)
have written: 'Two points stand out: first, minimal intergroup
discrimination is not based on incompatible group interests; second, the baseline conditions for intergroup competition seem
indeed so minimal as to cause the suspicion that we are dealing
here with some factor or process inherent in the intergroup situation itself.'

Tajfel and Turner's theory which attempts to explain this
phenomenon is effectively a translation of Festinger's (1954)
theory of social comparison processes into the social psychological realm. Whereas Festinger proposed that individuals have a
drive to compare themselves with others (that is, to evaluate their
own abilities and characteristics against other people's) and to do
so in ways that will preserve their own self-esteem, it is suggested here that there is an equivalent need for every social group
to create and maintain a positive social identity *vis-à-vis* other
social groups. Irrespective of the objective characteristics of these
groups, some positive evaluation of the ingroup (and, on the
other side of the coin, some negative evaluation of the outgroup)
can be achieved through the construction of their relationship as a
competitive one and discriminatory behaviour which ensures
'superiority' on at least that dimension.

The behaviour of the subjects in the minimal group experiments could then be interpreted in the following way: faced with
a situation where they have been categorized into nominal
groups, the subjects attempt to impose a 'real-life' construction
on this artificial situation. They behave 'as if' the groups were
meaningfully distinct and 'as if' ingroup norms were operating,
even though they are not actually in contact with their fellow
group-members. Perhaps *because* the relationship between the
two groups is ambiguous and undefined there is a greater need to
make social comparisons, establish a valued ingroup identity–devalued outgroup identity, than in real life where these
values are more defined by objective factors. In any event, discriminatory behaviour against the outgroup is one available
means of expressing these dispositions. Whether, as Billig (1976,
p. 352) puts it, 'social identity is achieved through showing
ingroup favouritism, rather than ingroup favouritism following
from the acceptance of social identity' remains an open question;

whether it is psychologically meaningful to separate these two cause–effect sequences as alternatives, is another.

For our purposes the very considerable importance of this research and theory lies in (a) its highly plausible account of basic social psychological processes originating in the need to organize and categorize our social as well as our physical world and the concomitant processes of social comparison, social identity formation and intergroup discrimination; and (b) following from our acceptance of these fundamental dispositions, the evident implication, as we move from the 'neutral' laboratory to the cauldron of everyday life, that discrimination between social groups distinguished by definite physical and cultural characteristics, with a history of competitive relations and accompanying intergroup ideologies, and tangible economic, social or political reasons for continuing conflict, is, to say the least, 'overdetermined' and almost inevitable. Race prejudice is a case which includes all these ingredients.

3   The nature of prejudice

Until now we have taken for granted that we understand what prejudice *is*. G. W. Allport's (1954) classic work *The Nature of Prejudice* offered several definitions, and Ehrlich (1973) marshalled some 15 alternatives, without difficulty one imagines, for there are almost as many definitions of the term as writers who employ it. In so far as we can synthesize some definition that encompasses the ways in which the term is consensually used it would include the following features:

1   Prejudice is 'an attitude that predisposes a person to think, feel and act in favourable or unfavourable ways toward a group or its individual members' (Secord and Backman, 1964).
2   It is 'based upon a faulty and inflexible generalisation' (G. W. Allport, 1954).
3   It is a 'preconceived judgement' (McDonagh and Richards, 1953) which is developed 'before, in lieu of or despite objective evidence (Cooper and McGaugh, 1963).
4   It is 'an emotional, rigid attitude' (Simpson and Yinger, 1965), 'not easily changed by contrary information' (Krech, Crutchfield, and Ballachey, 1962).

5   It is bad. This is not a frivolous aside, but expresses the
    overall value connotation which attaches to the term,
    because the prejudiced person is deemed to depart from
    certain ideal norms. Harding *et al*. (1969) describe these as
    the norms of *rationality* (which 'enjoins a persistent attempt
    to secure accurate information, to correct misinformation, to
    make appropriate differentiations and qualifications, to be
    logical in deduction and cautious in inference'; the norm of
    justice, which requires that 'in all areas of public concern
    individuals be treated equally'; and the norm of *'human-
    heartedness'* which quaintly expresses that norm which
    'enjoins the acceptance of other individuals in terms of their
    common humanity, no matter how different they may be
    from oneself' (Harding *et al*., 1969, p. 5).

It is convenient to regard prejudiced racial attitudes within the
traditional three-component structure of attitudes model (for a
discussion of this and alternative models of attitude structure,
see, for example, Jaspars, 1978). Thus the affective component of
the prejudiced person's racial attitudes will consist in feelings of
dislike, antipathy or even hatred for, say, black people. The cognitive component will include the perceptions beliefs and
stereotypes concerning black people's characteristics that the person has absorbed (often selectively, often secondhand, and thus
with no necessary relation to objective fact – for discussions of
stereotyping and other cognitive aspects of prejudice, see
Brigham (1971), Tajfel (1973) and chapter 5). Finally, the conative component comprises the individual's disposition to behave
in negative ways towards black people, from social rejection and
discrimination to outright aggression. It is important to stress that
this is a readiness to behave in these ways, rather than referring
to the behaviour itself. The actual behaviour will be a function of
specific situational factors quite as much as individual factors (see
Wicker, 1969).
    The relation between prejudiced attitudes (and particularly the
conative component) and discriminatory behaviour raises the
perennial issue of the extent to which attitudes are directly translated into behaviour. While Deutscher (1966, p. 247) has argued
that 'no matter what one's theoretical orientation may be, one has
no reason to expect to find congruence between attitudes and
actions and every reason to expect to find discrepancies between

them', we nevertheless argue for the utility of attitude studies for the information they give us concerning enduring dispositions towards attitude objects, rather than the more limited information we can derive from observing the behaviour, which may simply reflect the exigencies of a specific situation.

Actual examples of these components 'in action' in the case of racial prejudice and discrimination are too familiar to bear repetition here. What is interesting, however, is the way in which the content of people's prejudices may alter as a function of changes in the wider society such as the changing image and reality of black people in the last two decades, or the introduction of anti-discrimination legislation designed to not only outlaw discrimination but also to influence attitudes.

It could be argued with some justification that traditionally our concept of race prejudice has been static and somewhat undifferentiated. We have always 'known' that it is characterized by a set of beliefs concerning the nature of black people which usually include notions of intellectual inferiority, suspect morality and a variety of other individual and cultural attributes which distinguish them from the white majority and are viewed in a pejorative light. Ashmore and Del Boca (1976) have pointed out that this conception has persisted despite substantial changes in the nature of black–white relations and evidence that some of these beliefs have declined in significance for the prejudiced person. However, while it seems that whites less readily endorse stereotypes of intellectual inferiority and moral depravity, there does not appear to have been a concomitant reduction in anti-black feeling. Other factors, it is argued, have superseded these beliefs and they can be traced directly to the 'state of open competition' between blacks and whites that was initiated in the mid-1960s and 'has posed a threat to almost all white Americans. . . . The type and degree of threat perceived, however, is affected by a number of factors . . . [which vary] as a function of the individual's position in the socio-economic system' (Ashmore and Del Boca, 1976, p. 100). Three threat-related constructs are proposed to describe these developments: perceived racial threat, symbolic racism and tokenism.

Perceived racial threat involves the belief that blacks are now powerful and threatening (in contrast to the traditional stereotype of black submissiveness) and the fear that attaches to this belief. 'In contrast with prejudice as it has been conceptually and operationally defined, however, perceived racial threat has a larger fear and smaller contempt component and involves beliefs that blacks are trying to usurp the position of whites in this society rather than notions about black inferiority' (Ashmore and Del Boca, 1976, p. 102). Clearly, white reactions to desegregation and busing, affirmative action and positive discrimination, and above all to the urban insurrections of the 1960s, give some credence to this construct. While black penetration into previously white institutions and status positions has undoubtedly provided a more realistic basis for such feelings, it would be wrong to regard perceived racial threat as an entirely new construct and ignore its role in the very earliest stereotypes surrounding 'the negro's' savage and barbaric nature.

Ashmore *et al*. (1973) found that items tapping perceived racial threat in the areas of housing, employment, economic resources and personal safety correlated well with each other. They also showed that perceived racial threat correlated highly with evaluative ratings of blacks, higher in fact than does the F-scale. Other studies (Caprio, 1972; Feagin, 1970) have shown this fear–threat syndrome to correlate with behavioural indices, like willingness to make repairs to houses in areas threatened by black residential migration, and dispositions to buy guns in defence against black crime. If the argument appears circular it is clarified by the finding (Groves and Rossi, 1970) that 'urban policemen who scored high in perceived threat also tended to view ghetto residents as hostile; this perceived hostility was apparently more related to the policemen's perceived threat level than to actual hostile acts by ghetto residents' (Ashmore and Del Boca, 1976, p. 104).

Symbolic racism is an altogether more abstract system of beliefs, 'a combination of the generalised feeling that the social, economic and political *status quo* should be maintained with the belief that blacks are somehow responsible for threatening this *status quo*, and by implication, the whole American way of life – that is, blacks are seen as threatening values that are quite important to suburban whites' (Ashmore and Del Boca, 1976, p. 106). It is portrayed very much as a phenomenon amongst white middle-class suburb dwellers, who have little contact with blacks, but who are nevertheless well-socialized into antiblack, *pro-status quo* orientations, and have been exposed via the mass media to images of black activism and sociopolitical advances. These are experienced as threatening at a symbolic level, challenging the system as a whole rather than their positions as individuals. These people are not markedly antiblack on traditional measures (Sears and Kinder, 1971) and do not necessarily display the conventional antiblack beliefs about intellectual inferiority, etc. They also recognize the discrimination blacks suffer and may even favour integration in principle. They nevertheless maintain a resistance to actual black advancement even though they are effectively insulated from its consequences.

Tokenism refers to the practice of reverse discrimination by whites, particularly those of high-status, college-educated backgrounds, who go out of their way to favour blacks in individual encounters, for the purpose of protecting an egalitarian self-concept. While this may increase their standing in their own and other's eyes, it may also operate so as to diminish their propensity for more meaningful contributions to interracial harmony and minority progress. Their 'token' antiracism obviates the need for a more wholehearted commitment. Dutton and Lennox (1974) submitted college students to a procedure whereby they were led to believe that they might be prejudiced through false autonomic feedback on their reactions to interracial slides. Subsequently they were divided into three groups, the first and second being approached by a black or a white 'beggar', and the third group serving as a control were not approached. On the following day when all the subjects were asked to give some time to an 'interracial brotherhood' campaign, those who had given money to the black beggar volunteered less time than either of the other groups.

Clearly, symbolic racism and tokenism are the milder forms of racism, which may be more racist in effect than in intention. Both are intuitively familiar phenomena which fall outside the conventional conceptions of prejudice, but are nevertheless worthy of study. The practices described do not seem to connote the overt malevolence and the motivation to discriminate that is often associated with race prejudice. However, the pressures of antidiscrimination legislation and the encouragement of more liberal racial values have made prejudice more covert, to the extent that individuals may not be fully aware of (or prepared to recognize) what motivates their behaviour. Increasingly 'implicit' prejudice may replace the more overt forms with which we are familiar, and we should not overlook these developments or conclude that because prejudice is less obvious it has diminished. There is

not yet a sufficient body of evidence to enable us to say that there
has been a wholesale change in the nature of prejudice, in the
direction of these new forms proposed by Ashmore and Del Boca.
Much more research is needed before we can evaluate the practical and theoretical importance of these new departures.

They do, however, raise the important issue of how we come
to terms with assessing forms of prejudice which are more subtle
and less accessible to scrutiny than the explicit statements of antiblack feeling with which we have dealt in the past. There is a
parallel here with our neglect of 'institutional' racism which is
often not apparent in the behaviour of individuals and has therefore seemed to fall outside our domain. This is the form of racism
that is built into our institutions, in the broadest sense, whether
we are talking about housing policy, educational opportunity,
career and promotion structures or immigration legislation, each
of which may be discriminatory in effect, if not, apparently, in
purpose. Prejudice theory has concentrated primarily on individual racism, secondarily on wider group expressions of racism,
and almost never on the institutionalization of racism. Clearly,
there is a very complex relationship between individual prejudices and, say, discriminatory immigration laws in Britain. It is
certainly a dialectical relationship; on the one hand these laws are
a reflection of individual prejudices, in the sense that politicians
have sought to assuage their constituents' anxieties about black
immigration by supporting legislation designed to reduce or end
it; on the other hand, the laws legitimate the prejudices, giving an
official seal of approval to rejecting attitudes, a tacit encouragement to prejudice that has not been lost on a receptive audience,
from the person in the street, through the conservatives of the
major political parties, to National Front members.

If we are serious in our attempt to encapsulate the racial climate
in our society then we have to take account of these factors. Our
neglect of them leaves an enormous credibility gap between our
accounts of masses of prejudiced individuals and the actual
experience of racism *in toto* by black people. At the simplest
level, while individual acts of rejection and discrimination in
face-to-face encounters with whites may be very painful for black
people, it is not solely these factors which consign them to their
inferior status in our society. Equally, as we come to consider the
development of racial attitudes in children, we must bear in mind
that our institutions and social arrangements beam powerful

messages about racism which complement those they receive in person-to-person encounters.

4 The development of prejudice

4.1 Racial attitudes in children

Researchers within the developmental perspective have taken for granted the existence of prejudice in particular societies (on the basis of good evidence), and looked at the ways in which children develop an awareness of these issues and begin to form racial attitudes themselves. Ever since the late 1930s when this research tradition began, the same basic methodology has been employed, and one that has not escaped criticism as we shall see later. Given that the subjects of these experiments have sometimes been as young as 3 years old, it has been impossible to use attitude scales, questionnaires or any verbally sophisticated measure. Instead, the researchers have employed dolls or pictures representing the various racial groups in the child's environment; these are made the basis of a series of questions put to the child, the idea being that the child responds as if they were real people, and in that way reveals his or her feelings towards the groups that the figures represent.

Some 40 years' accumulation of research in this tradition has aggregated into a fairly coherent picture of racial attitude development in children, a picture which is not specific to the United States where most of this work originates, but has been replicated in a variety of other cultural settings, for example New Zealand (Vaughan, 1964a) and Britain (Milner, 1973). Goodman (1964) originally described this process as involving three stages, racial *awareness*, where the child first becomes aware of racial differences, racial *orientation*, when the first positive and negative evaluations of different racial groups appear, and finally racial *attitude*, when the child's more elaborated attitude begins to approximate to the adult form. More recently Katz (1976) has taken issue with this simple schema, suggesting that eight overlapping but separable stages can be distinguished:

1   early observation of racial cues, starting well before the age of 3; leading to
2   formation of rudimentary concepts about black people,

labels for which may be provided by adults, and often
accompanied by some evaluative information;

3   conceptual differentiation: the stage in which the learning
    of racial concepts and labels is reinforced, through encoun-
    tering positive and negative instances of the concept, the
    child testing his/her grasp of the defining characteristics of
    the concept against adult feedback. For example, the child
    will learn that skin-colour is not the only determinant of
    'race' because this person is called 'black' as a result of her
    hair-type and facial features, even though her skin is light-
    coloured;

4   recognition of the irrevocability of cues: the child's mastery
    of the notion that certain person-cues, like size and age, are
    subject to change while others are immutable, like race or
    sex;

5   consolidation of group concepts: by this stage the child can
    identify and label positive and negative instances and
    understand the permanence of group membership; con-
    solidation, then, is the further development of stages (3)
    and (4) and completes the functional interrelationship of the
    perceptual and cognitive aspects, together with the evalua-
    tive content; this process typically begins somewhat before
    5 years of age and continues for some time;

6   perceptual elaboration then takes places, proceeding from
    the 'us' and 'them' categorization of groups, involving
    greater differentiation between groups, while intragroup
    differentiation is less pronounced, particularly in the case
    of the outgroup;

7   cognitive elaboration: 'the process by which concept
    attitudes or preferences become racial attitudes' (Katz,
    1976, p. 150); this simply refers to the elaboration of the
    'incipient attitude' into a fully fledged attitude through
    school experiences, contact with other-race children, and
    contact with the attitudes of teachers and peers;

8   attitude crystallization, in which the child's attitudes fall
    increasingly into line with those in the immediate environ-
    ment, thus becoming supported, stable and rather resistant
    to change.

'Although this schema is not supported in every detail by
empirical evidence, it is broadly descriptive of the mainstream of

research findings in this area. Research has repeatedly shown the onset of racial awareness at or before 3 years of age, accompanied or shortly followed by the first indications of positive or negative feelings towards white and black people. As Harding *et al.* (1969, p. 19) wrote:

> In what sense then, can we speak of an ethnic attitude, inchoate or otherwise in the very young child? The fact is that his ethnic awareness is by no means affectively neutral. He reveals clear preferences for some groups while others are rejected. Thus a fundamental ingredient of an intergroup attitude is present: an evaluative orientation that is expressed in ingroup-versus-outgroup terms.

Empirically these orientations have been evident through children's choices of playmates or companions for various activities, and although these are essentially measures of preference, and do not automatically imply hostility towards the black figures not chosen by the child, there is plentiful evidence from the reasons that are given for the choices and from spontaneous comments made that indeed they involve markedly negative, rejecting feelings. These may be simple statements of dislike based on real or imagined group characteristics (the child rejecting a black figure 'because he's a darkie', 'because he's got messy hair', 'because he kills people') or they may be apparently sophisticated; in one study a 6 year old white child maintained that the black figure was the 'bad' one 'because he should have learned the language before he came over here' (Milner, 1973). A more macabre example is provided by Pushkin (1967) who enquired why a child had not selected any black dolls for an imaginary tea-party, to be told that 'If I have to sit next to one of those I'll have a nervous breakdown'. It matters little that these statements are made well in advance of any real understanding of the concepts involved. For it is clear that while the children may not fully comprehend this 'adult' language, they can nevertheless reproduce it in the sense in which it was intended, with the affective message intact.

The child now has an affective foundation for attitude development, an evaluative framework within which subsequent learning about racial groups and adult attitudes towards them can be fitted. By the age of 7 or 8 these rudimentary attitudes are elaborated with the addition of more information about the wider social connotations of racial group membership, particularly with regard to social roles and status: 'concepts and feelings about race frequently include adult distinctions of status, ability, character, occupations, and economic circumstances. . . . Among the older children stereotyping and expressions of hostility are more frequent and attitudes more crystallised than among the young children' (Trager and Radke-Yarrow, 1952, p. 150). Detailed accounts of the very substantial literature concerning racial attitude development in the first 10 years of life can be found in Harding *et al.* (1969), Pushkin and Veness (1973), and Milner (1975). However, it is a noticeable feature of the literature that the process of further development through adolescence receives meagre coverage. To some extent the methodological tail wags the dog, for while the doll and picture tests are appropriate for younger children, and attitude scales and questionnaires are used with young adults, neither are satisfactory for adolescents. The relatively few studies that have been conducted with this age-group suggest that there is a gradual intensification of prejudice which levels off as adolescence progresses (Minard, 1931; Muhyi, 1952). Wilson (1963) shows that the attitudes become increasingly stable, show less variance and exhibit more consistency between the ages of 13 and 18. There is development whereby the components of the attitude become more integrated, such that, for example, the behavioural component may fall more into line with the affective and cognitive components; thus a child who had previously had interracial friendships may not now entertain them, in line with basically negative attitudes. There is evidence of greater awareness of and conformity to prevailing social norms of behaviour which may account for this. At the same time it has been suggested that any or all of these components become more differentiated during this period. The cognitive component may become more sophisticated in admitting both the good and the bad characteristics of a group or individual; similarly the affective component may alter so as to allow a positive feeling towards a particular individual while maintaining an overall negative disposition towards the group as a whole. Both integration of components and differentiation within them assist the adolescent in handling the more complex information about racial groups (and situations involving them) which he or she now encounters.

The doll and picture methodology which has traditionally been employed in the studies of younger children is far from perfect.

These are essentially projectively based methods which require the use of the child's imagination so that he or she responds to the stimulus figures as though they were real people. It could be argued that the encouragement of this 'fantasy' is not conducive to reality-based responses; and of course, the less realistic are the stimulus figures, the more the child is required to suspend disbelief. Certainly there has been tremendous variation in the kinds of figures employed, and the argument that these studies involve the application of a rather blunt measuring instrument to a sensitive and volatile phenomenon appears to have some force. And yet, despite all the variation in materials, questions and situations that have been employed, the overall pattern of responses that has been elicited has been remarkably consistent. This might be taken as evidence of validity and reliability, that a wide variety of methods has nevertheless succeeded in tapping a constant underlying disposition.

Teplin (1974), however, interprets it otherwise; in a long critique of methodology in this area she argues that 'projectively-based methods' suffer from serious shortcomings as compared with 'reality-based methods', namely sociometric techniques based upon the child's choices of real people as opposed to unreal figures; the former, she suggests, have been less responsive to real changes in the social milieu over the years than have the latter. In fact this argument is not supported by recent developments in the area; since 1970 child studies of the projective type have consistently evidenced the effects of wider social changes, particularly with respect to the attitudes of minority-group children, as will be discussed in some detail later. While sociometric studies clearly have utility for specific purposes, they also have their shortcomings as indicators of racial attitudes *per se*. The child's choices of friends or companions on these tests reflect personality variables and idiosyncrasies quite as much as any other characteristics; while these are important and may well cut across racial group membership in particular cases, they confuse the picture of the child's overall disposition towards the racial group as a whole. It is worth pointing out that neither are sociometric tests 'pure' tests of behaviour, and methods which tap an overall group attitude which may or may not be translated into behaviour in individual instances have a more general utility.

One of the more cogent criticisms of research in this area has concerned the influence of the race of the tester. When we consider Dreger and Miller's (1960, 1968) reviews of comparative studies of blacks and whites across the whole of psychology, and we see how influential is the race of the tester in, for example, intelligence testing, then it is difficult to see how it could not be a factor in the sensitive area of racial attitude testing. And, of course, it has proved to be influential in some studies – but not in others. Where is has occurred, it has been in the predictable direction, operating to produce responses from the children which are more favourable to the experimenter's own ethnic group. Jahoda, Thomson, and Bhatt (1972) found this in their work in Glasgow, as have a number of the American studies (for example, Trent, 1954). Equally, several studies have found no effect or a negligible one that did not attain statistical significance (such as Hraba and Grant, 1970). Sattler (1973) reviewed all the available evidence and came to the conclusion that 'young black and white children do not appear to be affected by the experimenter's race in their preferences for dolls which vary in skin-colour'. This seems too emphatic a conclusion, but there is a separate question as to the real significance of this experimenter effect, if and when it does appear. Implicit in the criticisms which have drawn attention to this factor is the notion that the racial group of the experimenter is somehow distorting the child's 'true' response, and that the true response is the one that is elicited by an experimenter of the same race as the child. If we accept that there is this source of influence, it does not necessarily have to be seen as a distortion or bias, displacing the child's expressed attitude from one fixed point on a unidimensional scale to another. It might be better to conceive of a locus of responses which may be affected by a variety of situational factors, including the race of the interviewer, and that this is a far better correlate of real-life behaviour than the idea of rigid cross-situational consistency, any departure from which is portrayed as an artifact.

4.2 Racial attitudes in the socialization process

Where prejudiced racial attitudes have become widespread in a society it seems almost inevitable that the child will begin to absorb these attitudes as an integral part of the socialization process. All the socializing agencies with whom the child interacts will contribute to this: parents, siblings, peers, teachers and the schools, literature and the mass media. Of course there is not a single homogeneous message that is retailed by all these agencies, but to the extent to which prejudice has entered into the culture, so will it be reflected in the values and norms of behaviour that they encourage. In later years the child will encounter alternative values, and through secondary socialization may adopt different perspectives, but in the early years these choices do not exist. Clearly, the onset of racial awareness in the preschool years suggests that early experience within the family is the primary stimulus to these developments. The family defines the child's world, both in the sense of defining its outer limits, and in defining social reality. Jones and Gerard (1967, p. 127) have put the point forcibly:

> Because of his lack of ready access to non-social sources of information the child is peculiarly vulnerable to those social sources appearing and re-appearing in his immediate environment. Parents and siblings find themselves in positions of great power, the power that comes with having the answers (right or wrong) to resolve the child's uncertainties. In the early years ot socialisation this power is almost monopolistic. Alternative answers or explanations are absent and the child's earliest contacts with the broader universe are filtered through all the biases and distortions in his parents' conception of reality.

This conception of reality is based upon the parents' experience of perceiving people, objects and events, categorizing them and understanding them as best they can, evaluating them and reacting to them. This aggregate of experience coheres in a symbolic representation of the world, but one that is coloured by their values, attitudes and beliefs about the world. For the child there is no basis for objectivity about their perspective; it is not one view of the world, it is *the* world.

It is difficult to obtain direct evidence of the concrete ways in which race attitudes are taught and learned; three overlapping processes seem to be involved, direct tuition, indirect tuition and role-learning. Parents undoubtedly do make explicit statements about their beliefs and attitudes on a variety of social issues, and there is usually an implicit encouragement for the child to feel likewise. Parental reactions to black people face-to-face or in the mass media, and their comments about them are a case in point. There may be explicit guidance of the child's choice of friends, or their choice of school for the child may be influenced by racial considerations. This begins to shade into the category of indirect

tuition, where attitudes are not consciously taught but are implicit in what the parents say or do. Information on emotive
issues like race can seldom be conveyed without some flavour of
the parents' own attitudes, however unconsciously, and there is
evidence that it is precisely these evaluative overtones which are
most readily absorbed. Children may simply imitate and model
statements, as we have seen earlier, but in a wider sense, their
identification with the parents helps us to account for the absorp-
tion of their whole value-system, rather than discrete attitudes or
behaviours. Identification promotes the desire to emulate the
parents, to appear grown-up by spouting adult ideas, and simply
to gain approval by being like them. In a similar way, the process
of role-learning involves children in attaining a view of the world
appropriate to each role; they must learn to 'behave, feel and see
the world in a manner similar to other persons occupying the
same position' (Secord and Backman, 1964). Role-learning, by
definition, takes place in relation to other people; in the preschool
years these 'others' are principally the parents, which further
underwrites their influence over the child's conception of reality.

Even when children expand their horizons and their social
world they are likely to encounter similar versions of reality to
that within their own family. It is not only that they learn from
other people with a somewhat similar view of the world; it is also
that they validate that picture in their perception of the concrete
world. They learn that black people tend to live in the poorer
urban areas, in cheaper housing, and are concentrated in menial
employment and unemployment. These things can be adduced
as further reasons for prejudice against them, given that society
places a negative evaluation on each of these aspects of their
situation. In addition to direct experience, children increasingly
elaborate their world-view from the printed page and the mass
media. The world of children's books and comics has come under
close scrutiny in recent years in an effort to identify the material
which might contribute to negative racial attitudes. While
analysis of books and comics (see, for example, Dixon, 1977;
Laishley, 1975) has shown that the portrayal of black people is
frequently stereotyped and derogatory, there is little direct evidence of a causal link between this material and children's racial
attitudes (not least because of the ethical problems in initiating a
controlled study, and the difficulty in isolating the effects of literature from every other influence on the child's attitudes).

It is arguably true that television is now the most important non-human socializing agent, and the criticisms of omission and stereotyping of blacks levelled at other media have relevance here too. Greenberg and Atkin's (1978) analysis of American television describes how:

> Until the late 1960s blacks and other minorities were most notable for their invisibility in the mass media. . . . When these sub-groups were portrayed, it was usually in an unflattering fashion. . . . The growth of the civil rights movement was eventually accompanied by a trend towards more frequent and positive media representation of minorities. By 1969 half of all TV dramas contained a black performer . . . since that time about 6 to 9% of all characters in TV shows have been black. (p. 6)

The authors argue that although the overall portrayal of black people improved markedly in both quality and quantity, the picture has remained static for a number of years now. British television has been slower to respond to these demands and still does not approach the American level of utilizing blacks. British television news and current affairs programmes share with the newspapers a common perspective on race and immigration issues, one which implicitly assumes that black people constitute a problem. Husband (1975) has shown how the style of media treatment of these issues originates not only in implicitly racist values but also in conventional values about the nature of news items ('bad news makes good copy'). It is interesting in this connection to note that the 'problem' perspective is built into the very terms of the debate about race; invariably, public discussion of the issues will be couched in terms of 'prejudice' versus 'tolerance'. Clearly, 'tolerance' itself implies that there is something *negative* to *be* tolerated. Thus nuance is more obvious if we consider alternative terms to tolerance, like 'acceptance' or even 'mutual respect', which, however idealistic in the present climate, nevertheless constitute more genuine *opposites* to prejudice. This is also important because the terms are used to define the climate of race attitudes we would hope to create, and mere 'tolerance' sets that goal far short of any very positive ideal. Certainly the continuing 'problem' perspective and the negative connotations it carries can only assist the process of negative racial attitude development in the child's contact with these media.

4.3 *Race and colour*

In all the foregoing discussion it has been assumed that society's teachings about race were the main determinants of children's racial attitudes, as reflected in the studies described. However, in recent years it has been suggested (J. E. Williams and Morland, 1976) that part of the explanation for these attitudes may lie elsewhere; that children learn an evaluative orientation towards the *colours* black and white, and these influence their attitudes towards those groups of people designated by the same colour-names.

In a long series of studies, Williams and his associates have convincingly demonstrated that the colours black and white have a very strong evaluative connotation (black-negative, white–positive), and that these meanings hold good for a wide spectrum of people. Originally working with American college students (J. E. Williams, 1964), he later found that essentially the same colour-meaning system existed for students from Germany, Denmark, Hong Kong and India (J. E. Williams, Morland, and Underwood, 1970). Further cross-cultural replication of these findings (Osgood, 1967) across 23 different settings runs counter to any explanation of the phenomenon in terms of the conventional usage of black–white evaluative symbolism in the language, art and literature of a particular culture. Rather there would appear to be some pan-cultural influence at work to explain the consistency of the phenomenon across very diverse cultural settings. This view gains more credence when we take into account the findings with preschool children in the United States which show the same colour-meaning system operating before there could have been very much contact with literary or other sources of colour symbolism (J. E. Williams and Roberson, 1967). Several studies (such as Boswell, 1974a; J. E. Williams and Roberson, 1967) have shown a positive correlation between scores on tests of colour-meanings and those on tests of racial attitudes; in the main, however, they are not strong correlations, suggesting that 'the degree of racial bias shown by a child cannot fully be explained by reference to the strength of his tendency to view the colour white as good and black as bad, and vice versa' (J. E. Williams and Morland, 1976, p. 223) Nevertheless, in their summary of relevant research findings (J. E. Williams and Morland, 1976) the burden of their argument is that colour-

meanings do have an important role to play in the development
of racial attitudes, laying an evaluative foundation on which the
latter may build. They show, for example, how people who rate
the colour black negatively also rate the concepts 'black person'
and 'negro' negatively (J. E. Williams, 1970), with the implication
that the latter evaluations somehow proceed from the former.
Indeed, they demonstrate how easily this association can be
made by showing how the connotative meanings of colour names
can be conditioned to terms with which they are associated. For
example, subjects were conditioned to associate the colour black
with particular stimuli, and thereafter rated those stimuli negatively, even though at face values they had nothing whatever to
do with blackness (Harbin and Williams, 1966). How much more
easily, then, might these negative connotations become associated with a group of people whose skin-colour is referred to as
black and whose racial group is described in the same way?

Williams and Morland have arrived at a developmental theory
of colour and race bias which is based upon these findings and
related work. They argue that other theories have placed too
much emphasis on cultural, subcultural and familial influences in
shaping the child's racial attitudes. These theories, they suggest,
cannot account for some of their findings, for example, the cross-
cultural replication of colour-meanings, the lack of correlation
between race or colour bias and IQ in their young subjects and
the absence of clear age-progression in pro-white bias in the early
years; if these biases were solely a function of cultural learning,
they would be likely to increase with greater exposure to information sources from year to year, and show a correlation with IQ.
The authors prefer a theory which recognizes three distinct
determinants of children's race bias: (a) experiences in infancy
common to all members of the species which interact with certain
'biological' dispositions to produce a fundamental white-positive,
black-negative association; (b) subsequent exposure to 'the cultural practice of employing the color white (or light) to symbolise
goodness and the color black (or darkness) to symbolise badness.
Such symbolism abounds in the mass media, in children's literature, in Judeo-Christian religion, and, through idiomatic speech
in the very fabric of human communication' (J. E. Williams and
Morland, 1976, p. 267); (c) the interaction of factors (a) and (b)
with specific cultural teachings about race *per se*. For the individual child the nature of these influences will vary according to

his racial membership, socioeconomic status and family background (in terms of parental attitudes, personality dispositions and child-rearing practices).

Clearly it is the first of these categories which is both novel and controversial. J. E. Williams and Morland (1976, p. 262) propose:

> that virtually every child has experiences early in life which lead to the development of a preference for light over darkness. This is based primarily on the child's visual orientation to his environment and the disorientation which he experiences in the dark, and may be further strengthened by the fact that his major need satisfactions occur during the daylight hours. In addition to a learned preference, one can speculate that the young human may have an innate aversion to darkness, perhaps based on an evolutionary history in which avoidance of the dark was an adaptive characteristic.

Not only is this proposed to be the basis of the child's individual orientation it also explains the wider phenomenon of cultural colour meanings:

> Color symbols are not seen as arbitrary conventions but as cultural elaborations of shared human feelings. Further, there is little danger of the symbols losing their meanings because . . . [they] . . . are continually being re-established in successive generations of young children. . . . We believe that the main impact of the cultural symbolism is to confirm the child's own feelings regarding light and darkness and to consolidate this learning in conceptual form. Prior to the cultural messages the child *feels* that white is good; following the cultural messages, the child *knows* that white is good. (p. 267)

Onto this evaluative foundation is built a superstructure of information and attitudes that is specifically *racial*; but within this racial learning Williams and Morland continue to stress the importance of *colour* and explicitly counsel against the use of colour-names to distinguish between racial groups precisely because of the association with this established evaluative system.

The authors concede that the first proposition of the theory, concerning the effects of pan-cultural experiences and innate biological dispositions, is speculative. They also wish to avoid the implication that 'the light–dark preference of the young child is the sole – or even the principal – determinant of his race and color biases' (p. 266). However, it inevitably assumes an important role within their theory, if only because of its novelty and the need to argue for its acceptance.

The difficulties their proposition presents are to some extent acknowledged by the authors. As regards the biologically based component of the child's aversion to darkness, they allow that 'although the demonstration of other innate fears in children . . . makes such speculation plausible, we know of no empirical findings with children which require such a theory' (p. 262). The suggestion that the dark comes to be associated with fear and disorientation, and the day with better visual orientation and need satisfaction, is more persuasive; these are indeed universal cultural experiences, and the learning process involved may account for why children do not evidence fear of the dark from birth – a fact which detracts somewhat from the 'innate' part of the theory. However, there can be equally plausible speculations within this almost impenetrable realm of experience which would make quite opposite predictions. Perhaps the most compelling of these would be the argument that the child's earliest experiences take place in the total *darkness* of the womb, in perhaps the most favourable environment for warmth, security and immediate need-satisfaction that the individual will ever enjoy; subsequently thrust into the 'booming, buzzing confusion' of daylight, the infant only ever approaches his previous state when warm, relaxed and sleeping in the darkness of his bedroom. Later fears of the darkness may be learned from a variety of sources, including the simplest of childhood stories. This line of argument has its own shortcomings, but it does illustrate how this kind of 'biologism' can be adduced in support of diammetrically opposed theses. There is also something in the very nature of untestable biologism which counsels caution – particularly in this controversial area: 'innate biological dispositions' as explanations of human behaviour, like instincts, tend to prevail over other kinds of explanation. As Ashley-Montagu (1968, p. xiii) wrote: 'if no other rational explanation appeals, or even when it does, instinct is likely to trump every other card in the pack because it appears to be so fundamental, so recondite, so all-embracing and so simple'.

'Innate biological dispositions' not only have the connotations of 'basic', 'root' causes (which can elevate their importance over and above subsequent learning experiences), their influence can appear to be both inevitable and intractable. Having witnessed the sociopolitical repercussions of Jensen's theories concerning heredity, race and IQ, it seems unwise to argue for an innate component to racism without compelling proof. However, such a theory might be hedged with reservations in a scientific context, its simplification and translation into a public arena would inevitably provide a buttress and a justification for racism, which is not the authors' intention.

5   Prejudice and black identity

We now turn to consider the other side of the prejudice equation, namely the effects of prejudice on black people. This has always been an emotive issue, and, in recent years, one that has become increasingly controversial. Once again we shall approach it within a developmental perspective.

In the very first of the doll-studies of children's racial attitudes, Clark and Clark (1947) uncovered an unexpected phenomenon which subsequently entered the folklore of social psychology and even influenced national political decisions. They had presented each of their black subjects with a pair of black and white dolls and simply asked 'Which of these two dolls looks most like you?'; around a third of the black children indicated the *white* doll as looking more like them, and this finding was regularly repeated in many subsequent studies. Now there is no question about this 'misidentification' being in any sense a mistake; the children had shown themselves to be able to correctly label which doll was supposed to represent which group on other tests. Nor is it likely that this response represents any real belief that the white doll does indeed look more like them, except perhaps in a minority of disturbed cases. Rather it has been taken to signify that the child feels unwilling or ambivalent about identifying with the correct figure because of the inferiorized, derogatory connotation attaching to black people. As Goodman (1946, p. 626) wrote: 'The relative inaccuracy of Negro identification reflects not simple ignorance of self, but unwillingness or psychological inability to identify with the brown doll because the child wants to look like the white doll'. This interpretation tends to be confirmed by those studies that have found the misidentification response to be accompanied by a general prowhite orientation, which often involves the children expressing the wish that they would 'rather be' white if they could.

Naturally these results aroused much concern; here was distressing evidence that racism was so intense and pervasive that it had penetrated the psychological defences of young black children, to taint their picture of their group and, by implication, themselves. However disturbing this picture, it nevertheless married well with an overall conception of black mental health which held sway for many years. Kardiner and Ovesey (1951) wrote that for the negro: 'The central problem of adaptation is the discrimination he suffers and the consequences of this discrimination for the self-referential aspects of his social orientation. In simple words it means that his self-esteem suffers . . . because he is constantly receiving an unpleasant image of himself from the behaviour of others to him'. They went on to argue that the 'basic Negro personality' is essentially an unhappy, stressful one, suffering more and enjoying less than white men. The need for vigilance and personal control is ever-present which is 'destructive of spontaneity and ease . . . and it diminishes the total social effectiveness of the personality'; black people, in the title of Kardiner and Ovesey's book, bear 'the mark of oppression'. This perspective was based on interview material from a very small number of people in therapy and was thus hardly representative of black people as a whole. However, it was representative of psychology's view of black people, even though there was little evidence to demonstrate that black people were indeed less mentally healthy than their white counterparts. The argument took the following form: living within a culture dominated by white people and their values, black people introject white attitudes which hold them to be inferior. Feelings of inferiority are entirely natural, for the role of the black person as it is conceived by the majority and depicted in the culture simply *is* an inferior one. Moreover, the social and material environment to which racism relegates them is further cause for such feelings: 'Many Negroes . . . accept in part these assertions of their inferiority . . . when they employ the American standards of success and status for judging their own worth, their lowly positions and lack of success lead to further self-discouragement' (Pettigrew, 1974, p. 9). This image of their race makes for difficulties in identification with a despised and rejected group. They may identify with their own group but then it is difficult to escape the implications of that derogatory identity for their own self-image. Alternatively, they may identify with whites which denies their true identity and is unrealistic and fraught with anxiety. The problem is presented as a choice between two evils. They may resolve it in one direction or the other, or they may stay in conflict over their identity; in each case they suffer anxiety and lowered self-esteem.

There are a number of problems with this formulation; for example, it supposes that there is a perfect correlation between the individual's evaluation of the ingroup as a whole and his/her evaluation of himself/herself as a member of that group. This flies in the face of evidence of the ways in which individuals may psychologically distance themselves from other group members, accepting the devaluation of the group as appropriate to all except themselves. Then again, the formulation has a Catch-22 flavour to it; there seems to be no route to human happiness available to the black person, whatever psychological course is chosen, there lies anxiety and lowered self-esteem; there is, then, no place for the normal, well-adjusted black person in this scheme of things, which simply does not square with reality.

Above all else, this conventional view of the black person's personality and adjustment was firmly grounded in an era when the social status of blacks was uniformly inferior and relatively static. But as that social reality became subject to rapid change, through the civil rights movement and subsequently the various movements for black consciousness, identity and power, so did the conventional view appear more and more outdated. Cohorts of young, apparently proud blacks were making social, educational and political demands in an assertive way which was anything but anxious, inferiorized and self-abnegating. In time these developments were reflected in psychological research. In the late 1960s and early 1970s came the first evidence of any substantial change in black self-attitudes since psychology had first engaged with these issues. Hraba and Grant (1970) reported a virtual reversal of the pattern of references for, and identification with, whites that had so frequently been found amongst black children. Similarly, related studies of black children's self-esteem showed a significant shift in the direction of improved self-esteem; indeed some demonstrated higher self-esteem in black children than in whites, an apparently unthinkable prospect until quite recently (Zirkel and Moses, 1971).

One consequence of these new developments has been a tendency to rewrite history. Banks (1976) has gone back to re-examine some of the earlier studies of racial identification and preferences among black children, and taken together with more

recent studies, concluded that white preference in blacks 'has yet
to be definitively demonstrated' (p. 1185). He indicates a number
of factors which might undermine the validity of the measures
employed, for example the novelty and attractiveness of the
stimulus figures (see also Brand, Ruiz, and Padilla, 1974), but
more importantly, he questions whether black children's
responses as a group have departed significantly from 'chance'
levels of white-choices. It is arguable as to whether the studies he
cites are fully representative of the whole body of work in the
area, in that he overlooks some of the earlier studies where outgroup choices were more prevalent, and thus draws more heavily
on studies conducted since the phenomenon has diminished. He
also omits reference to any studies conducted outside the United
States which are congruent with the American findings, for
example in New Zealand (Vaughan, 1964b), South Africa
(Gregor and McPherson, 1966) and the United Kingdom (Milner,
1973; Jahoda, Thomson, and Bhatt, 1972). However, Banks' contention that, amongst the studies he has cited, 'the predominant
pattern of choice behaviour among blacks towards white and
black stimulus alternatives has conformed to simple chance',
while perhaps literally correct, disguises as much as it reveals.
'Chance' implies a random, arbitrary level of choice biased in
neither one direction nor the other. But unless one can show that
the nature of the task is ambiguous and misunderstood (and the
evidence is decidedly to the contrary), then choosing across racial
lines (on identification tasks, thus contradicting objective
reality) would seem to involve a somewhat more deliberate
choice than 'chance' implies. This is not, after all, a 'heads' or
'tails' situation, rather an attempt to call 'heads' as 'tails'. At the
simplest level, if these choices of racial identification and
preference responses were truly operating at or about the
chance level, and were affected by no other factors, then we
would expect the same pattern of choices among white children.
It is when we go beyond the statistical consideration of chance
levels, to make interracial comparisons, that we see the fallacy in
Banks' analysis, as indeed J. E. Williams and Morland (1979)
have pointed out.

Banks is by no means the first writer to take issue with 'traditional' views of black self-attitudes and identity (see, for example,
Nobles, 1973). This view has perpetuated a somewhat negative
picture of black people and the argument that it is now outdated

is well-supported by empirical evidence, as we have seen. How-ever, it seems a little quixotic to reject outright the earlier research paradigms and methods when these same procedures are now yielding a picture of more positive black identity which is entirely acceptable; indeed the same writers have adduced this evidence in support of the new perspective. Banks himself cites a number of studies (for example, Gregor and McPherson, 1968; Hraba and Grant, 1970) which are directly based upon the original Clark and Clark (1947) study and give a more positive picture of black identity, yet castigates their forerunners which do not.

Some of the force behind the arguments of Banks and other critics derives from their concern with the simple question that has conventionally been made between 'misidentification' responses on the doll and picture tests, and lowered overall self-esteem; they are right to point out that very few studies have measured both simultaneously, and that the relationship be-tween them has never been reliably established. Turning to the earliest studies of children, we discover that 'lowered self-esteem amongst black children' was frequently an 'interpretive' finding, that is, based upon an interpretation of the doll-test results (and in some cases, additional interview material; see, for example, Goodman, 1952) rather than tests of self-esteem *per se*. Where evaluation of self-esteem did take place it was in this specifically racial context. In contrast, the later studies of black self-esteem included a broader range of subjects (adolescents as well as young children) and employed standardized measures of overall self-esteem, not simply race-related 'tangential' measures. Most of these studies were conducted in the 1960s and early 1970s and demonstrated comparable self-esteem levels in blacks and whites (for a review see Rosenberg and Simmons, 1972). The strands of the argument appear to draw apart, because of the difficulties in comparing different studies of different subjects with different methodologies. They are brought together somewhat in a study by Ward and Braun (1972) which combined a conventional doll-test of racial preference and a standardized self-concept test. With 7 and 8 year old black children, the authors found a majority favouring the black figures, *and* higher self-concept scores amongst those children, as against the lower self-concept scores of the children who showed more white-orientated preferences. These findings would seem to be in lines with both the studies showing increasing black-orientated racial preferences (such as

Hraba and Grant, 1970) *and* those showing higher levels of self-esteem amongst blacks than had previously been acknowledged, while also admitting the possibility of a relationship between the two.

There is no doubt that the published literature on (a) black identification and preference, and (b) black self-esteem is converging on a more positive view of black identity and its implications for self-esteem. This reflection of social change in these studies might be taken as evidence of the relevance of social psychological research and the responsiveness of the measures to real-life developments in the wider society. A somewhat more cynical view of the issue has been taken by Adam (1978). He argues that the changing view of black psychology reflects changing ideology superimposed on research findings which may not be so very different from what went before. Whereas the traditional view of black inferiorization served a purpose as an academic lever in the struggle for civil rights, it increasingly 'acquired the taint of racism' (Adam, 1978, p. 48) as it seemed to connote pathology, and even imply some inherent incapacity, rather than just a response to oppression. Adam detects a rather too hasty attempt to set aside previous conceptions and embrace a new one that is more acceptable to current racial sensibilities. Thus, on the basis of relatively few studies showing no significant differences in black–white self-esteem, McCarthy and Yancey (1971, p. 591) described their aims as 'putting to rest' the lower-self-esteem-in-blacks-tradition, adding that 'discrediting this tradition is, we believe, necessary'. Though Adam somewhat overstates the case, he is right to identify the alacrity with which theory seemed to jump on the new bandwagon, leaving its inconvenient baggage behind. He is also right to point out that amongst that baggage, the concept of inferiorization is not so easily despatched.

Naturally Adam's implication of ideological influence has not passed unchallenged; Simmons (1978) was quick to point out that Adam, too, had his own bias which seemed to be more in line with the earlier findings on black self-esteem: 'he seems to believe that the oppressed must have lower self-esteem no matter what the studies show'. The acrimony of the debate rather reinforced Adams' argument in revealing the personal investment in particular positions. In the meantime, the question of whether racism does indeed psychologically harm minorities was somewhat obscured. Thomas Pettigrew attempted to resolve the competing claims in the following way (1978, p. 60):

(1) Oppression and subjugation do in fact have 'negative' personal consequences for minority individuals that are mediated by behavioural responses shaped through coping with oppression.

(2) There are also some 'positive' personal consequences for minority individuals as well as 'negative' consequences for majority individuals; but these effects of a repressive societal system have not received the research attention they deserve.

(3) Many of the 'negative' consequences for minority group members are reflected in personality traits that in a range of situations can act to maintain rather than challenge the repressive societal system.

(4) Not all minority group members will be so affected nor are most traits of most minority members so shaped, since a sharp disjunction between the 'real' personal self and the racial self is generally possible.

(5) Thus, proud strong minorities are possible despite the 'marks of oppression'. And this strength becomes increasingly evident as the minority itself effectively challenges the repressive societal system.

It is the fourth of these propositions that seems to provide some understanding of how the weight of 'inferiorizing' forces on the minority individual may nevertheless be withstood. The argument would be that blacks will tend to have lower self-esteem when evaluating themselves against whites, according to white standards, that is, when they are evaluating themselves in a racial context. The question remains as to whether that racial dimension is in fact an important one that affects the individual's overall feelings of self-esteem. As Simmons (1978, p. 56) wrote:

One major line of reasoning is that an individual's positive or negative attitude towards himself is influenced less by the larger society and more by the opinions of significant others in his immediate environment. The black, particularly the black child, tends to be surrounded by other blacks. Thus, those persons who matter most to him – parents, teachers and peers – tend to be black and evaluate him as highly as white parents, teachers and peers evaluate the white child. In addition, although his race, family structure or socioeconomic status may be devalued in the larger society, in his immediate context most others share these characteristics. Comparing himself to other economically disprivileged blacks, the black child does not feel less worthy as a person on account of race or economic background . . . encapsulated in a segregated environment as are most urban black children, they may be less aware of societal prejudice than is assumed. Even if aware, they may attribute the blame to the oppressor rather than themselves. Militant black ideology is aimed at just this end, encouraging the disprivileged to externalise rather than internalise blame for their low societal rank and thereby protect their self-esteem.

While the major part of the argument, concerning the sources of overall self-esteem in the black child is convincing, the latter part is less so. Even in segregated environments the climate of attitudes around black people would be evident to children in any number of ways, indeed the very environment in which they find themselves is a constant reminder of the valuation placed on their group by white people. And as we have discussed, race attitudes enter into the whole spectrum of cultural media with which they have contact whether in a segregated or non-segregated environment.

At this point we should perhaps review the various accounts of black people's reaction to the 'inferiorizing' pressures of prejudice:

1   the conventional view that some black people accept white society's devaluing portrayal of the group, and by implication, themselves; this leads to lowered self-esteem, and to strategies which avoid this conclusion, for example (a) misidentification or identification with whites, and/or (b) intragroup comparisons, whereby individuals distance themselves psychologically from other members of their group, believing the 'group characteristics' to apply to all except themselves (see also Klineberg and Zavalloni, 1969).
2   Pettigrew's suggestion that despite inferiorizing pressures, overall self-esteem may be protected by maintaining 'a sharp disjunction between the "real" personal self and the racial self'.
3   Simmons' argument that the inferiorizing pressures may be less severe than has been suggested in their consequences for self-esteem, because the individual's main sources of self-esteem are intragroup comparisons with other blacks who are similarly placed, and largely isolated from white society and its values about black people.

There are two main objections to these accounts: they describe only *individual* strategies (and are necessarily reductionist) and they do not account for the *changes* in black self-attitudes we have witnessed; they impose a further static picture on a dynamic situation. A more parsimonious account is provided within Tajfel and Turner's (1979) theory of social comparison processes, one which recognizes *group* coping strategies as they unfold in a changing situation. These strategies emerge when individual attempts at assimilation with the majority are perceived to have failed because of constraints imposed by the majority. As Tajfel (1978, p. 16) writes:

> . . . for the black Americans, this kind of movement (has developed) after the attempts to obtain a straightforward integration into the wider society have been perceived by some as a failure. This means that, in the eyes of some people, the expectation or the hope that there is a chance to integrate *as individuals* and on the basis of individual actions alone has more or less vanished. The remaining alternative, both for changing the present 'objective' social situation of the group and for preserving or regaining its self-respect, is in acting in certain directions not as individuals but as members of a separate and distinct group. . . . In addition to obtaining some forms of parity, efforts must also be made to delete, modify or reverse the traditional negative value connotations of the minority's special characteristics. In social competition for parity, the attempt is to shift the position of the *group* on certain value dimensions which are generally accepted by the society at large. In the simultaneous attempts to achieve an honourable and acceptable form of separateness or differentiation, the problem is not to shift the group' position within a system of values which is already accepted, but to change the *values* themselves.

In other words, the need for every social group to create and maintain a positive social identity *vis-à-vis* other social groups (as Tajfel and Turner posit) is frustrated, as is the strategy of leaving 'their existing group and joining some more positively distinct group' (Tajfel and Turner, 1979, p. 40). Thus parity, both 'objective' and psychological, can only be obtained through *positive* social differentiation (that is, positive social comparison) from/ with the outgroup, in this case the white majority. Tajfel and Turner (1979, pp. 43–6) outline a number of forms this may take; these include (a) 'individual mobility', which is constrained by the factors mentioned already; (b) 'social creativity', a group strategy that may focus upon (i) 'comparing the ingroup to the outgroup on some new dimension; (i) changing the values assigned to the attributes of the group, so that comparisons which were previously negative are now perceived as positive';

that is, creating a new identity through altering the valency of various characteristics associated with the group (for example, the celebration of blackness and the cultivation of African roots); (iii) 'changing the outgroup . . . with which the ingroup is compared' (which may be part of the stimulus to black antisemitism in the United States and anti-Asian attitudes among West Indians in the United Kingdom); (c) 'social competition', where 'group members may seek positive distinctiveness through direct competition with the outgroup. . . . To the degree that this may involve comparisons related to the social structure, it implies changes in the groups' objective social locations. . . . We can hypothesise . . . that this strategy will generate conflict and antagonism between subordinate and dominant groups insofar as it focusses on the distribution of scarce resources'. Certainly black demands for equal shares in the scarce resources of housing, employment and educational opportunity are preceived as social competition by whites, if we recall Ashmore and Del Boca's (1976) suggestion of 'perceived racial threat' as an emerging factor in contemporary racism.

This formulation describes and explains the evolution of various black reactions to racism, as evidenced both in 'real-life' and in research studies. To the extent that black individuals do indeed deem their racial membership as an important facet of their self-concept, and to the extent that the above strategies have been effective, so would we expect to find increasing willingness among blacks to identify themselves with a more valued social group, with concomitant positive effects on both their racial and overall self-esteem. While there is, or has been, some value in the accounts of individualistic strategies, they are inadequate to explain the wider group phenomena; and of course, the success of the group strategies in creating a positive social identity largely removes the need for individual ones.

6   Conclusion

After 70 years social psychology has seen racial prejudice move from the periphery towards the centre of our concerns, both as social scientists and ordinary citizens. The early theories of prejudice, like the scapegoat theory and the authoritarian personality theory, sought explanations in the 'externalization' of inner needs and conflicts within *individuals*. They are valuable in their own right, for example in explaining why particular individuals or subcultural groups may be more susceptible to absorbing the prevailing climate of prejudice in a particular context, but cannot in themselves explain the origin and maintenance of that climate *per se*, without recourse to (a) improbable equations between individual and group behaviour, or (b) supplementary social and cognitive factors. In line with Durkheim (1938), explanation of the wider social phenomenon requires an appropriate level of explanation in the sense that the determining cause of a social fact must be sought in social facts and not in the effects of individual consciousness. Sherif and Sherif's intergroup studies were an attempt to ground an explanation of intergroup behaviour and attitudes in the 'social facts' of competition and cooperation; though the Sherifs' analysis of their own observations was incomplete, the work was truly seminal, not least for the stimulus it provided to the subsequent work of Tajfel and Billig and their colleagues on intergroup discrimination. The research and some of the ideas it has stimulated are described elsewhere in this chapter and volume, and need not be reiterated here. There seems little doubt that Tajfel and Turner's theory of intergroup conflict, deriving from this work, is an important contribution to research on racial prejudice.

Before we become carried away with enthusiasm for these new developments we should perhaps indicate some shortcomings in theory in the area as a whole. It is easy and usual to pay lip-service to the idea that the study of prejudice is necessarily a multidisciplinary enterprise; there continues to be scant regard paid to this ideal in practice. Multidisciplinary cooperation is a two-way street, and social psychology is not solely responsible for the lack of traffic; however, the example set by Gurr (1970) in translating frustration–aggression theory into a political science context is one that should be followed. There is perhaps one incidental danger in the multidisciplinary approach – in encompassing the full spectrum of economic, historical, political and social determinants of prejudice we may be deterred from considering any ameliorative strategies, that is, attempts to combat prejudice short of wholesale social change. This is itself a neglected area of research, work being confined to small-scale experimental studies of techniques to induce racial attitude change in young children in preschool or inschool contexts (see

Best *et al.*, 1975; Litcher and Johnson, 1969). Hopefully we will see further developments of this kind; in so far as we can gain any purchase on the problem, the school as an important socializing agent affords an opportunity for intervention in the socialization process to foster more positive racial attitudes before prejudice has become too firmly established. This is not simply to propose 'education' as a panacea, but to argue for a philosophy and practice of multiracial education, which, while not in itself eradicating prejudice, can nevertheless foster a value-system which offers some resistance to the pressures towards prejudice from the world outside.

We have argued that our conception of what prejudice *is*, and the forms that it takes, has been a rather static one. Ashmore and Del Boca (1976) have attempted to refine the picture in their description of some contemporary forms of racism which are altogether more subtle than openly avowed prejudice. While it is too early to evaluate the utility of their particular contribution, we should welcome any trends to bring into focus the more covert forms of racism. Antidiscrimination and positive discrimination legislation, together with the perception of black socioeconomic and political advances, are all likely to militate against the kind of overt expressions of prejudice we have conventionally measured, and we require more refinement in our concepts and methods if we are not to conclude from this, perhaps mistakenly, that prejudice has diminished.

The issue of black reactions to prejudice has been a vexing one for many years, though it is capable of resolution. To reject, on the basis of contemporary studies, the notion that a *minority* of black people (though a significant one) has coped with the imposition of a devalued identity by various individual strategies including 'disidentification' or 'misidentification', seems, to the present writer at least, to be an overreaction to an unpalatable phenomenon. It discounts wholesale a considerable body of research evidence from children, which despite some methodological shortcomings, is persuasive, and reinforced by accounts of 'real life' behaviour patterns pointing in the same direction. Neither should we discount a number of literary accounts by black writers which testify to these same conflicts and strategies. The very fact that the evidence *now* points to a more unequivocal identification with blackness, in parallel with the substantial socioeconomic advances made by blacks and efforts to cultivate a positive black identity, seems to give more rather than less credence to the argument. Evidence of a similarly changing picture in 'black' minorities outside the United States (for example, Vaughan, 1978a, 1978b) also supports this point of view. As regards the relationship between racial identification and self-esteem, one of the more recent studies, by Ward and Braun (1972), showed that higher black preference was accompanied by higher overall self-esteem. This suggests that there is indeed a relationship between the two, and implies that, although the 'interpretive' equation of white preference and low self-esteem was too readily made in the earlier studies, it nevertheless had some validity. In any event, while the issue of identification and self-esteem obtaining in an earlier era cannot now be empirically resolved, there is currently a reasonable consensus in the literature as to the contemporary picture, one in which black preference and self-esteem on a par with whites has become the norm. It remains theoretically interesting to tease out the precise relationship between racial identification/preference, 'racial' self-esteem and overall self-esteem; and although these problems appear to have diminished for black Americans, there remain many racial minorities for whom they are all too relevant.

While both the 'conventional' view of black identity, and the contemporary critique of that view, are essentially 'static' accounts wedded to particular periods of history, Tajfel and Turner's theory subsumes the empirical evidence relevant to each, while also accounting for the transition from individualistic to group coping strategies. This effective resolution of the debate in the context of a more general theory of intergroup behaviour and attitudes seems to provide the most promising theoretical basis for future research.

CHAPTER 5

Social Stereotypes and Social Groups

HENRI TAJFEL

1 Introduction: stereotypes and social stereotypes

The *Oxford English Dictionary*, in its definition of 'stereotypes', draws a tight circle in admitting only that they 'make {things} unchangeable, impart monotonous regularity . . . fix in all details, formalize . . .'. This static formality of the semi-officially recognized use of the term contrasts nicely with the awareness of its social significance shown by the late Oliver Stallybrass, co-editor of *The Fontana Dictionary of Modern Thought* (1977). He wrote in it that a stereotype is

> an over-simplified mental image of (usually) some category of person, institution or event which is *shared*, in essential features, by large numbers of people. The categories may be broad (Jews, gentiles, white men, black men) or narrow (women's libbers, Daughters of the American Revolution) . . . . Stereotypes are commonly, but not necessarily, accompanied by prejudice, i.e., by a favourable or unfavourable predisposition towards any member of the category in question. (p. 601, my emphasis)

This definition will do for our purposes. By using the term 'shared' as a central part of his statement, Stallybrass went further than many social psychologists have done in encompassing the *social* psychological significance of stereotypes and of the processes on which their functioning is based. He was not unique in doing so. The important social functions of unfavourable stereotypes were at the forefront of the discussions held at the Edinburgh International Television Festival in August 1978. Some extracts of the statements made at the Festival by various playwrights, producers and executives, and reported in *The Times* (30 August, 1978), are worth quoting:*

---

*These statements are not *verbatim* reproductions of what was said at the Festival, but quotations from the account of the proceedings as published by *The Times*.

. . . stereotyping should be seen as a part of the comic method by which we tried to diminish what we feared: in the case of contemporary Britain, not only the Irish but also Afro-Asians and Arabs. (John Bowen)

It was appalling . . . to find programmes like the *Black and White Minstrel Show* or *Mind Your Language* being broadcast in a multiracial society under strain, when what they did was reinforce stereotypes of black and brown people as being lovable but ridiculous. (Brian Winston)

A socially damaging caricature becomes a stereotype. (Fay Weldon)

. . . a distinction [needs to be made] between the creation of a dramatic 'type', which meant achieving the subjectivity of another person or group, and the creation of stereotypes, which were essentially weapons in the struggle for power constantly being waged in society. (John McGrath)

It is clear from all this that some of the people whose jobs put them in daily contact with the creation and diffusion of social stereotypes are keenly aware of the variety of social functions served by these stereotypes. After some years of relative neglect, we have also recently seen a revival of interest amongst social psychologists in the study of stereotypes. Their approach stands, however, in stark contrast to the awareness of the social dimension of the problems shown by the practitioners of the media. This will become clear from our second series of quotations:

Illusory correlation refers to an erroneous inference about the relationship between two categories of events. [The hypothesis] suggested that the differential perception of majority and minority groups would result *solely* from the cognitive mechanisms involved in processing information about stimulus events that differ in their frequencies of co-occurrence. (Hamilton and Gifford, 1976, p. 392, my emphasis)

. . . there is no theoretical or empirical reason to assume that forming generalizations about ethnic groups is radically different from forming generalizations about other categories of objects. (S. E. Taylor *et al.*, 1978, p. 778).

The present writers believe that stereotypes are not a unique structure or process but exist and operate in the same manner that cognitive processes in general influence an individual when he deals with any aspect of his environment. (D. M. Taylor and Aboud, 1973, p. 330)

... the group's impression may depend on the way in which data on individuals are organized in memory .... Specifically, the proportion of extreme individuals in a group was retrospectively overestimated; this was true for both physical stimuli (height) and social stimuli (criminal acts). (Rothbart *et al.*, 1978, p. 237)

All this is a consistent echo of earlier views:

These judgemental effects of categorization {of physical objects} are probable fairly general .... It is likely that the same is happening in the use of more abstract social judgements which are implicitly quantitative, such as, for example, those concerning the relative frequency of crimes in various social groups .... (Tajfel, 1957, pp. 202–3)

Or:

One of the aims of the investigations reported here was to show that evidence for the essential unity of judgement phenomena, social or physical, can be slowly accumulated and that ... it is possible to attempt an understanding of seemingly varied phenomena in terms of the same general judgement principles. (Tajfel and Wilkes, 1963, p. 114)

These quotations do not stress the social functions of stereotypes but consider them as aspects of general cognitive processes, products of the basic ways in which individuals perceive and interpret their environment. An important point must be stressed at this juncture. It is emphatically *not* the argument of this chapter that general cognitive processes can be neglected in the study of the formation, diffusion and functioning of social stereotypes. On the contrary, as will be seen later, we fully agree with the views expressed in the above quotations that the understanding of the cognitive 'mechanics' of stereotypes is essential for their full and adequate analysis. The question that arises is whether such a study is all that is needed – a view which, as we have seen, seems to be adopted in some of the recent (and also earlier) work on the subject.

Two definitions of stereotypes were provided at the beginning of this chapter, the 'formal' one from the *Oxford English Dictionary*, and the more 'social' one formulated by Stallybrass (1977). The difference between the two illustrates (albeit rather crudely) the difficulties which are bound to arise in an approach to the study of stereotypes which remains exclusively or primarily cognitive. 'Stereotypes' are certain generalizations reached by individuals. They derive in large measure from, or are an instance of, the general cognitive process of categorizing. The main function of this process is to simplify or systematize, for purposes of cognitive and behavioural adaptation, the abundance and complexity of the information received from its environment by the human organism (see Bruner, 1957; Bruner and Klein, 1960; Bruner and Potter, 1964; Tajfel, 1959, 1972b, 1978d). But such stereotypes can become *social* only when they are *shared* by large numbers of people within social groups or entities – the sharing implying a process of effective diffusion. There are at least two important questions which cannot be answered if we confine our interest to the cognitive functions alone. The first concerns an analysis of the functions that stereotypes serve for a social group within which they are widely diffused. The second question concerns the nature of the links between these social or group functions of stereotypes and their common adoption by large numbers of people who share a social affiliation. It is the asking of these two questions which defines the difference between the study of stereotypes *tout court* and the study of *social* stereotypes.

1.1   *The four functions of social stereotypes*

The cognitive emphasis, just discussed, in the recent revival of interest in the study of stereotypes is but one instance of a much more general trend of work and thought in social psychology. This is based on two assumptions, implicitly adopted or explicitly made in some of the highly influential traditional texts in the subject (for example, Berkowitz, 1962; Jones and Gerard, 1967; Kelley and Thibaut, 1969). The first is that the analysis of individual processes, be they cognitive or motivational, is necessary *and* also (very often) sufficient for the understanding of most of social behaviour and interactions. The second assumption follows from the first: such an analysis need not take into account *theoretically* the interaction between social behaviour and its social context. The latter is seen as providing classes of situations in which the general individual laws are displayed. Alternatively, the social context is conceived as providing classes of stimuli which 'impinge' upon social interactions, in other words, they selectively activate certain individual 'mechanisms' or modes of functioning which are already fully in existence. These 'individualistic' views have recently been contested in a number of publications (for example, Doise, 1978; Moscovici, 1972;

Perret-Clermont, 1980; Stroebe, 1979; Tajfel, 1972a, 1978a, 1979; see also chapter 2), so the detail of the arguments will not be rehearsed here once again. It is enough to say that, in the case of social stereotypes, 'social context' refers to the fact that stereotypes held in common by large numbers of people are derived from, and structured by, the relations between large-scale social groups or entities. The functioning and use of stereotypes result from an intimate interaction between this contextual structuring and their role in the adaptation of individuals to their social environment.

The remainder of this chapter will be concerned with outlining these individual and social functions of stereotyping and with the nature of the interaction between them. In the case of individual functions, stereotypes will first be discussed (as they have been in the earlier and recent work mentioned in the previous section) in relation to their cognitive aspects; this will be followed by a consideration of stereotypes as tools which help individuals to defend or preserve their systems of values. Two social functions of stereotypes will then be considered: first, their role in contributing to the creation and maintenance of group 'ideologies' explaining or justifying a variety of social actions; and, second, their role in helping to preserve or create positively valued differentiations between one's own and other social groups. Finally, we shall attempt to specify the links that possibly relate these two social functions of stereotypes to their individual counterparts.

2 The cognitive functions of stereotypes

The basic cognitive process in stereotyping is categorization, the structuring of sense data through grouping persons, objects and events (or their selected attributes) as being similar or equivalent to one another in their relevance to an individual's actions, intentions or attitudes. The essential cognitive function of stereotyping is thus to systematize and simplify information from the social environment in order to make sense of a world that would otherwise be too complex and chaotic for effective action. When G. W. Allport discussed the categorization process in his classic (1954) book on prejudice, he assigned to it the following 'five important characteristics' (pp. 20–2):

1 It forms large classes and clusters for guiding our daily adjustments.
2 Categorization assimilates as much as it can to the cluster.
3 The category enables us quickly to identify a related object.
4 The category saturates all that it contains with the same ideational and emotional flavour.
5 Categories may be more or less rational.

In his later discussion in the same book of 'the cognitive process' in prejudice, Allport assigned to it the characteristics of selecting, accentuating and interpreting the information obtained from the environment. He distinguished, however, between a category and a stereotype (p. 191). The latter was 'an exaggerated belief associated with a category. Its function is to justify (rationalize) our conduct in relation to that category'. In this way, Allport combined the cognitive and the 'value' functions of stereotyping. But his definition of stereotyping located the phenomenon as no more than an adjunct to his fourth 'important characteristic' of the process of categorization (see above), as something which itself 'is not a category' but an 'image' which 'often exists as a fixed mark upon the category' (p. 192). Since then, we have gone beyond Allport's static conception of a 'fixed mark' or an image.

This section is concerned with the details of the functioning of categories which, as Allport put it, guide 'our daily adjustments'. As it is not possible to describe in detail the extensive literature on the subject, we shall summarize the issue of 'adjustments' by a few statements followed by a lengthy quotation of a general hypothesis. Categorizing any aspect of the environment, physical or social, is based on the adoption of certain criteria for the division into (more or less inclusive) separate groupings of a number of items which differ in terms of these (and associated) criteria and resemble each other on the same (or associated) criteria within each of the groupings. The 'differing' and the 'resembling' need not necessarily be based on any easily ascertainable concrete similarity or dissimilarity. A common linguistic labelling may be sufficient, as in Wittgenstein's (1953) example of games: 'for if you look at them you will not see something that is common to all, but . . . we see a complicated network of similarities overlapping and crisscrossing' (see Billig, 1976, chapter 9, for an extensive discussion of this issue as it applies to social categorization). It might be argued that, for example, the social category of 'nations' represents some of the characteristics attributed by Wittgenstein to the category of 'games'.

Whatever these classifying criteria may be, *some* of the attributes of the items separated into, for example, two categories may present varying degrees of bimodal correlation (or subjectively experienced bimodal correlation) with the division into categories. In turn, these correlated attributes, which are associated in an orderly fashion with the categorial division *need not* be the original criteria for the categorization. For example, if oranges were to be classified as being of Spanish or Californian origin, and at the same time it turned out that the Spanish ones tended to be larger than the Californian ones (or vice versa), the size would be an attribute correlated with the categorization, but not a criterion for it. (It should be noted that in chapters 2 and 3 the term 'criterial attribute' is used in a broader sense which includes both criterial and correlated attributes as defined here.) Starting from this basis, the following general hypothesis has been formulated:

> When a classification in terms of an attribute other than the physical dimension which is being judged is superimposed on a series of stimuli in such a way that one part of the physical series tends to fall consistently into one class, and the other into the other class, judgements of physical magnitude of the stimuli falling into the distinct classes will show a shift in the direction determined by the class membership of the stimuli, when compared with judgements of a series identical with respect to this physical dimension, on which such a classification is not superimposed. When a classification in terms of an attribute other than the physical dimension which is being judged is superimposed on a series of stimuli, and the changes in the physical magnitudes of the stimuli bear no consistent relationship to the assignment of the stimuli to the distinct classes, this classification will have no effect on the judged relationships in the physical dimension between the stimuli of the series. (Tajfel, 1959, p. 21–2)

This hypothesis was later elaborated to predict that when a classification is correlated with a continuous dimension, there will be a perceptual tendency to exaggerate the differences on that dimension between items which fall into distinct classes and to minimize these differences within each of the classes (Tajfel, 1969a; Tajfel and Wilkes, 1963). In this form, the same hypothesis and some others related to it were extended to explain cognitive aspects of social stereotyping. These aspects which follow directly from the hypothesis are the perceptual accentuation of differences between people belonging to different social groups or categories (on those personal attributes which are subjectively correlated with their division into categories), and the perceptual accentuation of the corresponding similarities between people belonging to the same social group or category. To create the fullblown stereotype, we need only assume that the physical dimension described above stands for some personal attribute such as 'intelligent', 'lazy', or 'dishonest' which has become subjectively associated with some social group through personal or cultural experiences and that the classification itself is in terms of some racial, ethnic, national or other social criterion. It seems likely that the categorization process, as described in the hypothesis, is responsible at least in part for the biases found in judgements of individuals belonging to various human groups (some recent extensions of the categorization process to social phenomenon are described in chapters 2 and 3).

Secondary hypotheses were concerned with the effects of the amount of past experience with the correlation between the classification and the stimulus dimension, the strength of the correlation, and its salience in any particular social situation (see Tajfel, 1959; Tajfel and Wilkes, 1963). Most of these hypotheses were subsequently confirmed in experiments using both physical stimuli and categorizations of people into social groups (see Billig, 1976; Doise, 1978; Eiser, 1979; Eiser and Stroebe, 1972; Irle, 1975; Lilli, 1975; Tajfel, 1969a, 1972b for general reviews of the earlier work). Some of the same hypotheses have been rediscovered and retested in very recent experiments (for example, S. E. Taylor et al., 1978, pp. 779–80).

In one sense, some of these recent reformulations represent a theoretical retreat from the earlier work. This is so for two reasons. The first concerns the crucial role played in stereotypes by value differentials associated with social categorizations. This 'value' aspect of categorizations, to be discussed in the next section, was one of the cornerstones of the earlier theories (see most of the references mentioned above). It has lost its explicitness through the emphasis in the more recent work upon the near-monopoly of 'pure' cognitive processes in the functioning of stereotypes. The second reason for the theoretical retreat is a lack of specification in some of the more recent work of the *nature* of the dimensions on which differences between social groups, or similarities within such groups, would or would not be accentuated. As was seen above, clear specifications of this kind were amongst the principal aims of the earlier hypotheses. The understanding of the use of categorizations in simplifying and ordering the social environment clearly depends upon these specifications. They help us to predict when and how various aspects of these categorizations fit or do not fit requirements posed by the need to systematize the information which individuals receive or select from their environment. What is equally important, they provide predictions as to when and how the various social differentiations or accentuations will or will not occur.

Rothbart *et al*. (1978) point out that: 'Research on the nature of group stereotypes has focused far more on the description of social stereotypes than on the mechanisms or processes implicated in their formation . . .', (p. 237) and that: 'Traditionally, research and theory on stereotypes have emphasized the motivational functions of group stereotypes, with particular attention paid to the inaccuracy, irrationality and rigidity of such judgements' (p. 254). It can be seen from the work described above that there has also been a long tradition of cognitive research into stereotypes, done and multiply reported from the late 1950s onwards. At present there seems to be a resurgence of such research (both in stereotyping and in social psychology at large). Unfortunately, some of the more recent work seems to be almost completely unaware of the earlier tradition. There is a danger that the frequent complaints about the non-cumulative character of much social psychological research will find here, once again, their unwelcome vindication. We seem sometimes to be working by a series of successive starts or jerks, separated from each other by a few years during which a topic drops more or less out of sight; each of the new starts then claims in turn to be the harbinger of a fresh and previously neglected approach.

The research of Rothbart *et al*. (1978) and Hamilton (1976) and Hamilton and Gifford (1976) and their colleagues draws our attention to another cognitive aspect of the functions of social stereotyping. This has to do with the subjective inflation or exaggeration of the significance of social events which either occur or *co*-occur with low frequency in the social environment. Rothbart's research is concerned with the fact that impressions of *groups* of people are affected by 'the way in which data on [some individual members of these groups] are organized in memory' (Rothbart *et al.*, 1978, p. 237). Extreme events or extreme individuals are more accessible to memory retrieval than are more average instances. In turn, following Tversky and Kahneman (1973), Rothbart *et al.* argue that this affects judgement in the sense that those instances from a class of events which are the most available for retrieval serve as a cue for judging the frequency of their general occurrence in the class as a whole. In this way, *negative* behaviours of members of *minority* groups are likely to be over-represented in memory and judgement. (This is a brief summary of a more complex argument made by Rothbard *et al.*) The attitudinal aspects of these interactions between social categorizations and memory have recently been studied by Eiser, Van der Pligt, and Gossop (1979).

There is a family resemblance between some of this research and the work on 'illusory correlations' reported in Hamilton (1976) and Hamilton and Gifford (1976). As the latter wrote, the concept of 'illusory correlation' was introduced by Chapman (1967) who defined it as 'the report by observers of a correlation between two classes of events which, in reality, (a) are not correlated, or (b) are correlated to a lesser extent than reported' (p. 151). Experiments conducted by Hamilton and Gifford show that this kind of processing of information (associating, as in Rothbart's views, 'infrequent' events with 'infrequent' people) is directly related to the formation of stereotypes about minority groups.

In sum, there exists a long and reputable tradition of work which shows that the formation and use of social stereotypes cannot be properly understood without a detailed and painstaking analysis of the cognitive functions they serve. We must now turn to the second major function of stereotypes: the role they play in the preservation of an individual's system of values.

3 *Social stereotypes and individual values*

Much of the argument in the previous section and the studies mentioned in it referred to a general cognitive process which can be briefly restated as follows: once an array of stimuli in the environment has been systematized or ordered through their categorization on the basis of some criteria, this ordering will have certain predictable effects on the judgements of the stimuli. These effects consist of shifts in perceived relationships between the stimuli; these shifts depend upon the class membership and the relative salience of the stimuli in the total array. The resulting polarization of judgements and the special weight given to some of the stimuli serve as guidelines for introducing subjective order and predictability into what would otherwise have been a fairly chaotic environment.

But this is not enough if one is concerned with the issues of social categorization and stereotyping. Many of the categorizations applying to objects in the physical environment are neutral, in the sense that they are not associated with preferences for one category over another, with one category being 'bad' and another 'good', or one being 'better' than another. When, however, this does happen in the physical environment, certain clear-cut effects appear which distinguish between 'neutral' and 'value-loaded' classifications.

In the heyday of the 'New Look' in the study of perceptual processes, some of these effects were considered to consist of an overestimation of the magnitude of the stimuli which had some value relevance to the individual judging them (see particularly Bruner, 1973, Part I). In a pioneering paper Bruner and Rodrigues (1953) drew attention to the possibility that what appeared to be a simple overestimation may have been in fact a *relative* increase in the judged subjective differences between stimuli (such as coins) which varied simultaneously in their size and value to the subjects. This notion was elaborated and developed a few years later (Tajfel, 1957) and confirmed in a number of subsequent experiments (see, in particular, Eiser and Stroebe, 1972, for a general review and analysis of the theoretical considerations and the earlier empirical work).

Three consequences followed. The first was that there was no reason why what appeared to be true for judgements of physical magnitudes of individual stimuli should not also apply to judgements of differences between individual people on various dimensions of person perception (see Tajfel and Wilkes, 1964). The second was that the model of increased polarization of judgements relating to value differentials between *individual* stimuli should also apply to *classes* of stimuli which differed in their respective value to the people making the judgements. The third consequence was a combination of the first two: the increased accentuation of judged differences, due to value differentials, between classes of stimuli and of judged similarities within each of the classes should apply, once again, to value differentials not only in the physical environment but also (and much more importantly) to social categorizations of people into differing groups (see Doise, 1978; Eiser and Stroebe, 1972; Tajfel, 1959,1963).

It is at this point that it is important to state the clear-cut *functional* differences between the 'purely' cognitive processes manifested in the shifts of judgement applying to neutral categories, which were discussed in the previous section of this chapter, and the social value differentials with which we are now concerned. Two of these differences are particularly relevant to the present discussion.

The first concerns the nature of the feedback obtained from the environment when the use of categorizations as a guiding device for judgements leads to shifts or biases which are in accordance with the *assumed* characteristics of the stimuli belonging to the different classes. In the case of judgements applying to the physical environment, it can be expected that shifts leading to erroneous responses which are maladaptive will be quickly eliminated. Exaggerating the differences between two coins of different value is a 'good error' as long as it provides an additional guarantee that there will be no confusion between them. But any errors or shifts of judgement which do lead to misidentification or a confusion between objects which should be clearly discriminated will have as a direct consequence the correction of the errors. The speed and accuracy of these corrections will depend upon the degree of clarity of the information received after the response has been made.

In the case of the social environment, it is not only that the information received (about, for example, the personal characteristics of people) is generally much more ambiguous to interpret and lacking in clear-cut criteria for its validity. If we now return to the shared nature of social stereotypes, discussed in the first section of this chapter, the judgements made of people who belong to one or another social groups or categories which are stereotypes in certain ways are likely to receive, by definition, the positive feedback of general social consensus. Less information than is the case for physical categories will be needed to confirm these judgements, and considerably more to disconfirm them in the face of what appears to fit in with what is generally accepted as a social reality.

The second of these two issues is perhaps even more important. It concerns once again a difference between social categorizations which are neutral and those which are value-loaded. A neutral social categorization means that certain stereotyped traits may be applied to certain social groups ('Swedes are tall', for instance) without having a positive or negative value connotation. It is not that the trait 'tall' is necessarily value-free; it is the category 'Swedes' which may be neither positive nor negative, and therefore meeting a Swede who happens to be short will not present much of a crisis – if there are enough short Swedes around, this may even modify the general stereotype. But the story is very different if and when a social categorization into groups is endowed with a strong value differential. In such cases, encounters with negative or disconfirming instances would not just require a change in the interpretation of the attributes assumed to be characteristic of a social category. Much more importantly, the acceptance of such disconfirming instances threatens or endangers the value system on which is based the differentiation between the groups. As we have seen, for G. W. Allport (1954) the cognitive process in prejudice consisted of 'selecting, accentuating and interpreting' the information obtained from the environment. It is in this way that the process fulfils its function of protecting the value system which underlies the division of the surrounding social world into sheep and goats. There are many and varied daily social situations which enable us to select, accentuate and interpret in accordance with our value differentials information about different 'kinds' of people; but we shall select here only two instances of the process since both have been subjected to fairly systematic study by social psychologists.

The first of these can be discussed very briefly, as it is no more than a simple extension of the earlier discussion in this and the previous sections about value differentials magnifying *still further* the accentuation of differences between classes, and similarities within classes, which is characteristic of neutral categorizations. Just as the judged differences in size between individual items in a series of coins tend to be larger than the corresponding differences in a neutral series of stimuli (Tajfel, 1957), so the judged differences on certain dimensions correlated with the classification tend to be larger in the case of social categorizations related to value differentials than they are in neutral categorizations (Tajfel, 1959, p. 21). One way to test this hypothesis has been to compare the ratings of personal attributes of people belonging (or assigned) to two different social categories and made by two groups of subjects; one of these groups of subjects was previously ascertained to be prejudiced against one of the two categories while the other group of subjects was not. The underlying assumption was that the categorization presents a stronger value differential for the former than for the latter group. The results usually showed that the prejudiced group judged the differences on certain dimensions between the members of the two categories to be larger than the non-prejudiced group (Doise, 1978, for a recent review of some of the earlier studies). We shall return later, when discussing the group functions of stereotypes, to this issue of intergroup differentiation. For the present, it will be enough to point to the value-preserving function of differentiations of this kind. The ordering by individuals of their social environment in terms of social groups, some of which are viewed favourably and some unfavourably, becomes more efficient and stable if and when various relevant differences between these groups (and similarities within them) can be conceived to be as constant and clear-cut as possible.

The second line of social psychological evidence concerns the identification in ambiguous conditions of members of disliked social categories. Bruner, Goodnow, and Austin (1956, chapter 7) presented an early and detailed analysis of the conditions in which individuals will commit errors of overinclusion or overexclusion in their assignment of ambiguous items into one of two categories which are available for such assignments. The first of these errors consists of including into a category an item which, on specified criteria, does not belong to it; the second, of excluding an item which does belong.

In their analysis, Bruner, Goodnow, and Austin related the frequencies of the type of errors to their perceived consequences, that is, to the weighing up of the respective risks entailed by making one or the other kind of mistake. This analysis of risk can be extended to the subjective consequences of misidentifying the group membership of individuals when the social categories to which they belong are related to a strong value differentiation for the person making the category assignments. The risks are that a

'bad' person could be assigned to a 'good' category or a 'good'
person to a 'bad' one. If this happens too often, it could threaten
or even invalidate the value differential. From the empirical evidence we have, it looks as if the former of these two kinds of
errors is avoided more persistently than the latter. In other
words, there seems to be a preference for not having the wrong
person inside an exclusive club over the risk of having the right
person out of it. This conclusion can be can be drawn from a
group of studies conducted in the 1950s in the United States in
which comparisons were made in the accuracy of recognition of
Jews by antisemites and non-antisemites. The prejudiced subjects showed greater accuracy in recognizing Jews. This was due
to a response bias; they labelled a relatively larger number of
photographs as Jewish (for example, Scodel and Austrin, 1957).
'The mistakes committed by [this] group . . . tend in the direction
of assuming that some non-Jews are Jewish rather than the other
way round' (Tajfel, 1969b, p. 331).

Here again, the value differentials guide the use made of
ambiguous information. As in the previously discussed case of
accentuation of differences and similarities, the maintenance of a
system of social categories acquires an importance which goes far
beyond the simple function of ordering and systematizing the
environment. It represents a powerful protection of the existing
system of social values, and any mistakes made are mistakes to
the extent that they endanger that system. The scope, frequency
and enormous diversity of witch-hunts at various historical
periods (including our own) of which the basic principle is not to
miss out anyone who might be included in the negative category,
bear witness both to the social importance of the phenomenon
and to the importance of the psychological processes insuring the
protection of the existing value systems or differentials. In this
section we discussed a few rather undramatic instances of this
process. It must not be thought that the value aspects of the
functioning of social stereotypes remain equally undramatic in
periods of high stress, social tensions and acute intergroup conflicts.

4   *The ideologizing of collective actions*

The witch-hunts just mentioned above bring us to a discussion of
the role of collective actions in the functioning of social

stereotypes. Tens of thousands of 'witches' were tortured and killed in Europe in the sixteenth and seventeenth centuries. As Thomas (1971) wrote:

> It was the popular fear of *maleficium* which provided the normal driving-force behind witch prosecution, not any lawyer-led campaign from above . . . . Even when the courts ceased to entertain witch-trials, popular feeling against witches continued, as the periodic rural lynchings demonstrated . . . . The reason for the new popular demand for witch-prosecution cannot be found in the changing attitude of the legislature and the judiciary. It must be traced to a change in the opinion of the people themselves. (pp. 548, 550, 551, 1973 edition)

Thomas's point about witch-hunting having been a massive and widespread phenomenon in the population at large is important, since it is likely that it applies to many social situations where causes of distressful social events are sought in the characteristics, intentions or behaviour of outgroups. In his early functionalist analysis of witchcraft, Kluckhohn (1944) characterized witches as being generally 'outsiders'. It is interesting to see that the social psychological parallels to the hotly contested functionalist views in social anthropology have mainly stressed the individual motivational processes rather than their social equivalents. They consisted, in the main, of adopting perspectives on mass violence or mass hatred which extrapolated from individual displacement or redirection of aggression to the large-scale instances of social aggression or violence (see Tajfel, 1972a, 1978a, for a discussion of this issue and of the theoretical difficulties presented by extrapolations of this kind).

In contrast, the large-scale diffusion of hostile or derogatory social images of outsiders do not seem to have been the subject of explicit applications of cognitive theories in social psychology, although such theories might have made a useful contribution to our understanding of the large-scale acceptance and resilience of social stereotypes. These theories would include, for example, the 'justification of behaviour' aspects of cognitive dissonance, the work within attribution theory on the attribution of responsibility and intentionality, the research on internal versus external locus of control, etc. The traditions of social psychological research on stereotypes originate primarily from two sources: the descriptive one, consisting of a detailed analysis of the contents of stereotypes; and the cognitive one which emphasizes, as we have seen, the *individual* cognitive processes.

These two traditions have not, however, come together to work towards the construction of a theory of *contents* of stereotypes as shared by social groups. The outer limit of the social psychologists' interests resided in manipulating the salience of social categorizations in natural or laboratory conditions and finding that, as a result, intergroup stereotypes became more 'active', intense or extreme. As I wrote elsewhere (Tajfel, 1979, p. 188):

> . . . there are undoubtedly some social contexts in which these salient social categorizations are generally induced in many individuals, for one reason or another; there are other social contexts in which they are not. But all the rest remains a deep mystery to the social psychologist. Thus, social categorization is still conceived as a haphazardly floating 'independent variable' which strikes at random as the spirit moves it. No links are made, or attempted, between the conditions determining its presence and mode of operation, and its outcomes in widely diffused commonalities of social behaviour. Why, when and how is a social categorization salient or not salient? What kind of shared constructions of social reality, mediated through social categorizations, lead to a social climate in which large masses of people feel that they are in long-term conflict with other large masses? What, for example, are the *psychological* transitions from a stable to an unstable social system?

It is quite obvious that an approach to a social psychological theory of the contents of stereotypes would address itself to no more than a small corner of the large issues raised by the questions above (see Tajfel, 1978a). We have, however, at our disposal all the elements needed to make a modest beginning, and we can trace some general directions that could be taken. This will be done in two steps. The first consists of a rough classification of the psychological functions that stereotypes can serve for social groups; and the second, of pointing to some potential developments which could provide a theoretical and research articulation for these functions.

The classification of functions is not presented here as an *a priori* or deductive exercise. It is a rough attempt to bring together what is generally known from social psychology, social history, social anthropology and common sense. It appears, from all these sources, that outgroup social stereotypes tend to be created and widely diffused in conditions which require: (a) a search for the understanding of complex, and usually distressful, large-scale social events; (b) justification of actions, committed or planned, against outgroups; (c) a positive differentiation of the ingroup from selected outgroups at a time when such differentiation is perceived as becoming insecure and eroded; or when it is not positive, and social conditions exist which are perceived as providing a possibility for a change in the situation. We shall refer to these three functions, respectively, as those of social causality, justification and differentiation.

No more can be done here than to cite a brief selection of examples in order to illustrate or clarify the nature of each of these categories. To start with causality: something was 'needed' in the seventeenth century to explain the plague, but as Thomas (1971) wrote, its incidence 'was too indiscriminate to be plausibly explained in personal terms'. Thus, 'the Scots were accused to have poisoned the wells of Newcastle in 1639', Catholic sorcery was held responsible for an outbreak of gaol fever in Oxford in 1577, and the local Independent congregation was blamed for an outbreak of plague in Barnstaple in 1646 (Thomas, 1971 (1973 edition), pp. 667–8). An even clearer example can be found in antisemitism. This is carefully and brilliantly traced in Norman Cohn's (1967) description of the persistence of the myth about the Protocols of the Elders of Zion. As Billig (1978, p. 132) wrote:

> The emotional ferocity of the crudest anti-Semitism makes it easy to forget that anti-Semitism can provide an extensive cognitive interpretation of the world. Above all, crude anti-Semitism is based upon a belief that Jews have immense powers of evil in the world. Modern anti-Semitic dogma asserts that Jews control both communism and capitalism and that they aim to dominate the world in a régime which will destroy Western civilization. All facts are explained in terms of this pervasive and perverse belief.

The 'justification' principle is well documented throughout Kiernan's (1972) work. Two examples, taken almost at random, illustrate the principle:

> The idea of Europe's 'mission' dawned early, but was taken up seriously in the nineteenth century. Turkey, China, and the rest would some day be prosperous, wrote Winwood Reade, one of the most sympathetic Westerners. 'But those people will never begin to advance . . . until they enjoy the rights of men; and these they will never obtain except by means of European conquest'. (p. 24)

> An ex-soldier from Tonking whom W. S. Blunt talked to in Paris exclaimed against his government's folly in sending armchair

philosophers to run the colonies, who fancied that all men were brothers – it was the English in India who were realistic – *'en agissant avec des brutes il faut être brutal'*. (p. 97)

The 'differentiation' principle could be considered as a part of the general syndrome of ethnocentrism understood in Sumner's (1906) sense of the term, but this is an oversimplification. It is a dynamic process which can only be understood against the background of *relations* between social groups and the social comparisons they make in the context of these relations. The creation or maintenance of differentiation, or of a 'positive distinctiveness' of one's own group from others which are relevant to the group's self-image seems to be, judging from the accounts of social anthropologists, a widespread phenomenon in many cultures. As this intergroup differentiation has been discussed recently and extensively elsewhere (see Tajfel, 1974, 1978a, 1978c, 1979; Tajfel and Turner, 1979; Turner, 1975a; see also chapter 3) we shall simply note it here as the third of the major group functions served by stereotyping.

5   Links between the collective and the individual functions

Two points remain to be made, concerning the relationship of this discussion to the potential development of a properly *social* psychological theory of stereotyping. The first of these two points has to do with the social functions of stereotypes – social causality, justification and differentiation or some combination between them – as they relate to the contents of a stereotype. The analysis of such a relationship cannot be done in psychological terms alone. The competitive and power relations between groups will largely determine the nature of the psychological functions which need to be fulfilled by the groups' reciprocal images. But when this is taken for granted as the indispensable background for any social psychological analysis, such an analysis should then be able to make theoretical sense of the contents of ingroup and outgroup stereotypes. This can be done through identifying one or more of the major group functions that the stereotype may be serving. A perspective of this kind would undoubtedly be a significant advance upon the descriptive tradition of work which often did not go much further than eliciting a cultural consensus about certain 'traits' attributed to certain groups and, at times, monitoring the stability or changes over time of these collective descriptions.

The second and final point concerns the links between the group functions of stereotyping discussed in the previous section of this chapter and the individual functions discussed in the preceding sections. It seems that, if we wish to understand what happens, the analytical sequence should start from the group functions and then relate the individual functions to them. As we argued in sections 2 and 3 of this chapter, an individual uses stereotypes as an aid in the cognitive structuring of his social environment (and thus as a guide for action in appropriate circumstances) and also for the protection of his system of values. In a sense, these are the structural constants of the sociopsychological situation; it is the framework within which the input of the socially derived influence and information must be adapted, modified and recreated. No doubt, individual differences in personality, motivation, previous experiences, etc., will play an important part in the immense variety of ways in which are shaped these adaptations, modifications and recreations. It remains equally true, however, that – as we argued at the beginning of this chapter – a stereotype does not become a *social* stereotype until and unless it is widely shared within a social entity. As long as individuals share a common social affiliation which is important to them (and perceive themselves as sharing it), the selection of the criteria for division between ingroups and outgroups and of the kind of characteristics attributed to each will be directly determined by those cultural traditions, group interests, social upheavals and social differentiations which are perceived as being common to the group as a whole. As Berger and Luckmann (1967) so cogently argued some years ago, social reality is not 'out there' to be comprehended or assimilated in some manner which asymptotically approaches to its faithful reflection in individual attitudes and beliefs. It is constructed by individuals from the raw materials provided to them by the social context in which they live. If this were not the case, the selection and contents of social categorizations and social stereotypes would have to be conceived as arbitrary and random occurrences, capriciously varying from one society to another, from one historical period to another. As it is, the restricted variety of the combination and recombination of their common elements can be attri-

buted to the restricted number of the major group functions that
they generally seem to be serving; and their common structure to
the two major psychological functions they serve for the individual.

As was mentioned earlier, social psychological theories of
stereotypes have not been much concerned in the past with
establishing the links between these collective and individual
functions. This is why no grand theory can be offered in this
chapter – or perhaps an all-encompassing theory is not possible,
or even desirable. Theories in social psychology have often been
characterized by a strong positive correlation between the scope
of their ambitions and the bluntness of their predictions or explanations. As Hinde (1979) recently argued in relation to another
area of social psychology, we are still at a stage in which a strong
dose of theoretical criticism is not only unavoidable, but is
perhaps the most useful way to proceed.

The suggestion made here is that future research in social
psychology could relate the group functions of explanation, justification and differentiation to the individual functions of cognitive structuring and value preservation by using two recent
theoretical and research initiatives. These concern the study of
social groups conceived as social categories, each immersed in a
complex and wider structure of many social categories which are
defined as such by the individuals involved and are related to each
other in a variety of definable patterns (such as those of power,
status, prestige, majority–minority, perceived stability or perceived possibility of change, flexibility or rigidity of group boundaries, etc.). The first of these two research initiatives relates an
individual's self-respect or self-concept (or his 'social identity') –
through the process of intergroup social comparison – to the relative position of his group on a number of dimensions in a multi-
group social system. This idea helps to account for the ways in
which individuals shape the realization of the group functions of
differentiation and justification. It is not possible to review here,
even briefly, the substantial amount of recent research on this
subject (see Tajfel, 1978a, 1982; Tajfel and Turner, 1979; and
chapters 3, 4 and 7 in this book). An apt one-sentence summary
has been provided by Commins and Lockwood (1979, p. 282):
'The social group is seen to function as a provider of positive
social identity for its members through comparing itself and distinguishing itself, from other comparison groups, along salient
dimensions which have a clear value differential'.

There is a clear theoretical continuity here with some of the processes of accentuation of differences occurring when certain criteria of classification are combined for individuals with value differentials between those categories which have been selected as important in systematizing the social environment (sections 2 and 3 of this chapter). Thus, a social psychological theory which relates the group differentiation function to social representations of the macrosocial context has at the same time direct implications for the individual functions of categorization and value-preservation in stereotyping. This continuity is consonant both with the general argument of the chapter and also much empirical research on the role of social categorization in structuring our views of the social environment (see Tajfel, 1978d). The social context of values and requirements for adaptation to the environment helps the individual to seek out, to select for special attention, to exaggerate, and, if necessary, to create, those similarities and differences which fit in with the general consensus about what matters and what does not matter in the potentially infinite number of possible structures of social divisions and social equivalence.

The second of the two initiatives mainly concerns the social or group function of explanation, but it also has important implications for the two other functions of justification and differentiation. It consists of some recent attempts to draw attention to the fact that traditional attribution theory has remained largely individualistic and has neglected both the social determinants and the social functions of the processes of attribution (see Apfelbaum and Herzlich, 1971; Deschamps, 1977, 1978; Duncan, 1976; Hamilton, 1978; Hewstone and Jaspars, 1982; Mann and D. M. Taylor, 1974; Stephan, 1977; D. M. Taylor and Jaggi, 1974).

The remainder of this brief excursion into 'social' attribution is a paraphrase of some of the arguments put forward by Hewstone and Jaspars (1982) – to whom I am grateful for first drawing my attention to the synthesis that can be made of some of the ideas outlined in this chapter with their attempts to 'socialize' traditional attribution theory. As they wrote:

> . . . the main point is that traditional attribution theory has failed to introduce the fact that *individuals* may belong to different social *groups* . . . . In this alternative perspective . . . an observer attributes the behaviour of an actor not simply on the basis of individual characteristics, but on the basis of the group or social category to which the actor belongs and to which the observer belongs.

Hewstone and Jaspars provide a number of recent empirical examples of this kind of social attribution, although perhaps the earliest instance can be found in the famous study of rumour by G. W. Allport and Postman (1947). As Hewstone and Jaspars argue, this is a dynamic interaction, in the sense that perceptions of the causes and reasons for the behaviour of members of the ingroup and the outgroup are determined by the existing relations between the groups, they are interdependent, and they contribute in turn to the future course of the intergroup relations. Following Buss (1978), Hewstone and Jaspars define causes as 'that which brings about a change' and reasons as 'that for which a change is brought about'. They also expect that 'reasons' would tend to be used to explain the behaviour of ingroup members and 'causes' would apply to outgroup members. At the same time, this hypothetical dichotomy would be strongly affected by the positive or negative evaluations of the behaviour to which the explanation is applied. The results, such as those from the study of D. M. Taylor and Jaggi (1974) in which internal attributions were made of socially desirable acts performed by ingroup members and external attributions to the socially undesirable acts performed by them (with the opposite pattern applying to members of the outgroup), are not too far removed from the 'reasons–causes' dichotomy. It is obvious that this kind of a model can lead to useful predictions of a number of complex interactions in the perception or attribution of social causality.

To return to the main argument of this section, it is also quite obvious that these 'internal' (that is, dispositional) explanations are an instance of the functioning of social stereotypes. But the static, stable consensus implied by the older descriptive studies of stereotypes is replaced here by shifting perspectives closely related to the individuals' evaluation of the equally shifting social situations which are perceived *in terms of the nature of the relations between the groups involved*. It is in this way that the potential development of a *social* attribution theory provides the second of our links between the group and the individual functions of stereotyping. Just as the previously mentioned social identity perspective helps to transpose the differentiation and justification group functions of stereotypes to the level of individual functioning, so the social attribution perspective seems to be a promising tool for a similar link from the group functions of justification and explanation.

6 Conclusion

In this chapter we moved from the individual to social functions of stereotypes, and then reversed directions in proposing a sequence of analysis which would start from the social functions to reach the individual ones. This is not the usual sequence in social psychological texts. It is, however, justified on two grounds at least. The first is that, in this way, we come closer in our work to a healthy respect for the social realities of intergroup relations, including social conflict, than is often the case in the study of stereotypes focusing exclusively or predominantly upon cognitive or motivational processes 'inherent' in the individual. At the same time, the resulting individual processes of stereotyping are not conceived as some mystical offshoot of a 'group mind' – the theoretical and empirical integrity of moving from one researchable perspective to another and of linking them explicitly seems to be preserved. Much of what has been proposed here is no more than a hazy blueprint for future research. But if we wish our discipline to become more directly and theoretically involved in the study of the tough realities of our social functioning we need to make a start, even if it consists, for the present, of no more than speculations and blueprints. As I recently wrote elsewhere (Tajfel, 1979, p. 189): 'The point is that we shall never be able to formulate adequate guidelines for research on collective social behaviour if we do not go beyond constructing sets of independent variables seen as functioning in a social environment which is assumed to be psychologically unstructured in its homogeneous and all embracing "inter-individuality"'.

CHAPTER 6

Intergroup Bargaining and Negotiation

GEOFFREY M. STEPHENSON

1 Introduction

'Haggling over the terms of give and take' is one dictionary definition of bargaining, and conveys well the flavour of the processes
involved. There is disagreement – why else the 'haggling'? – but
the bargainers seek agreement over the terms of their exchange –
the 'give and take'. Bargaining occurs in everyday commercial
and legal transactions, it occurs within marriage, it characterizes
much of what goes on in international and industrial relations.
For example, shop stewards as representatives of the workforce
of a company wish to obtain increased material rewards for their
members in exchange for their labour. Management, representing the owners, wish to resist or modify the demands. Together,
by haggling, they may negotiate the terms which should govern
the future relationship of those parties they represent. Both sides
are able to close the factory, the one by withdrawing labour, the
other by locking it out, but not without each side incurring heavy
costs. Such costs may of course be considered bearable if the
rewards of agreement are sufficiently poor, and the likelihood of
ultimate victory sufficiently high.

Bargaining or negotiation (and these terms are here used
synonymously) refers to the process whereby the two sides agree
on how they will determine their relationship in the future. This
chapter is about *intergroup* bargaining, and it is necessary to consider briefly what we understand by that term. *Intergroup* bargaining may be contrasted with *interpersonal* bargaining. Bargaining in industrial relations is a good example of intergroup, or
'collective' bargaining as it is more commonly called, where
wages are negotiated collectively on behalf of employees, by their
representatives in conjunction with managerial representatives of
the employers. *Interpersonal* bargaining might be said to occur
when no representation is involved: for example, a parent
negotiates the allowance a teenage son or daughter should have.

It should, however, be noted that even at these two extremes, the division between 'intergroup' and 'interpersonal' cannot be rigidly upheld. If the parent concerned has more than one child, then agreement with one has implications for the other. Moreover, the children may wish to compare themselves with children who fare better, and maybe force the parent into a like stratagem. In this case, both parent and child may have the experience of being a representative somewhat akin to that of the shop steward or managerial negotiator in industrial relations.

For industrial bargainers, too, there may well be interpersonal *and* intergroup considerations. The representative of a trade union may be a professional negotiator, or she/he may be negotiating on behalf of a group of which she/he is a member, and, hence, may benefit directly as a result of her or his own efforts. Either way, perceptions by the individuals of what constitutes an appropriate settlement will affect their attitudes towards group goals, and what is perceived as appropriate interpersonally does not necessarily coincide with collective interests. In particular when negotiators repeatedly meet each other 'across the table', their understanding about what constitutes appropriate 'give and take' from one negotiation to the next may lead to startling discrepancies between interpersonal and intergroup expectations on any one occasion. They may perceive it in their interests to 'collude' – or negotiate secretly – with their fellow negotiators, in which case processes of interpersonal and intergroup negotiations cannot easily be disentangled (see Walton and McKersie, 1965).

1.1   *Reasons for neglect of the relation between interpersonal and intergroup processes*

This chapter suggests reasons why the inter-relatedness of interpersonal and intergroup factors has been ignored. It will be argued that theories of both interpersonal and intergroup behaviour have been inappropriately applied. However, it will also be argued that current theories of intergroup relations have some limitations when they attempt to explain behaviour in this context.

Research on bargaining and negotiation has been largely concerned with the conditions which lead to 'successful' outcomes. 'Success' has been defined in commonsense terms as that which maximally satisfies both sides, or may be supposed to have satisfied both sides (see McGrath, 1966). This pragmatic approach has led to the examination of the personality, historical and situational factors which are readily manipulable in laboratory simulations of real negotiations. The effect, for example, of 'dogmatism' of negotiators, or their training, and of the physical circumstances of their interaction, have all been examined for their effect on the outcome, and less frequently, the process of negotiations (see Morley and Stephenson, 1977). The theoretical underpinnings of much of this work have been primitive, reflecting what has been, by and large, a rather crude concern with outcomes. Theories of interpersonal bargaining have relied largely on ideas derived from theories of social exchange (Homans, 1961; Thibaut and Kelley, 1959), and have assumed that individuals should adopt strategies which are likely to maximize their joint profits. As far as intergroup bargaining is concerned, the emphasis has been on the lesson to be drawn from Sherif's (1967) conclusion that superordinate goals are necessary for the avoidance of conflict and the emergence of cooperation. Consequently a principal aim of research has been to discover the circumstances in which perceived common interests are maximized, and perceived divisive interests minimized.

The concern with conditions leading to 'successful' negotiations has, it can be suggested, diverted from what should have been the principal question – examination of the strategies whereby negotiators achieve a reconciliation of their interpersonal and intergroup relationships. McGrath's 'tripolar' model of the forces acting upon collective bargainers draws attention to the problem, but his analysis of the process of negotiation was again geared to illumination of the conditions of 'success'. Morley and Stephenson (1969, 1970b) observed that the behaviour of negotiators has implications for relations between individuals, *and* between the parties they represent, and in their later work (Morley and Stephenson, 1977, following Douglas, 1962) they examine the extent to which the emergence of *stages* in negotiation represent one answer to the principal question posed above. As we shall see, for rather different reasons the main theories of intergroup relations have as yet failed to throw much light on this question.

2   *Interpersonal approaches to bargaining*

Although this chapter is concerned with intergroup bargaining in which *representatives* of groups bargain with one another over the terms on which the groups will coexist, the contribution of interpersonal approaches must not be ignored, precisely because the behaviour of representatives has both interpersonal and inter-party (or intergroup) implications. No doubt it would be possible, and sometimes asserted by those they represent, that representatives cynically conduct their negotiations as if they were of only interpersonal significance, and without regard for the true interests of their respective parties. Indeed, it is claimed by some critics that negotiators who meet frequently together develop a consistent emphasis. Walton and McKersie (1965) suggest that bargaining relationships in industry vary from a situation of 'armed truce' to one of 'collusion', according to the tradition prevailing in a particular factory, or industry. In terms of our present discussion this suggests that negotiators may act at one extreme more or less purely as group representatives, their personal feelings and interests being submerged, or identified completely with the collective interests of their party. In such circumstances, negotiations are protracted and frequently bloody, both sides being prepared to exploit every weapon at their disposal. At the other extreme of collusion, the interpersonal relationship is so strong that the interests of their respective parties play a minor role. Deals are struck privately and irresponsibly by representatives whose primary concern is their own personal convenience. In any event, and especially between those who repeatedly bargain with one another, there may well develop an interpersonal bargaining relationship which impinges on the formal process. Bargainers while formally representing their groups' interests are also, to varying degrees, more or less explicitly, and more or less privately, agreeing on how best to 'manage' the relationship between their parties.

When no such interpersonal understanding develops, or private 'deals' are struck, then the formal process of negotiation is hazardous. The problem is largely one of trust – trust that if you as a representative of your side are cooperative, and perhaps concede a point of agreement to the other side, your opponent will be suitably responsive, and not take advantage of your good nature. This problem has been highlighted in laboratory experimental studies of the Prisoner's Dilemma (PD) and other 'matrix games'. In matrix games, players, normally two, in isolation from one another, are required to choose one of two alternative strategies, X or Y, which together determine the 'outcome' of the game, in other words, how many points or how much money they will be awarded. Consider the example of a PD game in figure 6.1.

If both players choose X, a reward of three 'points' is obtained. If one chooses X, the other Y, the one who has chosen X receives no points, and the other four. If both choose Y then each receives one point. The dilemma arises from the fact that if one can rely on the other to 'cooperate' by choosing X, then it is most profitable oneself to choose Y (the 'competitive' strategy), and hence gain the maximum available four points. However, if both players adopt that strategy then one point each is the reward, rather than three points each which could be obtained if both 'cooperated'.

A great deal of work has been directed to the question of the conditions which facilitate the emergence of mutually cooperative or competitive strategies in interpersonal bargaining, as it is frequently called – although its resemblance to 'haggling over the terms of give and take' is not immediately obvious. There is no haggling, no joint decision-making; subjects know exactly what alternatives they may choose and precisely what effect those alternatives will have, and there is customarily no social relationship

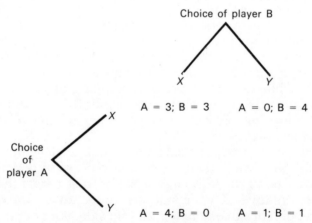

Figure 6.1   A Prisoner's Dilemma game: payoffs for players A and B are determined by their independent choice of strategies X or Y.

between participants. However, it may be said that representatives of competing groups when negotiating face the same strategic dilemma that subjects face in the PD. Over time, by cooperation, they may achieve more than by pursuing jointly competitive or exploitative strategies. Generally speaking, in gaming research interest focuses not on the strategy adoped in a single play, but in *repeated* plays, and such research may have something to say about the development of bargaining relationships, or, indeed, of other relationships in which strategic interdependence is a significant factor. Pruitt and Kimmel (1977) summarize 20 years of gaming research and conclude that, 'How the parties behave at any given point depends on whether they take a short-range or long-range perspective – whether they are only concerned with options and outcomes in the current situation or are trying to achieve some future goal'. (p. 375)

More particularly the evidence suggests that short-range thinking leads to competition in the PD. If the other is about to cooperate, he can be exploited, and if he is not likely to cooperate, then the immediate aim should be to defend oneself against exploitation. Cooperative behaviour, on the other hand, results from long-range thinking, and is designed to achieve the goal of establishing or maintaining mutual cooperation. This goal will elicit cooperative behaviour when the actor has reason to *expect* that the other will him/herself respond cooperatively. In general, this goal-expectation theory of strategic choice in the PD gives a good account of the findings. For example, consistent cooperative or non-cooperative behaviour by one party, not surprisingly itself elicits correspondingly consistent behaviour in the other. Other factors influencing expectations of the other's cooperation include knowledge that she/he has cooperated in the past, receipt of message implying cooperative intent, and so on. A number of studies have explicitly tested the hypothesis that there will be an interaction between determinants of a goal to cooperate, and expectation of other's cooperation. For example, it has been shown that communications about what one expects from the other have greater effect in the later stages of game-playing (when the *goal* of cooperation is presumed to be greater).

Such conclusions from experimental gaming studies are relevant to intergroup negotiations to the extent that strategic interdependence is an important factor in both. More properly, they are relevant to the development of *bargaining relationships* over time – when parties may have to do business repeatedly with one another, in the same way that subjects make repeated plays in experimental games. In short, the goal-expectation theory gives an account of the conditions in which cooperative interpersonal relationships may be established.

For the elucidation of the *process* whereby parties settle disputes or decide on what terms they will cooperate we may turn to another review by Magenau and Pruitt (1979). They define bargaining as a 'process by which two or more parties who cannot dominate one another attempt to reach an agreement that reduces a difference of preference', and negotiation refers to occasions when this is accomplished verbally. In all the studies they review, there is, in other words, communication which may lead to *agreement* between the opposed negotiators about how they should proceed in the future. As opposed to work on experimental gaming, the focus moves from a concern with abstract strategic choice, to discussion of concrete policy on particular issues. The emphasis is then on the process of influence, whereby two individuals with opposed viewpoints come to agreement on that which divides them.

Anyone who has bargained over the price of a second-hand article she/he is buying or selling is aware of the possible tactics that may be employed. An offer can be rejected out of hand and negotiations discontinued, the owner may agree to drop her/his higher price marginally, she/he may attempt to justify the price, or a discussion may be initiated as to the true value of the article concerned. Following Walton and McKersie's (1965) discussion of management–union negotiations, Magenau and Pruitt suggest that at any point in a negotiation, a bargainer may adopt one of four such tactics. Besides deciding to *break off* negotiations, she/he may *concede* a point or two, she/he may try – by either straightforward, devious or deceitful means as she/he so chooses – to *persuade her/his opponent* to concede, or finally, she/he may seek to *coordinate* concession-making between the parties. Figure 6.2 represents their interpretation of the (largely experimental) data that is available on what influences choice of tactics. The material has for the most part come from studies of two-person exchanges in distribution games, games of economic exchange, and to a lesser extent, role-playing and substitute debates, to use the distinctions made by Morley and Stephenson (1977). All the studies have attempted in one way or another to throw some light on

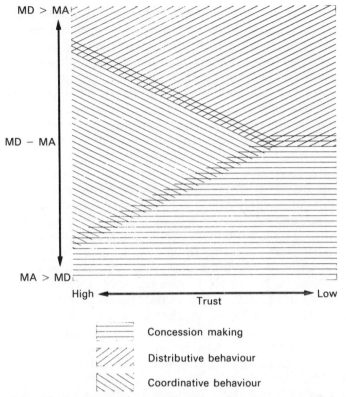

Figure 6.2 Choice of strategy as a function of motive to maintain demand (MD), motive to reach agreement (MA), and trust in the other's cooperative intentions (from Magenau and Pruitt, 1979).

which of the various available strategies will be chosen. On the horizontal axis is represented the *relationship* variable – trust in the opponent's cooperative intentions – which we have seen is the main factor at issue in the Prisoners' Dilemma. This may vary from 'high' to 'low'. Independently of this, on the vertical axis the bargainer is shown at one extreme to be determined to maintain her/his demands (MD) in preference to reaching agreement (MA), and at the other extreme to be more concerned with reaching agreement than with maintaining demands. The various shaded areas indicate what strategies follow from the interplay of these two dimensions, of *trust*, on the one hand, and degree of concern with *maintaining demand* on the other. *Concessions* follow from the strong MA and *distributive* (competitive) behaviour from a strong MD, with evident attempts to coordinate concession-making when these two motives are more evenly balanced, and when trust is high. Given the initial assumption that the negotiators value agreement, this model can account for many of the principal research findings. For example, level of aspirations, the existence of a minimally acceptable outcome, the introduction of a 'fair' alternative by a mediator, and many other factors, have all been shown to influence the adoption of strategies in ways which are consistent with this model.

There are, of course, many factors – in the personalities of the bargainers, history of the relationship, the nature of the task, and the circumstantial constraints – which may determine positions on the main dimensions of this model, and which will determine the extent to which bargainers may deem it necessary to adopt a highly distributive or competitive approach, or judge it worth-while to attempt to develop a joint, coordinated strategy for coming to agreement, or merely to give in, or concede. Research has thrown some light on these, but predominantly in the context of interpersonal relationships. In distribution games, for example, money or some other reward has to be divided between two competitors, or in games of economic exchange, a price negotiated in a simulated buyer–seller transaction. Role-playing debates, and substitute debates may ask the participants to imagine themselves to be representatives of groups, but only in rare instances have players genuinely represented a group, or been required to report back to their principals. The underlying theme of this work, and of Magenau and Pruitt's model, is individualistic. Individuals' relative concern with agreement or with success (from whatever source their concerns come), in relation to the perceived trustworthiness of their opponent, will determine choice of strategy, and consequently, the chances of achieving satisfactory outcomes. The bargainers are haggling over the terms of *interpersonal* exchange.

This is not to say that such considerations are irrelevant to the process of intergroup, or collective bargaining, for, as we have seen, in practice negotiations are unlikely to be purely interpersonal or purely collective. In some instances, as we shall discuss later, the interpersonal bargaining relationship is a highly salient feature of the interaction between established negotiators. The fact is, however, that in the bargaining which concerns us, in negotiations between representatives of groups, the negotiators have an explicit representative role to fulfil. We now turn to the implications of this.

3 *Intergroup negotiation*

In rare circumstances – in the school playground for example – negotiations may take place between *all* members of groups in dispute, as an alternative to fighting it out, tossing a coin, taking a vote, or whatever. Some groups (see Sherif, 1967), however, use such intergroup conferences as an occasion for stepping up the conflict, not as an opportunity to agree about its management. A negotiated compromise – which may be perceived as betrayal of group interests – is more readily accomplished by delegated representatives, and this is the form of 'collective bargaining' or intergroup negotiations, which concerns us here.

What is distinctive about *intergroup* negotiation? We have already suggested that conclusions from research on interpersonal bargaining do not tell us all we need to know about collective bargaining. In collective bargaining, the dispute about which the bargainers must come to agreement does not concern the rate at which the bargainers will swap resources between *themselves*. What the bargainers personally get from the encounter is not strictly germane to the question of what they have secured for those persons whom they represent.

How have psychologists examined processes of collective bargaining? By and large, they have been content to treat collective bargaining as an instance of interpersonal bargaining, but have tried to graft on the collective factor, as just one of many factors which may affect the outcome. Recent reviews (Druckman, 1977; Klimoski, 1978; Magenau and Pruitt, 1979; Rubin and B. R. Brown, 1975) have summarized the results of studies which have adopted the 'grafting' procedure. In all of them, no distinction is made between interpersonal and intergroup or collective bargaining; it is merely established that, in Druckman's words (1979, p. 31), 'The research completed to date has made us aware of the importance of role obligations in negotiation. The way in which a negotiator responds to these obligations influences the negotiation process'. What factors determine his responsiveness? Druckman (1977, pp. 30–1) summarizes the work as follows:

... responsiveness (to role obligations) legitimizes a pattern of behaviour that prevents a negotiator from responding spontaneously to his opposite number. These effects are most pronounced under certain conditions, such as (1) when a negotiator has little latitude in determining either his position or his posture, (2) when he is held accountable for his performance, (3) when he has sole responsibility for the outcome, (4) when he is obliged to a constituency that is present during the negotiation, and (5) when he is appointed rather than elected. Under these conditions, a negotiator's behaviour is constrained by his obligations. The more latitude a negotiator has in formulating his positions, the more dispersed the responsibility for the outcome, the more abstract the constituency (e.g. cultures, ideologies), the less is the impact of his role obligation on negotiating behaviour. The 'uncommitted' representative is relatively free from constituent or administrative demands; instead, he is free to respond to the demands of his opposite number.

Now, while it may be legitimate to ask, as does Druckman, how variations in the salience of role obligations affect the behaviour of the collective bargainer, it is fallacious to argue, or to assume, that role obligations impinge – more or less detrimentally – on an otherwise interpersonal negotiation, and that collective bargaining is merely a particular form of interpersonal bargaining. Yet that is precisely what the majority of psychological researchers have done, as the quotation from Druckman illustrates. There are signs that investigators (including Druckman) are recognizing the problem. For example, the explicit concern of Klimoski (1978) is to elucidate the resolution of intergroup conflict by negotiations, and he is rightly concerned that investigators have not systematically examined the effectiveness of different methodologies in accomplishing this. Druckman (1978) attempts to solve the problem by suggesting that an interpersonal bargaining model may apply to the bargainer's dealings with his/her opposite number, and suggests that an additional 'negotiator-as-representative model' is required to deal with his accountability to a constituency. This merely acknowledges the problem, and, as Druckman admits, does not provide 'a more general model, incorporating both processes'. (p. 110)

Druckman (1977) states that responsiveness to role obligations reduces the spontaneity of interpersonal exchange. What implications is this said to have for choice of tactics in negotiation? In terms of Magenau and Pruitt's model, the effects of increasing responsiveness to role obligations would be to increase MD (motive to maintain demand), and hence to encourage distributive behaviour, with predictably unfavourable consequences on time to agreement, deadlocks and so on. Responsiveness to role obligations, in other words, is adjudged to *hinder* the process of effective interpersonal decision-making. As we shall see, this is a thoroughly unsatisfactory approach to the problems of intergroup negotiations, pervasive though it may be. Let us examine a major drawback of this tradition.

3.1 *The attempt to transcend intergroup aspects of negotiation*

One consequence of this approach to collective bargaining (intergroup negotiation) has been to reinforce a comfortable illusion in the psychological treatment of conflict, stemming – paradoxically – from the work of Sherif (1967, see chapter 4): That representatives of groups may be expected to perceive the higher interests which their respective groups have in common, and to act as if the conflicting interests they are entrusted with pursuing do not exist. This approach is seen perhaps at its most blatant in the theoretical position adopted by McGrath (1966). McGrath suggests that outcomes of negotiations are determined by the interplay of three sets of forces: R (role) forces, directed towards the position of the party the negotiator represents; A (adversary) forces, directed towards the position of the opposing party; and C (community) forces, directed towards the position of 'the broader organization or social system in which all parties participate'. R forces are regarded as especially important determinants of success, that is, they are *detrimental* to success. R force pressure is regarded as inversely related to success. Strong R forces produce conflict that prevents negotiators perceiving those outcomes which would respectively satisfy *both* sides (*and* the 'community'). Vidmar and McGrath (1965) state: 'Conflict arises not as a result of the task *per se*, but rather from a conflict-producing role structure derived from member commitments to reference groups outside the actual negotiation situation and from perception of a contrient reward situation'.

The illusion is clear: that intergroup relations *distort* the process of bargaining. Rogers (1969) exemplifies this in his suggestion that negotiations should be divided into two parallel sets: one normal and publicly committed, and one 'free' – an anonymous shadow group which discusses issues rationally without prior commitment. The unfettered negotiation group, of course, is supposed to emerge with the appropriate solutions, the implication being that negotiations best take place *independently* of relations between groups. In truth, of course, negotiations are a *consequence* of intergroup relations, and have no independent validity.

Ann Douglas (1957) recognized this. She saw clearly that the representative role was the integral element that had to be fulfilled and could not be discarded without betraying constituents' trust. She observed a number of mediated disputes and concluded that negotiators fulfilled their representative role principally in the first and final stages of negotiations, and she averred that emphasis on disagreement in the first stage enhanced the prospect of ultimate success: 'To the extent that the contenders can entrench their seeming disparity in this period, the more they enhance their chances for a good and stable settlement in the end.' (p. 73) Such a view cannot easily be reconciled with accepted wisdom, which dictates that role obligations – and their accompanying 'entrenched' positions – are detrimental to successful resolution of disagreement. Far from being detrimental to success, the chances of success are apparently enhanced when negotiators fully vent their opposed views.

Camouflage of the intergroup basis of collective bargaining has been accomplished partly by psychologists restricting their experimental investigations to studies of dyadic negotiations. Collective bargaining by negotiating teams is, of course, standard procedure in real life, but the exigencies of experimental niceties and necessities have prompted psychologists to restrict their attention to two-person debates. This has had the entirely predictable consequence of heightening interpersonal considerations and fostering the illusion that the representative role structure is an unfortunate intrusion. Where two persons interact they are likely to be concerned about what impact this behaviour has, or is likely to have on the other. Even though their discussion may be directed towards a particular task, interpersonal considerations are likely to be prominent. This is perhaps less likely to be the case when a larger group discusses a problem or issue. In a larger group *sides* are frequently taken, and, as representatives of a *position*, individuals may more recklessly attack another's position without the risk that the attack will be taken personally.

An experiment by Stephenson and Brotherton (1975) demonstrated what might happen when group size is increased beyond a two-person discussion. When two mining supervisors on one side of an issue which concerned their work role were required to argue with two persons on the opposing side, both the character of debate and the outcomes were distinctly different from what occurred when one person was opposed to another. Not only was there less overt conflict in the dyad, but whereas two persons tended to agree on a *compromise* position between their starting positions, in the four-person group, one side or the other tended to *win*, that is, the group as a whole would polarize. Compromise was eschewed, and debate continued until victory was secured for one side or the other. Increased size had the effect of making discussion more oriented towards the task of arguing about the issues. Argument and conflict was welcomed as a contribution towards performance of the task, not avoided because it might offend another whose viewpoint was subject to attack.

We have already noted that a number of investigators attempted to introduce 'role obligations' towards a 'constituency' in experimental studies of negotiation using two-person groups. Nevertheless, the dyadic model, despite the introduction of role obligations, may have effectively masked the intergroup basis of collective bargaining by emphasizing processes of *interpersonal* exchange. There is reason to believe that this may have led not only to a misrepresentation of the style of interaction, but also of the outcomes of interactions in intergroup negotiations. One way of minimizing the interpersonal component in interaction is to make individuals less aware of another by placing them at a distance. Milgram's well-known experiments on obedience (Milgram, 1974) offer a good example of how the role occupied by a participant may then be more readily fulfilled. When the 'learner' is not visible, the 'teacher' is more likely to punish his errors, as instructed. Similarly, bargainers may more readily exploit their strategic advantage when an opponent is not visible, as in negotiations conducted by telephone rather than face-to-face (Morley and Stephenson, 1970a, 1977). As Morley and Stephenson argued, considerations of reciprocity or equity may prevail when conditions favour interpersonal exchange, and compromise between respective positions will become the favoured settlement-point. When interpersonal factors are minimized, as in telephone negotiations, compromise solutions are less likely to materialize, and victory more frequently goes to the party with the stronger case. Part of the bargainer's skill lies in so manipulating the circumstances of his/her interaction that the advantages of an interpersonal or intergroup orientation may at any one time be maximally exploited. More attention should be given in experimental research to those factors, like size of negotiation team, and the physical circumstances in which the negotiation is conducted, that may systematically affect the inter-personal orientation of the participants. The intergroup basis of collective bargaining may then be more effectively revealed and examined.

3.2 Further limitations of current intergroup analyses of negotiation

3.2.1 Equating negotiation with problem-solving groups

Douglas's (1957) approach acknowledges that integration of a negotiator's responsibilities as a representative with the interper-sonal task of securing an agreement cannot be achieved by relegating role obligations to the status of an unwelcome ideolog-ical intrusion in an otherwise impartially conducted discussion of a shared problem.

Morley and Stephenson (1977) suggested that it is important to elucidate the important characteristics of negotiation groups, and to highlight how they diverge from problem-solving groups. Bales and Strodtbeck (1951) showed how problem-solving groups progress through stages which are determined primarily by the need (a) to collect evidence, (b) evaluate it, and (c) to decide to act on the basis of those evaluations. This rational sequ-ence gives rise to three stages in which presentation and discus-sion of evidence predominates in the first stage, evaluation in the second and decision-making in the third. Conflict arises from disagreements which arise within these phrases, and is some-thing to be 'managed' lest it upset the smooth progress to agree-ment. Such a model is inappropriate for the study of negotiation groups, not least because disagreement defines the problem, and cannot appropriately be viewed as an intrusive element in an otherwise amicable discussion. In fact, one may seriously ques-tion how far the problem-solving model as evolved by Bales and Strodtbeck extends beyond the confines of the laboratory group of unacquainted individuals discussing novel problems prescribed by the experimenter.

It is important to study the content of debate closely if the way in which bargainers fulfil their representative role is to be effectively studied. Douglas (1957) suggested that bargainers are more or less identifiable as belonging to one side or another at different stages in the total negotiation. Morley and Stephenson (1977), Stephenson, Kniveton, and Morley (1977) and Stephenson (1978) have shown in different case studies that, indeed, bargainers are predictably more identifiable as management or union representatives in the early stages of a negotiation. Moreover, behaviour indicating conflict and disagreement did not increase with time, as occurs in problem-solving groups. Rather, it started high and progressively decreased from one bargaining session to the next. The role of conflict sharply differentiates problem-solving from negotiation groups.

Both Douglas (1962) and Morley and Stephenson (1977), suggest that the stages observed in negotiation groups reveal the means whereby negotiators integrate their representative and interpersonal interests. Morley and Stephenson (1977) suggest that, in the first stages of the formal negotiations they observed, the relative position strength of the parties becomes established such that in general terms who should 'win' and by what margin becomes clear. The outcome of this intergroup struggle being more or less decided in the first place, the 'interpersonal' task of determining a detailed presentation of an acceptably polarized outcome is enlarged upon. They would agree with Douglas that an initial stage of high intergroup antagonism characterizes formal negotiations in which representatives come prepared with elaborate arguments for the (conflicting) positions their sides have adopted.

Not all negotiations are so stage-managed, and perhaps it is inappropriate to conceive of negotiations as being obliged to pass through a *particular* sequence of stages. In British industrial relations in recent years the use of joint consultative committees, in which shop stewards meet regularly with representatives of management, has increased substantially. Here, items for discussion and decision are introduced by both sides, but they may take time to develop as fully fledged issues for negotiation.

Harding and Stephenson (unpublished) have analysed data from observations of consultative committees obtained over a period of a year at a medium-sized food manufacturing concern in the East Midlands. One striking feature of these consultative meetings was the extent to which the atmosphere of debate changed dramatically from one item to the next. Items are normally discussed over a series of meetings, and it seemed sensible to treat the complete discussion of one item over several sessions as a negotiation in its own right. A consultative meeting may then be portrayed as consisting of segments of a dozen or so independent negotiations, each at a different stage of development. By way of illustration, figure 6.3 shows the role identifiability of negotiators when discussing a series of 12 items at a consultative committee meeting. 'Items' strongly affected our measures of identifiability (judgements of which side was speaking from unlabelled transcripts).

However, this independence of items is not in fact complete. In the first place, there is a linear effect *within* one meeting, such that

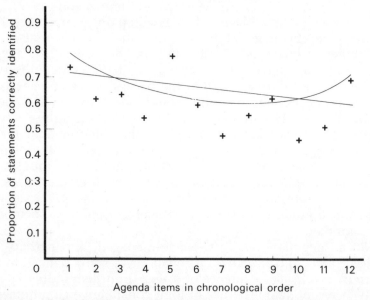

Figure 6.3   Role identifiability of management and union representatives discussing 12 items at one consultative meeting (from Harding and Stephenson, unpublished).

Key: 1 Christmas closing   2 Flies in the extract   3 Telephone   4 Car park   5 Sports or social club 6 Procedure for meeting   7 Christmas party   8 Manpower   9 Christmas closing   10 Bike shed   11 Leak in spraydrier   12 Telephone calls.

Overall effect $p < 0.001$ *linear* $p < 0.05$ *quadratic* $p < 0.005$.

identifiability decreased with time, although both starting and finishing high, as the significant quadratic effect indicates. But more importantly for this argument, when the total discussion of an item over several sessions is tested as an entity – as a single negotiation – those items that are successfully concluded showed a marked phase effect. On some occasions the issue gives rise to very high identifiability, whereas on others negotiators are indistinguishable in terms of party affiliation. Unsuccessfully concluded items, on the other hand, showed moderately high identifiability throughout. *Successfully negotiated items, therefore, may be said to embrace extremes of both partisanship and integration*. The precise pattern of alternation between the two varies according to how the issue originated, by whom and with what degree of preparation. But the rule that high differentiation must at some time occur in a successful intergroup debate is supported by our data.

Other writers have also argued that periods of high differentiation are essential to integration. In his discussion of third-party interventions, Walton (1969, p. 105) argued that:

> At least two phases of an effective conflict dialogue can be identified – a differentiation phase and an integration phase . . . . A conflict resolution episode does not necessarily include just one differentiation and one integration phase. It may be composed of a series of these two phases, but the potential for integration at any one point in time is no greater than the adequacy of the differentiation already achieved.

Our results from studies of consultative committees confirm this viewpoint. They also suggest that successfully concluded issues start with a period of high differentiation and finish integratively, but with wide fluctuation between times.

We can see that two main factors have contributed to the neglect of the negotiation group as a distinctive entity in which *intergroup* relationships are central. First is the tradition – paradoxically stemming from the influential intergroup theorist, Sherif – which views opposition between the parties as an unnecessary interference in the relationship, arising from misperceptions of reality. On this view, if a group mistakenly sees itself as divided, this must be rectified – by the introduction of, or an emphasis on superordinate goals which transcend the differences. That way, and this brings us to the second factor, it is suggested that the negotiation group may proceed as a problem-solving group, faced with a common problem, and to which the participants develop a common approach. On this view, negotiators are discussants, disagreement between whom arises only from difficulties encountered within the discussion. However, we have seen that negotiation groups do *not* proceed like problem-solving groups. The allegiance of the negotiators is not first and foremost to the negotiation group, but to their respective parties. Nevertheless we have also seen, as Douglas so eloquently described many years ago, that successful negotiators do *in time* come to speak with indistinguishable voices; at this stage it becomes appropriate to think of the group as in some senses an individual entity. This stage, however, is achieved not by masking differences, nor by avoiding conflict. Rather it is a consequence of having explored the differences and fought over them. The implications of the result of this first 'distributive' phase are subsequently explored in an increasingly 'integrative', or problem-solving manner.

3.2.2 *The role of interpersonal relationships*

Interpersonal relationships may be used to mitigate the tensions and misunderstandings generated in the formal intergroup relationship. Such a phenomenon is not limited to industrial relations, but occurs in international relations (for example the 'hot-line' between Washington and Moscow) and has more recently been demonstrated in relation to 'plea bargaining' in the legal process (see Baldwin and McConville, 1977), although in the latter case the apparent frequent neglect of the client's interests suggests collusion of the worst kind.

The negotiator's task of reconciling his obligations as a representative with the problem of securing agreement emerged strongly as an important dimension in a recent study of the behaviour and attitudes of shop stewards in a large manufacturing organization. In this notable study Batstone, Boraston, and Frenkel (1977) distinguish between the behaviour required by the formal relationship, and that which characterizes the interpersonal relationships which may or may not develop between particular stewards and managers. In some circumstances 'strong' (interpersonal) bargaining relationships develop. As they say (pp. 168–9):

> A strong bargaining relationship . . . involves the development of a relationship between steward and manager which goes beyond the minimum formal relationship which necessarily exists between

them. At the minimum, this relationship is specific in terms of goals, affectively neutral, and universalistic in the sense that people are substitutable within the relationship. A strong bargaining relationship exists where the negotiating relationship becomes particularistic and affectively positive. As a consequence, certain kinds of information confidential to each side are exchanged, 'off the record' discussions occur, and to a degree each is concerned with protecting the relationship and the other party. The basic opposition of interests which exists within negotiation is therefore mediated by personal relationships which facilitate the constructive resolution of problems.

Paradoxically, these strong interpersonal bonds develop in circumstances of greatest intergroup differentiation – in particular in relations of management with shop-floor stewards, rather than with *staff* stewards. Shop-floor stewards tended to be 'leaders', rather than followers of opinion amongst their members. Moreover, the organization of their work fostered a collective orientation which was somewhat alien to staff employees. In this more threatening atmosphere, strong bargaining relationships developed, although such relationships were not permitted to threaten the established conflict. As one manager said:

> It's important that you both accept you've got a job to do. [The steward] has got to look after his members. I've got to do what my masters tell me, but we will both try to change the minds of our masters. But, if I can't I've got to follow the company line, and the same's true of [the steward]. Because of our jobs, we could well find ourselves fighting, each against what we thought was right. (p. 175)

The importance of Batstone's analysis is two-fold. Firstly, it highlights the importance of distinguishing clearly between the interpersonal and interparty orientations of negotiators, and of recognizing that these may be separately indulged. Secondly, and perhaps most importantly, it confounds those theories of intergroup relations which posit a simple relationship between intergroup conflict and interpersonal relations. In this case, relationships between negotiators are clearly not straightforwardly predictable from knowledge of the extent of intergroup conflict. High intergroup conflict or confrontation may elicit strong interpersonal bargaining relationships between representatives.

3.2.3 *Not all conflicts are 'real'*

We have seen that 'real conflict' theory, as it has been called, encourages the attempt to camouflage the intergroup basis of negotiation, for it suggests that negotiators can only be successful when real conflicts between the groups no longer exist. Sherif, Blake and Mouton, McGrath, and others since (for example, Warr, 1973), have all effectively denied that representatives of competing groups can legitimately come to agreement unless either (a) superordinate goals integrate the groups, or (b) individual representatives abandon their allegiances. We have seen, on the contrary, that the most 'differentiated' groups have representatives who develop the closest relations in the interests of own group advancement. Partly this is effectively accomplished because bargainers in real negotiations are not *merely* representatives. They may well have taken a highly active role in fashioning and determining policy. They have, in Walton and McKersie's terms, ensured that *intra* group bargaining has furnished them with demands which they may reasonably pursue.

There is another way in which real conflict theory fails to do justice to the behaviour of industrial negotiators. It has been informally noted before that the most divisive issues in financial terms are not necessarily those which give the representatives most difficulty, or give rise to the greater antagonism. In the consultative meetings mentioned earlier, Harding and Stephenson nevertheless expected that those issues which were intrinsically divisive – in other words, concerning those questions of job regulation where commitment of considerable financial resources was involved, such as 'manpower', and 'Christmas closing' – would give rise to more overt conflict than mere 'problems'; the latter were those items where it could be assumed that both sides had common interests, matters concerning hygiene, efficiency and safety, such as 'flies (in the extract)' and 'leak in the spray-drier'. The appropriate allocation of items was sometimes problematic, but in principle the differences between the two groups of issues and problems was clear enough. It was expected, in accordance with the real conflict model of intergroup relations, that the behaviour of the negotiators would reflect the competition between the two groups more in discussion of 'issues' – where conflict of interests was apparent – than of 'problems', where common goals apparently prevailed. In practice, there was no difference in role identifiability of negotiators between issues and problems, i.e. there was no tendency for representatives to be more or less identifiable as belonging to one party or the other in the discussion of issues than in the discussion of problems.

In fact, a *safety* matter was a greater source of continuing controversy than any other. The joint management–union Safety Committee had recommended the purchase of safety shoes for the female packers, and the footwear had been purchased and distributed accordingly. There was, however, dissatisfaction with their comfort among some of the employees, and the shop stewards in question encouraged the senior steward to contact the factory inspector on their behalf, to ask whether or not they could be 'forced by management' to wear the shoes. The problem was fast becoming a matter of principle, and when the inspector's reply in the negative was conveyed to the women many forthwith refused to wear the protective shoes. This small practical matter was subsequently transformed into a moral issue of considerable proportions. Management 'had no right to dictate' what footwear should be worn, on the one hand; the senior steward 'had no right to bypass the Safety Committee' on the other. The senior steward was brought before the Committee to defend his actions against high-minded attacks from management representatives, and, more hurtfully, embarrassed and angry attacks from his fellow stewards on the Safety Committee. Securing the cooperation of the stewards in the humiliation of the senior steward was an achievement regarded with some pride by certain members of senior management, but the price was subsequently paid, for management was in turn subjected to ridicule. The factory inspector's judgement was taken by the mass of workers to imply that the purchase of the protective footwear had been an unnecessarily expensive mistake. In the general view, management had been made to look absurd; the shoes would never be worn because they served no purpose. Yet again management's incompetence had been made manifest!

In this case, the distortion, accusations, misperceptions and sheer hostility were directed towards demonstrating the moral superiority of one or other group, and the importance of the outcome rests in its symbolic significance. The underlying intergroup dynamic was not competition over the distribution of scarce resources, but seemed much more in line with the social identity theory of intergroup conflict (Tajfel, 1978a; Tajfel and Turner, 1979; see also Skinner, 1979, and chapters 1 and 3).

This theory states that individuals seek positive social identity (positive self-concepts based on their group memberships) through social comparisons between their own and other groups. They try to achieve 'positive distinctiveness' for their own group in order to protect and maintain their self-esteem as group mem-

bers. Thus, it predicts that intergroup competition or discrimination does not require real conflicts of interest but may be motivated solely by a concern to enhance identity.

This seems consistent with the above account. In the instance just
described, the safety problem was transformed into a moral
issue, each side seeking to condemn the conduct of the other. In
this way, the superiority of own group could be established, and
hence, by association, one's social identity be enhanced. Opportunities for scoring points in this way arise fortuitously and are
not associated straightforwardly with the intrinsic divisiveness of
the matter in hand. More likely, the appropriateness of the *manner* with which any matter is approached may often be of critical
importance. In the case of the safety footwear, the 'high-handed'
way in which the shoes were necessarily introduced probably
precipitated the unfortunate sequence of events, in which key
members on each side unnecessarily exploited the other side's
improprieties. The 'problem' became an 'issue' because it came to
threaten the identity and status of the various groups involved.
Social identity theory may often be a more convincing explanation than the real conflict model of the circumstances in which
overt antagonism may be expressed, and unproductive conflicts
prevail. It needs to be realized that not all difficulties in intergroup negotiations relate to the distribution of material resources.

4 Negotiation as the integration of interpersonal and intergroup relationships

It has been argued so far that intergroup negotiation is a consequence of intergroup relations. The issue therefore arises of the
contribution which current theories of intergroup behaviour (real
conflict, social identity) can make to understanding intergroup negotiation. At present, their main value is to explain why
intergroup hostilities may erupt: to specify the determinants and
effects of conflicts and the conditions necessary for their resolution. However, in some respects this is not very helpful.
Negotiators must take intergroup conflict for granted, both as
their point of departure and in their objective, which is not so
much to resolve conflict as to find a way in which the groups can
come to terms despite it. Thus far, intergroup theories have

tended to ignore the central problem for group representatives in negotiation: the integration of their intergroup and interpersonal relationships with the opposition.

To illustrate the problem, we can consider a recent theoretical statement by Tajfel (1978a). In this book, prior to outlining social identity theory proper, Tajfel discusses in general the psychological transition between interindividual and intergroup behaviour (pp. 27–60). He rightly and importantly highlights the distinction between intergroup and interpersonal behaviour. The former is the behaviour of two or more individuals towards each other determined by their membership of different social groups or categories, and the latter is any social encounter between two or more people determined by their personal relationships and individual characteristics (see chapter 2). These forms of social interaction are considered to represent theoretical extremes which define the poles of a continuum:

> We have therefore a continuum which goes from the probably fictitious outcome of 'pure' interpersonal behaviour to the rarely encountered extremes of 'purely' intergroup behaviour. All of the 'natural' (and also experimental) social situations fall between these two extremes, and the behaviour towards people who are categorized as members of the ingroup or the outgroup will be considerably affected by the individuals' perception (or other interpretation) of the situation as being nearer to one or the other extreme. (p. 43)

Thus, according to Tajfel, our actions depend on whether we perceive or interpret the social setting as interpersonal or intergroup. If we attempt to portray this notion schematically, something like the picture in figure 6.4 emerges.

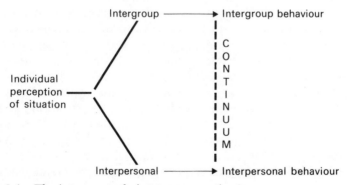

Figure 6.4   The interpersonal–intergroup continuum.

This picture is modified by the assertions that 'pure' inter-personal behaviour does not exist and that 'pure' intergroup behaviour is rare; most behaviour lies somewhere on the con-tinuum between the two extremes. Tajfel (1978a) makes two formally stated generalizations about how behaviour varies along the continuum. The first generalization concerns the similarity of ingroup members' behaviour towards outgroup members:

> The nearer is a social situation (as interpreted by members of a group) to the intergroup extreme of the interpersonal–intergroup con-tinuum, the more uniformity will the individual members of the groups concerned show in their behaviour towards members of out-groups. Conversely, the nearer is the situation to the interpersonal end, the more variability will be shown in behaviour towards mem-bers of outgroups. (1978a, pp. 44–5).

Moreover, in intergroup situations, members will also treat different outgroup members in an undifferentiated way:

> The nearer is a social situation to the intergroup extreme, the stronger tendency will there be for members of the ingroup to treat members of the outgroup as undifferentiated items in a uniform social cate-gory, i.e. independently of the individual differences between them. (1978a, p. 45)

Let us consider some possible difficulties that could arise with the 'continuum hypothesis', as we may call it. The first arises from the hypothesized correspondence between 'perceived situ-ation' and 'observed behaviour'. There is obviously a danger of circularity here unless some means is provided of recognizing the position of the situation on the continuum independently of the behaviour it is meant to explain. Tajfel implicitly recognizes this danger when he points out that some individuals ('the extreme outgroup haters') are likely to perceive all situations as relevant to intergroup relations, whereas, for most people, the simple appearance of outgroup members in a setting will not necessarily lead them to perceive it in intergroup terms or engage in inter-group actions (1978a, p. 43). The question arises, therefore, of the factors which lead individuals to perceive situations as relev-ant to their group memberships. Tajfel mentions personal (for example, extent of emotional investment in the group member-ship) and situational factors (for example, immutable and closed social boundaries between stratified groups). Some other factors which seem to enhance the salience of group membership in specific settings are described by Brown and Turner in chapter 2 of this book. Research to systematize our understanding in this respect is obviously important to make the continuum hypothesis really useful.

Another difficulty more directly relevant to problems of inter-group negotiation is the implication of the continuum hypothesis that identity of behaviour indicates identity of perception. The hypothesis seems to assume that, in a looting mob, a determined lynching party, or a chanting football crowd, the more or less identical behaviour of the participants reflects a common perception of the situation. However, this assumption is not always plausible. The same behaviour may mask an array of individual perceptions of a given situation. For example, conformity pressures are very strong in some of the real-life instances of depersonalization and subsequent dehumanization which Tajfel gives. How can we distinguish between intergroup situations in which an individual behaves inhumanly towards an outgroup member because (a) the outgroup member is not perceived as a differentiated person, or (b) the ingroup member simply feels constrained through loyalty to act like other ingroup members?

In general, it cannot be assumed that there is a direct one-to-one correspondence between perceptions (or attitudes, or cognition) and behaviour. Behaviour masks as much as it reveals our perceptions and understandings of what is appropriate. In inter-group negotiations, it will be argued presently, both interpersonal and intergroup goals may be strong; these may often conflict, and yet a choice between the two may still have to be made. Once the choice is made and either interpersonal *or* intergroup goals are furthered, it may appear from the outside that the situation was only perceived in one way. However, this inference would be fallacious. It cannot be assumed that negotiators perceive settings in interpersonal *or* intergroup terms or seek interpersonal *or* intergroup goals in an inverse ratio, simply because in some instances they may be forced to act in this manner.

This brings us to the central point. Tajfel's notion of the continuum suggests that in the case of both situations and actions, the interpersonal and interparty aspects are *alternatives*. This rules out the possibility of *conflict* between the different aspects. The continuum implies that as one factor increases in strength, the other decreases, a situation in mid-continuum being neither one thing nor the other but some mixture of both, and the same for behaviour. In truth, conflict between the two factors is of the essence, and no aspect of our social life can escape the problem of reconciling intergroup and interpersonal objectives. The continuum does imply that neither intergroup nor interpersonal factors are ever entirely absent, but suggests that the relative balance between them changes. Tajfel makes clear that the balance can and may usually be very lopsided when he states that 'much (if not most) of our social behaviour in many circumstances may have very little to do with this (ingroup–outgroup) membership' (p. 43). This contrasts with the present view that both intergroup *and* interpersonal considerations inform all social behaviour to a greater or lesser extent, and that they may vary in salience independently of each other. The study of negotiation bears ample testimony to this viewpoint. We have seen in the cases described by Batstone, Boraston, and Frenkel (1977) that strong interpersonal relationships may coexist with marked intergroup antagonism, and the same is true in the field of international relations. Indeed, it may be argued that strong intergroup hostility *necessitates* the development of strong interpersonal relationships if conflict is to be effectively contained. Relations between the 'superpowers' are not now so dangerous to peace as relations between unequally matched protagonists where informal mechanisms (for example, the Washington–Moscow 'hot-line') for the resolution of disputes have not developed to complement the formally antagonistic intergroup relationship.

Other studies of negotiation indicate that the view of intergroup and interpersonal behaviour as *alternatives* does not adequately depict reality. Negotiators may be intensely responsive to both interpersonal and intergroup considerations at one and the same time. This undoubtedly occurred in the negotiation at 'Demy Ltd', the transcript of which is reproduced in full in Morley and Stephenson (1977). There, managers and men in a co-ownership company negotiated directly a revision in the terms of employment of a group of electricians. The philosophy of the company militated against the open pursuance of redress of grievances to the detriment of the company. Such divisiveness ran counter to the spirit of cooperation which prevailed. Unused as they were to formal bargaining, it was difficult for those on either side to give adequate expression to intergroup attitudes without jeopardizing their previously harmonious interpersonal relationships. In this instance both intergroup and interpersonal objectives were critically important, and behaviour was attuned to both sets of considerations. The interpersonal embarrassment created by the necessity to treat one another as members of separate groups is painfully clear from the written record, and more so from the live recording.

Negotiators evolve a variety of strategies to overcome the *conflict* which necessarily stems from their commitment to one another as individuals, and from commitment to their respectively opposed groups' values and interests. They develop understandings about acceptable and unacceptable tactics: when to tell the truth, and when to lie; when to believe and when to be sceptical; when to trust and when to distrust; what to divulge in private, and what to confess in public; when to help one another, and when to obstruct; when to pursue intergroup, and when interpersonal objectives. This is a process which spans both the intragroup planning for negotiation, as well as the intergroup phase of bargaining. In the same way that negotiators when bargaining cannot lay aside their role obligations, neither can their bargaining relationship be set aside in their prenegotiation discussion with their fellow ingroup members. At all times negotiators must be aware of the interpersonal and intergroup implications of their behaviour. If intergroup objectives take precedence, this must be managed so as to minimize any possible harm to the interpersonal relationship, and vice versa.

It is difficult to think of any social situation which may not have both intergroup and interpersonal significance. Making love, for example, may seem unambiguously interpersonal, yet a consideration of the objectives achieved by James Bonds' sexual exploits should prevent our being overly sentimental about performance even in that sphere. In any interaction with another, our apparent membership of different social groups – be it male, female, old, young, English, black or European – is at least a potential allegiance which may be exploited by the other, such that we act in some sense as *representatives* of fellow members of those groups. When our nationality, sex or occupation becomes salient in the interaction, this does not necessarily obliterate the interpersonal significance of the encounter; indeed, it may enhance it. Similarly, as Bond shows us, the introduction of our interpersonal fancies into an intragroup transaction, does not necessarily render us disloyal to our group.

Some laboratory experiments alluded to earlier (Morley and

Stephenson, 1969, 1970a, 1970b) help to elucidate the main point that interpersonal and intergroup considerations are not alternatives. Subjects played the role of management and union negotiators in simulated bargaining sessions. One side or the other always had the 'stronger' case. Bargaining took place either face-to-face or by telephone. Intergroup objectives were constant in both telephone and face-to-face encounters, but it was antici-pated that face-to-face, the interpersonal significance of their behaviour would be enhanced. In that condition it was expected that interpersonal norms of reciprocity would prevail against set-tlements in favour of the side with the stronger case. Hence it was anticipated that victories for the side with the stronger case would occur more frequently in telephone rather than face-to-face conditions. Results conformed to the hypothesis, and have since been replicated a number of times (Morley and Stephenson, 1977; Short, 1975; Short, Williams, and Christie, 1976). There is no way in which it could be said that subjects in the face-to-face condition were less committed to the group task. Superimposed on performance of their role, however, was greater awareness of the interpersonal significance of their behaviour.

The diagram in figure 6.5 depicts how the intergroup and interpersonal salience of an encounter can vary independently of each other. It illustrates very simply that a social setting can be described in terms of its salience in both respects. Thus, in the

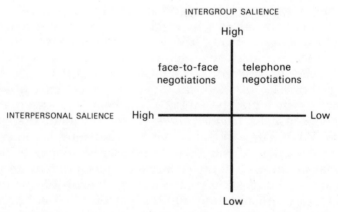

Figure 6.5   *Interpersonal and intergroup relations as independent dimensions.*

experiments just cited, telephone negotiations would be located in the upper right-hand quadrant, and face-to-face in the upper left. The diagram is suggested as a better representation than a single dimension of the possible social relationships between negotiators. It focuses our minds on the central issue of how group representatives integrate the development and employment of strong interpersonal and intergroup roles.

5 *Conclusion*

In conclusion, it is apparent that intergroup theories, while contributing to our understanding of what appears on the agenda, have not as yet added much to our knowledge of the process by which bargainers negotiate successful agreements. It can be argued that an adequate theory of intergroup relations should make an effective contribution in this area, because the task of the negotiator – as a representative to come to an acceptable accord with representatives of opposed groups – is in general terms one which faces all of us in many everyday transactions. In the past the intergroup basis of negotiation has tended to be camouflaged. The interpersonal or individualistic orientation has been so strong that even Sherif's real conflict theory was used to argue that negotiation must proceed regardless of intergroup relations and group allegiances. There may now be a danger that the influence of intergroup theories will be able to minimize the role of the interpersonal dimension. This would occur because such theories have been employed to explain striking examples of collective behaviour in which unusually pure processes of intergroup discrimination appear to be operating, apparently uncorrupted by interpersonal considerations. The latter tends in consequence to be legislated out of existence as of importance in our understanding of intergroup relations. While this may be a welcome corrective to the individualistic orientation which explains intergroup relations in terms of fictitiously pure interpersonal processes, the fact remains that in collective bargaining both interpersonal and intergroup allegiances coexist and the basic issue is to understand how these are reconciled. Moreover, in this respect, negotiation represents a microcosm of much other social behaviour: the integration of interpersonal and intergroup relationships with others is a general feature and problem of social life. The distinction between interpersonal and intergroup behaviour is valuable and important; it is, after all, fundamental to the basic issue posed above. However, it needs to be remembered that these theoretical extremes are to some extent fictitious in that they rarely occur in isolation. An advance in our general understanding of behaviour within and between groups, to which research on negotiation can contribute, now requires detailed consideration of various conceptualizations of this distinction and the actual interplay between its components.

CHAPTER 7

The Role of Language in Ethnic Group Relations

HOWARD GILES and PATRICIA JOHNSON

1 Introduction

Throughout history there have been instances where efforts at linguistic change and nationalist movements have coincided. In Turkey for example, the official language of the Ottoman Empire for the previous 400 years was repressed by the leaders of post-1922 Turkey in favour of a new form of the language (modern Turkish) in order to emphasize a linguistic identification with central Asia (Khleif, 1979a). In India, Sikh writers promoted a standard variety of their language in order to differentiate it from Hindi, since the two languages were originally very similar in spoken form. The two languages then grew further apart and there are now two distinct languages and peoples, with a separate Sikh state in India. Similarly, Macedonian writers in Yugoslavia sought words and grammatical structures from remote rural areas in order to establish a standard which would distinguish their language from Serbo-Croatian. The struggle for a separate Macedonian republic in Yugoslavia coincided with these efforts at linguistic differentiation. Weinstein (1979, p. 360) states that in these and other cases:

> Linguistic development furnished a point of reference for people pursuing their interests and protecting their beliefs. Acceptance of a standard form was the essential step in symbolisation; the living and the dead and the contemporaries over a geographical area had signed a pact . . . . The reinforcement or the creation of a cultural network around language transformed an unconscious language group into a selfconscious 'identity group'.

Language then is an important factor in interethnic relations, as at the same time it acts as a dependent variable reflecting the situa-

199

tion, as well as an independent variable actively creating and defining that situation.

In this chapter, we shall be concerned with the following problems: who in an ethnic group uses which language strategies, when and why? In order to provide a backdrop for answering these questions, we will need initially to address certain critical issues. First, what do we mean by ethnic group membership? Second, why is *language* important to interethnic relations anyway? Third, what have previous approaches contributed to our understanding of the relationship between language and ethnicity? These preliminaries will then allow us to introduce an integrative framework with the following components: social identity theory; the concept of perceived ethnolinguistic vitality; the concept of perceived group boundaries; and notions concerning multiple group membership. On the basis of this social psychological approach to language and interethnic behaviour, we shall be in a better position than hitherto to predict who in an ethnic group uses which language strategy, when and why. Finally, the chapter will conclude in propositional terms with the conditions necessary for ethnic ingroup members to differentiate linguistically from, rather than assimilate towards, members of an ethnic outgroup.

2   Ethnicity and its relationship to language

2.1   On defining ethnic group membership

The adequacy of different criteria for defining a collectivity as an ethnic group and the influence of different definitions on the composition of the group have been much discussed (see, for example, Eastman, 1974). J. Ross (1979, p. 3) has summed up some of the problems as follows:

> Ethnicity has proven to be a very difficult concept to define with much precision. Indeed those who have approached the task have not been able to achieve a consensus. Most usages are both vague and ambiguous in their application to empirical research. What some scholars consider to be examples of ethnicity, others would consider to be cases of such variables as regionalism, religious sectarianism, class conflict and even sheer opportunism. When ethnicity is at best a fuzzy concept, it becomes rather difficult to convincingly establish its relationship to language.

One definition of ethnicity which has been widely used is that of Barth (1969) who defines an ethnic unit as those individuals who say they belong to ethnic group A rather than ethnic group B, and are willing to be treated and allow their behaviour to be interpreted and judged as As and not Bs. This emphasis on self-identification and identification by others allows one to see that continuity (stability and persistence) of ethnic boundaries depends on their maintenance. Ethnic boundaries are seen as the distinctive feature of ethnic units, and though the form and content of the ethnicity experience may change, members and non-members are still distinguishable: 'The cultural features that signal a boundary may change, and the cultural characteristics of the members may change, but the continuing dichotomisation between members and outsiders allow us to specify the nature of the continuity and to investigate the changing culture form and content.' (Barth, 1969, p. 14) Further, individuals may *use* shared beliefs about ethnicity: 'in the process of self-definition, the group myths and cultural values, including language . . . may be substantially revised, altered and reinterpreted so as to fit with changed conditions. Clearly, ethnic identity is a distinctly modern phenomenon rather than a mere reiteration of primitive or traditional images.' (J. Ross, 1979, p. 8)

This manipulation of existing ethnic group culture and language may be seen as an attempt to maintain and clarify group boundaries in the face of increased dependence on and interaction with other groups in modern urban society (Eastman, 1974; Tajfel, 1978a). It seems then that group boundaries and contrast across these are necessary for an articulated selfconscious ethnic identity (Paulston and Paulston, 1980). Clear and distinct boundaries are necessary for individuals to become aware of their membership of a group and for identification to follow from this awareness: 'If boundaries define belonging, if identity itself is anchored in boundaries, then a decreasing emphasis on, or blurring of, boundaries would be regarded as a threat to group existence, that is to allegiance, social coherence and conformity . . . a harbinger of anonymity, anomie and marginality.' (Khleif, 1979a, p. 159)

The nature of these boundaries may be considered in terms of the internal and external criteria of group membership (Breakwell, 1979; Tajfel, 1978c). The external criteria are those objective standards which must be fulfilled for membership, such as skin colour, or fluency in the ethnic language. These criteria may be imposed on individuals from outside by a dominant group, who thereby define the minority (see Lyons's (1972) exclusive boundary). The internal criteria are the concepts members hold of what constitutes legitimate membership – their beliefs, expectations and aspirations with respect to their group membership (see Lyons's (1972) inclusive boundaries). Here we shall consider groups primarily in terms of the internal criteria, with the emphasis on self-identification with the ethnic group, in other words, on subjective rather than objective criteria (Harris, 1979). J. Ross (1979, p. 8) also views ethnicity in these terms as it:

> results from a mobilisation around an inter-subjectively shared sense of peoplehood. It does not matter if this sense of peoplehood has any historic–genetic basis; what is important is that the members of the ethnic group differentiate themselves from others because they believe they are unique. Ethnicity in this sense is a subjective reality rather than an objective characteristic.

Our preferred definition of an ethnic group is, then, a cognitive one following Turner (1982; and see chapters 1, 2 and 3), as those individuals who identify themselves as belonging to the same ethnic category. This group identification may be based on a common set of ancestral cultural traditions or may stimulate the creation of a unique set of traditions in other cases (Fishman, 1977). In both instances, we are concerned with the establishment and maintenance of distinct ingroup boundaries. This social psychological definition avoids categorization of individuals on the basis of supposedly 'objective' ethnic criteria, and does not rely on notions of physical proximity or similarity between members.

2.2   *The salience of language in interethnic relations*

Why then is language important to ethnic relations? There are different criteria for membership of an ethnic group. These may involve ancestry, religion, physiognomy, etc. and relate to the paternity (and perhaps maternity) dimension of ethnicity (Fishman, 1977). Most ethnic groups also have a distinct language or dialect and these ethnic characteristics can be a necessary attribute for membership of the group. This links up with the notion of paternity through concepts such as 'mother tongue', where language is seen as an aspect of ancestry. For example, one definition of an Arab (from Article 10 of the Constitution of Socialist Arab Resurrection Party) is: 'A person whose mother tongue is Arabic, who has lived or who looks forward to living on Arab soil, and who believes in being a member of the Arab nation' (cited in Fishman, 1972, p. 44). Similarly, it is common to hear in Hispanic communities in the south-west of the United States that: 'Mexican-Americans who can't speak Spanish should choke on their chilli beans'; such individuals may not be afforded full membership by other group members, and may themselves feel that their ethnic identity is incomplete. Even when there are other strong and clear criteria for ethnic group membership (such as skin colour), an ethnic language variety often remains a criterial attribute (see chapters 2, 3 and 5). An Afro-American member of the Peace Corps Volunteers was surprised and upset to find that when he met his African 'brothers' in Sierra Leone, they called him *oyimbo* ('white man') because of his standard American English and behaviour (Hancock, 1974).

For orientation in a complex and rapidly changing environment, individuals need to organize their world cognitively and this includes the social categorization of its inhabitants for order and simplicity. Language is central to these categorizations, having the social and personal importance, overt physical presence and flexibility to underlie a range of social categories (McKirnan and Hamayan, 1980). Although we may not necessarily have to listen to how West Indians speak to categorize them according to the appropriate ethnic group, certain linguistic characteristics are often necessary in other cases to distinguish, for example, an American from a Canadian, a Catholic from a Protestant in Northern Ireland (see the concept of 'telling', Frank, 1978), an Australian from a New Zealander and between certain ethnic minorities in the United States. The findings of a multidimensional scaling study in Puerto Rico suggest that language can be an important aspect of the social environment for an individual even when it is not salient to his or her personal identity (Giles *et al.*, 1979). Further, many language varieties (for instance, a broad ethnic accent) may be viewed as acquired characteristics rather than those given by virtue of birth. Therefore, language is also potentially a stronger cue to an individual's sense of ethnic belongingness than inherited characteristics (such as skin colour) in the eyes of others since acquired characteristics may be attributed internally rather than externally. In other words, while paternity (inherited characteristics) may be the key to ethnicity for the individuals themselves, patrimony (acquired characteristics, see Fishman, 1977) may be a guide as to *how ethnic* others perceive them to be (Giles, Bourhis, and Taylor, 1977; see also discussion of level 1 and 2 speech markers in Giles, Scherer, and Taylor, 1979). Moreover while there may be clear and unambiguous non-linguistic cues as to the ethnic group membership of individuals (such as skin colour, dress) at the same time their speech style can be used by others to make inferences about their strength of ethnic identification, and hence (via the ethnic stereotype) about their personality traits, job suitability (de la Zerda and Hopper, 1979; Kalin and Rayko, 1980; Sebastian and Ryan, in press), etc.

Language has been shown to be an important aspect of ethnic identity, more important even than cultural background for some individuals (see Smolicz, 1979). For instance, in a series of multidimensional scaling studies, it was shown that some French Canadians felt closer to an English Canadian who spoke French, than to a French Canadian who did not (Taylor, Bassili, and Aboud, 1973); analogous results have been obtained for Welsh bilinguals in their context too (Giles, Taylor, and Bourhis, 1977). Among Lithuanians in the United States, language is the variable on which the group shows least assimilation. Although they have become fully integrated into American life they have nevertheless maintained their language for use amongst themselves (Băskauskas, 1977). With a similar emphasis on the importance of language to ethnic identity, the Catalonian Cultural Committee stated: 'Our language, the expression of our people, which can never be given up, is the spiritual foundation of our existence . . . a people without a language of its own is only half a nation. . . .' (cited in Fishman, 1972, p. 46). Naturally enough, individuals are very emotionally attached to such a precious commodity which symbolizes their ethnicity (see Hudson-Edwards, 1980), and ethnic group members using a language and speech style other than that of their group may be labelled cultural traitors by fellow group members, their language behaviour being regarded as improper, insulting and disloyal. An example of such attitudes is the following from an interview with a Puerto Rican boy in New York:

I have to answer in Spanish. My father asks me a question in Spanish. He won't take it in English. I have to answer in Spanish 'cause he says I'm not Italian and I'm not a Negro but I'm a Puerto Rican and have to speak to him in my language. He says I was born in Puerto Rico and . . . I'm gonna raise you like Puerto Ricans. So if we speak in English in front of him . . . it's like cursing right in front of him.' (Wolfram, 1973, p. 171)

Indeed, Fishman (1977, p. 25) suggested provocatively that language: 'Can become the *ultimate* symbol of ethnicity, since in expressing, referring to, and evoking something else in addition to itself, it becomes valued in itself'. The use of an ethnic speech style is hence a reminder of a shared past, of a shared solidarity in the presence of a shared destiny in the future (Ryan, 1979) as well as a means of excluding outgroup members from within-group transactions (Drake, 1980).

It can be argued however that it is not necessary for members of an ethnic group to speak the language so long as they have it available; indeed: 'Ethnicity is frequently related more to the symbol of a separate language than to its actual use by all members of a group'. (De Vos, 1975, p. 15) Examples of this would be Gaelic, Welsh and Breton which are not spoken by the majority of those who identify with their respective groups, but which nevertheless are highly valued as aspects of ethnic identity. Moreover, it is not even necessary for an ethnic group to have a distinct language to value and maintain an ethnolinguistic identity:

Group identity can even be maintained by minor differences in linguistic patterns and by style of gesture. There are a wide variety of ways in which language patterning fluency or lack of fluency in a second language is related to identity maintenance. Changing patterns within groups are related to the sanctioning positively or negatively of specific dialects . . .'. (De Vos, 1975, p. 16)

Thus, for example, many people of Jewish origin speak their host language with a distinctive accent, and with words and phrases borrowed from their own ethnic tradition, culture and religion. Similarly, the Scots and the Irish have distinctive speech styles in English, together with the knowledge that their ethnic groups have a separate language, even though most members of the group cannot speak it.

As was argued earlier, language is frequently used to rouse the ethnic selfconsciousness of group members:

> Language is probably the most powerful single symbol of ethnicity because it acts as shorthand for all that makes a group special and unique. Many ethnic nationalist movements trace their roots to literary and philological revivals. Ethnic movements often find their organisational precursors in language and literary societies. It is around the issue of language that ethnic politicians and ethnic intelligentsia may organise and inter-relate. Language, given its affective potential, is a symbol that is very effective in fostering a mass mobilisation on ethnic lines. (J. Ross, 1979, p. 10)

In sum, language is important in interethnic relations because it is frequently a criterial attribute of ethnic group membership, a cue for interethnic categorization, and can readily become a primary symbol of ethnicity as well as being the ideal medium for facilitating intraethnic cohesion. Because of this emotional significance of language for ethnic groups, it is perhaps not surprising often to find language issues at the focal point of interethnic conflicts. In India for example, until about 40 years ago, language was not generally a salient criterion for distinguishing oneself from others. More recently however, some language groups have sought to have their variety recognized as the 'absolute' or 'standard' variety and have tried to gain language privileges in education and government, etc.: '. . . the tendency to struggle for language privileges in all walks of life has been mainly instrumental in promoting political discord among competing language groups'. (Khubchandani, 1979, p. 146) Similar friction between different language groups has been evident in Belgium, Catalonia, Brittany and elsewhere. The Soweto riots in South Africa were sparked off by attempts in 1976 to introduce Afrikaans as the language of the school curriculum. Before introducing our own theoretical framework concerning the role of language in interethnic relations, let us overview some important themes emerging from this multidisciplinary area.

3   Current approaches to the study of language and ethnicity

We shall identify three main orientations to the study of language and ethnicity and label them the 'sociolinguistic', 'sociological' and 'communication breakdown' approaches. The first has been concerned primarily with cataloguing differences in the speech of ethnic groups in contact, the second with examining why some ethnic minority languages 'survive' while others do not, and the third focuses on the factors resulting in the breakdown of interethnic communication. We will briefly discuss each of these, admittedly overlapping, approaches in turn.

3.1   *The sociolinguistic approach*

We have already seen that an ethnic group's language and style can function to symbolize the group's distinctiveness from other groups and provide a socially significant cue for ethnic categorization. The sociolinguistic approach focuses upon the large variety of ways in which individuals can manifest their ethnic membership through speech; such interethnic differences have been termed 'ethnic speech markers' (see Giles, 1979, for a more detailed review).

Clearly the most obvious ethnic speech marker will be the use of different languages by different ethnic groups. However: '. . . language can be an important part of ethnicity without its taking the form of the presence or absence of some particular language or dialect' (Dorian, 1980, p. 36). She suggests that a 'linguistic lag' can act as an ethnic speech marker with a group's linguistic distinctiveness taking different forms over time. For example, in east Sutherland, Scotland, Dorian found the fisherfolk were considered as a separate ethnic group in the past because they had remained monolingual in Gaelic when others in the population had become bilingual in Gaelic and English, later because they spoke imperfect English when mastery of English was the norm, and currently because they are bilingual while most of the population speak only English.

Intralingual ethnic markers may be phonological, grammatical, lexical, paralinguistic, or prosodic in nature. Phonological markers in the speech of different ethnic groups speaking the same language have been studied extensively, particularly in the United States (Feinstein, 1980; Laferriere, 1979). For example, while whites would tend to say 'thought' and 'then', blacks would tend to pronounce these as 'tought' and 'den' (Trudgill, 1974). There may be no apparent markers in the speech of members of a subordinate ethnic group who have attempted to assimilate into the dominant community (Giles and Bourhis, 1976). Yet sometimes, such individuals may *overcompensate* in the direction of the other group to such an extent that these 'hypercorrections' may in turn become new ethnic markers (Sawyer, 1973). Grammatical markers have also been well-documented in the American context, for example the more frequent absence by blacks than whites of -s in the third person singular present tense as in, 'he tell me'. An example of lexical marking between different ethnic groups speaking the same language is the use of *different* words for the *same* semantic concept. For example, Moslems, Croats and Serbs all speak the same Yugoslav language, but have different words for 'train' using *carsija, grad* and *varos* respectively (Trudgill, 1974). The creation of black American slang is another instance of lexical marking perhaps more common in the younger generations (Drake, 1980). Ethnic groups may also use the *same* word but have different semantic contents. The use of the word 'nigger' would be negatively valued and derogatory when used by whites, but positively valued when used by a subset of fellow blacks who have creatively redefined the negative referent more favourably. This 'linguistic inversion' (Holt, 1973) functions positively as it excludes the possibility of having self-debasing words in the group's vocabulary (Kochman, 1976).

Ethnic group membership may also be marked in speech through prosodic and paralinguistic features. Prosody refers to the way in which a sentence is broken into tone groupings which are signalled in speech through intonation and stress, while paralinguistic features are those such as pitch, register, rhythm, loudness and tempo. Gumperz (1978) analysed the speech of West Indian immigrants and British whites in interaction and suggested that the former adopt different prosodic and paralinguistic rules from the members of the host community, which may easily lead to misattributions of intent and negative ethnic stereotyping. A white listener may perceive a West Indian speaker's 'peculiar' paralanguage and prosody as rude, excitable or threatening, while the latter may interpret the negative feedback in terms of ethnic discrimination. Other ethnic speech markers lie at the level of different discourse patterns of which there are many varieties (Clyne, 1981). Examples would include: different use of irony by blacks and whites in their overstating and understating respectively (Kochman, 1979); different uses of degrees of indirectness in conversations, so that a particular question may be interpreted as a request for information by the ingroup but as expressing unstated meaning by the outgroup (Tannen, 1979); different rules for pause lengths which can lead to one ethnic group regrading an outgroup as dominating the conversation and talking all the time, while the other may be seen as withdrawn, surly or unfriendly (Scollon and Scollon, 1979).

The above are only *potential* markers and do not characterize all speakers with a group, or even any one speaker on all occasions. Just as there are variations in the degree to which individuals identify with an ethnic group, so there will be variation in the degree to which this is reflected in their speech. However, some speech markers are ambiguous in the sense that they may be used to mark not only ethnic identity but also class membership, or to signal a change in the formality of the situation. Thus for example, a speaker may broaden his Scottish accent in order to signal a more informal definition of the situation, although this may be interpreted by the listener as signalling ethnic affiliation (P. Brown and Fraser, 1979; Taylor and Giles, 1979).

3.2   *The sociological approach*

We have already seen that language can be a salient dimension of ethnicity, but we have also suggested that a distinct *language* is not necessary for the maintenance of ethnolinguistic distinctiveness. The review of the previous approach has revealed some of the complex ways in which ethnic groups can remain differentiated while speaking the same language. Nevertheless, the question remains as to why some ethnic groups maintain their own languages while other groups assimilate to a dominant group and lose them. This issue of so-called 'language erosion' has been a primary concern of language sociologists interested in ethnicity (Clyne, 1979a; Kloss, 1966).

It has been suggested that the establishment of definite functional roles for different languages in a society tends to create a stable bilingualism or multilingualism (Fishman and Giles, 1978; Muthiani, 1979). For example, in Kenya English has a stabilized role as the language of higher education, while Swahili is the language of wider communication and national solidarity. Thus, *both* languages have important distinct functions and are indispensable, with stable multilingualism being the result. However, if this functional differentiation changes, for instance if one langauge no longer has a separate functional domain, then another language may displace it or a new type of functional differentiation of the languages may be arrived at. In any case, the salience of the language erodes for the group.

In considering the influence of language contact on language erosion, Lewis (1979) suggests there are primary and secondary factors operating. Primary factors (for example, economic, demographic, and physical), are the conditions which go towards producing language contact with the operation of these factors being similar in different cases. Secondary factors (for example, ideological, educational, and religious), do not bring about language contact but will influence the specific outcomes in different cases. An example of an important primary factor is industrialization. The rapid development of large-scale industry which is labour-intensive is likely to lead to a saturation of the local area by immigrants as a supplement to the labour force. In Ireland, industrialization had little influence linguistically on the Irish-speaking areas since the industry was 'capital' rather than labour-intensive, and also its development was phased to take account of the available local labour. Industrialization in Wales, in contrast, was of the type requiring large numbers of unskilled labour and was more rapid in leading to an influx of large numbers of English speakers. This led to increased contact with English, and also meant that English became associated with economic advancement to a great extent (compare Veltman, 1979). Urbanization is also likely to lead to increased contact between members of different language groups and through its association with industrialization, may lead to polarization of rural and urban areas in the language spoken. In Wales for example, the growth of towns and cities was associated with industrialization and the influx of English speakers, leading to a polarization between the Anglicized urban and Welsh-speaking rural areas. Since there was greater social mobility in the urban areas, the English language gained in prestige and became associated with social and economic advancement, while the number of Welsh speakers dwindled as people from rural areas moved to the cities. In an interesting complementary fashion, J. M. Orvik (personal communication) has suggested that one factor operating in *favour* of non standard code or minority language maintenance is the 'differential out-migration' of members of the language community who are most motivated for upward social mobility. Their removal from the community will leave it more linguistically and socially homogeneous, favouring the survival of the minority variety.

Fishman and Giles (1978) consider implicitly a number of Lewis's primary factors in explaining the different outcomes for the languages of immigrants to the United States and French Canadians in Quebec. In the former case, the original ethnic languages have been largely eroded whereas in the latter, French has been maintained and even strengthened in recent years. It seems that one of the most decisive factors in language erosion is a revolutionary change in economic conditions leading to greater interaction between different language groups and to changes in the relative influence of one group over another (Lewis, 1979; G. Williams, 1979). This has also been shown to be the case in a bilingual Slovenian and German-speaking community studied by Gumperz (1978) where a gradual language shift to German was taking place. This was attributed mainly to a change in the village's primary economy from a mutually interdependent agricultural to an urbanized service economy, involving more interactions (and of a different order) with the German-speaking community. However, other primary factors besides the economic have been considered crucial in language maintenance and erosion, particularly the demographic ones (Anderson, 1979; De Vries, 1979; Lamy, 1979), of which differential fertility rates and intermarriage have been found to be important between ingroups and outgroups.

3.3   *The communication breakdown approach*

Thus far, some of the sociostructural factors influencing the maintenance of an ethnic group's language, and the ways in which the group can maintain its linguistic distinctiveness even after its language has been eroded, have been outlined. A related issue, overlapping with the sociolinguistic approach, is the study of factors involved in the breakdown or lack of communication between ethnic groups (Simard, 1980; 1981). Although there are many areas throughout the world which are shared geographically by two or more ethnic groups, there is often a marked lack of interethnic contact. In Montreal, it was found that 99.9 per cent of conversations reported by French Canadian (FC) and English Canadian (EC) students were with fellow ingroup members rather than with ethnic outgroup individuals (Taylor and Simard, 1975). Two hypotheses have been proposed to explain this lack of interethnic contact and communication. First, it has been suggested that the ethnic groups involved are not *able* to communicate and the lack of contact is related to bilingual abilities. Indeed, some researchers suggest that individuals fail to learn a second language as effectively as the first (see Macnamara, 1966). Others point to sociolinguistic deficits apparent in many people's use of another group's language; that is, they are unskilled in the ability to produce different forms of a language (for example, particular non verbal signals such as facial expressions and gestures, more colloquial phrases and less prestigious pronunciation) for different social contexts, topics and purposes, etc. (see P. Brown and Fraser, 1979). Interestingly, Segalowitz (1976) found that non fluent bilingual FCs who tried to match an EC's informal speech in English and inevitably failed, misattributed their own lack of sociolinguistic competence externally to a dislike for the EC recipient. Still other researchers, adopting a more or less Whorfian perspective, suggest that although members of different ethnic groups may share a common vocabulary (and perhaps even the necessary sociolinguistic skills), they may not share similar cognitive and cultural frames of reference. Hence, Tucker and Gedalof (1970) found that FC bilinguals who were professional translators were significantly better linguistic mediators with other FCs than with ECs despite their expert bilingual competence. However, some studies suggest that effective interethnic communication in a second language *is* possible at some level. Taylor and Gardner (1970a) showed that FC listeners were as efficient as EC listeners at decoding taperecorded messages from EC speakers; similar results were obtained from mixed ethnic interactions in the Philippines (Taylor and Gardner, 1970b). In a further investigation, mixed-ethnic pairs and same-ethnic pairs in Quebec were found to be equally proficient at performing a task and talking face-to-face in an unstructured atmosphere after it (Simard and Taylor, 1973). The fact that different language groups can communicate effectively, even if as measured only by certain objective criteria under laboratory conditions suggests that *motivational* factors may play the most salient role in interethnic communication breakdowns.

The second hypothesis then suggests that the lack of interethnic contact is due to ethnic groups *choosing* not to communicate or avoiding situations where they might have to, and a number of factors can be suggested to account for this. First, since language is generally a salient dimension of ethnicity (see section 2.2), communicating in a language other than that of one's own may lead to a sense of cultural anomie and threaten or subtract from one's sense of ethnic identity; this is particularly likely for groups occupying a low power position when using the dominant group's language (Lambert, 1979, 1980). Second, individuals may feel a lack of established norms for appropriate behaviour in an interethnic interaction and these uncertainties may lead to an avoidance of cross-cultural contact (see C. R. Berger, 1979). It seems that interaction with a member of another ethnic group requires to varying degrees, reorientations to a new set of cues for appropriate behaviour and a novel value system (Brein and David, 1971; see, however, Taylor, Simard and Papineau, 1978). When a person actually resides in a cultural context other than the one to which he/she is accustomed, this need for personal and interpersonal reorientation can precipitate reactions such as depression, loneliness and self-doubt. Moreover, individuals who value their former culture and identify highly may experience these reactions more intensely. This phenomenon has been termed 'cultural/transition shock' and is comparable in many ways to reactions after divorce, institutionalization, and other major changes in lifestyle and environment (Coffman, 1979). Third, the lack of contact, as well as the nature of it when it does occur, may be due to previous unfavourable experiences with members of the ethnic outgroup, brought about perhaps by misinterpretations of their language behaviour. For example, while Latins and Arabs tend to stand very close to the person with whom they are talking, other groups, say Britons, will tend to maintain a greater interpersonal distance (Collett, 1971; Hall, 1966). The Latins may therefore perceive the latter as unfriendly or self-important while the Britons may in turn regard the former as threatening or overfamiliar. A vast array of norms for verbal and non verbal behaviour differ between ethnic groups such as routines for persuasion and concepts of trust, honour and hospitality (Clyne, 1979b; Grayshon, 1980; see also section 3.1) all of which if misattributed by an outgroup can lead to negative stereotyping and dissatisfaction (Jaspars and Hewstone, 1981). Fourth, lack of contact and communication breakdowns can arise because of negative attitudes associated with the ethnic outgroup itself. Indeed, it has been shown that after interethnic communication an interaction is often *perceived* by participants as inefficient and unsatisfactory despite the fact that the communication objectively was just as effective as within-group encounters (Taylor and Simard, 1975). These subjective impressions of interethnic communication are likely to reinforce the already negative expectations held prior to interaction and lead to further avoidance of interethnic contact.

In general then, simply understanding the language and communicational norms of another ethnic group will not automatically lead to better interethnic communication if social, political and economic disparities between the groups still remain (Pettigrew, 1967; Taylor and Simard, 1975). Moreover, while acquiring the other's language may lead to an increased ability to make social comparisons across ethnic boundaries, it can also lead to an exacerbation of conflict if such social comparisons bring intergroup inequities to the fore.

3.4 *Problems with existing approaches*

The foregoing discussion has established that language plays an important role in intergroup relations: we have looked at some of the ways in which speech styles are used and valued differently between and within different ethnic groups; we have considered some sociostructural factors which may influence the maintenance or erosion of different linguistic varieties; and how differences in expectations about language use and ethnic varieties provide sources for ethnic stereotyping, lack of interethnic contact and potential communication breakdown. However, while the three approaches outlined above have provided fruitful lines of enquiry, they do not represent a basis from which *generalized* predictions can be made. In particular, the notion emerges that an ethnic group's perception and use of particular language and speech styles may be important indicators and transmitters of both social differentiation from, and integration with, another ethnic group. In other words, while a group in one place is using and thinking about its language varieties in one way, a group somewhere else appears to be doing and believing quite opposing things. A primary question would appear to be: who in an ethnic group uses which language strategies, when and why? There is as yet no coherent theoretical framework from which this can be approached. Part of the reason for the difficulties in making generalizations and non specific predictions from previous approaches may lie in the heterogeneity of interethnic situations, language strategies and attitudes towards the ingroup's language. A brief review of some of these problems highlights the contribution a social psychological approach can make.

First, different ethnic groups vary on many dimensions including their history, geography, territory, as well as in their economic and political relations with other contrasting groups. In addition, an important source of *linguistic* variation between ethnic groups is the degree of overlap of the speech repertoires of the ingroups and outgroups concerned. Thus, groups in contact may be monolingual in their own languages; possess one or more languages or dialects in common; or one of the groups may be bilingual or monolingual in the other contact group's language (see Giles, 1978 for a fuller discussion).

Second, and relatedly, ethnic groups use different linguistic strategies. While some groups *attenuate* their ethnolinguistic varieties – even to the extent of them disappearing without trace (complete assimilation) – other groups *accentuate* these features, create new forms, or even incite civil action on behalf of their neglected languages. Examples, respectively, are West Indians in Cardiff, Wales, whose speech has been found to be indistinguishable from that of working class whites 80 per cent of the time (Giles and Bourhis, 1975; 1976) whereas blacks and whites in the United States have been 80 per cent accurately distinguished from speech samples (Shuy, Baratz, and Wolfram, 1969). The latter reflects the retention, accentuation and even creation by blacks of their ethnic speech style. Similarily, in recent years, the Welsh, Bretons and Catalans, far from assimilating into the dominant ethnic groups with which they are in contact have attempted to foster the communicative and economic viabilities of their languages by pressing forcibly for their wider use in such domains as the media and education. Third, not only do differences in attitudes to language varieties exist between ethnolinguistic groups, but there is also, of course, heterogeneity between different factions and members of the *same* group (Ryan and Carranza, 1977). This is exemplified amongst Indians living in Britain whose ethnic language is Gujarati: 'If I didn't speak Gujarati, I would feel drowned in a bucket of water. I would suffocate if I didn't speak Gujarati. If an Indian tries to speak to me in English I always ask "can't you speak Gujarati?" If he can't, I feel distant from him.' Another member of the same group is quoted as saying: 'I was at a polytechnic in London and a year passed before I spoke any Gujarati. Even when I met a Gujarati from Leicester, we got to know each other in English and wouldn't dream of speaking anything else' (cited in Mercer, Mercer and Mears, 1979, p. 23).

Within-group heterogeneity has likewise been observed in the Soviet Union. Members of the same ethnic group (the Udmurts) vary in the value they place on different aspects of their ethnic identity such as the ethnic language, cultural traditions and ethnic selfconsciousness (Guboglo, 1979). In a similar vein, French Americans in Maine were found to value either the French language or the shared ethnic cultural background more as aspects of their ethnicity depending on whether or not they could speak French (Giles et al., 1976). Because of within-group differences in attitudes towards ethnicity and the group language, differences may also be expected in the linguistic strategies that group members adopt. Furthermore, ethnic groups in contact may not have discernible differences in their spoken language varieties but ingroup members may believe that they do (Parkin, 1977; Wolff, 1959), complicating any predictions regarding the likely linguistic strategies adopted by them.

In short, we require an approach which will begin to take into account between-group and within-group diversity in language and ethnic attitudes, speech repertoires and strategies, as well as structural features of, and influences on, groups in contact. The remainder of this chapter is aimed at providing a social psychological perspective which attempts to do just that. Armed with the principle that quite different linguistic strategies may be adopted for similar psychological reasons, our framework may enable us to better specify who uses which language strategy, when and for what purpose.

4   A social psychological approach to the study of language and ethnicity

The theoretical approach to be introduced here has four components which will be considered in relation to language behaviour: social identity theory, the concept of perceived ethnolinguistic vitality, the concept of perceived group boundaries, and notions of multiple group membership. Social identity theory is the framework to which all the other components relate and provides an analysis of strategies for positive distinctiveness as well as some hypotheses about when they will be adopted. The other concepts are then introduced and discussed as they specify more precisely some of the personal and situational factors enhancing the salience of ethnic identification for individuals and hence allow more concrete predictions concerning ethnolinguistic behaviours. The approach concludes in propositional terms with an outline of eight conditions considered necessary for individuals to maintain, accentuate or create a favourably valued ethnolinguistic distinctiveness.

4.1 Social identity theory

Social identity theory (Tajfel, 1974, 1978a, 1978c; Tajfel and Turner, 1979; and see chapter 1) is built around a sequence of processes which can be expressed as follows. Social categorization of the world involves knowledge of our membership in certain social categories. This knowledge of our category memberships together with the values, positive or negative, attached to them is defined as our social identity and has meaning only in social comparison with other relevant groups. Social identity forms an important part of the self-concept and it is assumed that we try to achieve a positive sense of social identity in such a way as to make our own social group favourably distinct from other collectivities on valued dimensions (such as, power, economic and political resources, intellectual attributes). Such a process of achieving positive distinctiveness enables individuals to achieve a satisfactory social identity and thereby enhances their own positive self-esteem (Oakes and Turner, 1980). Thus, when *ethnic* group identity becomes important for individuals, they may attempt to make themselves favourably distinct on valued dimensions such as language (Giles, 1977), and an accentuation of ethnic speech markers as a strategy for positive differentiation may be expected (Bourhis and Giles, 1977; Bourhis *et al.*, 1979; Drake, 1980; Taylor and Royer, 1980); a process termed 'psycholinguistic distinctiveness' (Giles, Bourhis, and Taylor, 1977).

It now becomes clear why a superordinate goal of a stable

world language such as Esperanto (see Lieberman, 1979) is unlikely to be realized (see Bragga, 1979). Similarities between ethnic groups on, for example, linguistic dimensions act as cues for comparison giving rise to competition between the groups for positive differentiation. Collaborative goals (like a universal language) are likely to heighten the perception of similarities between the groups in values, attributes and in language (see chapter 3). This in turn will lead to further comparisons, competition and linguistic differentiation between groups, illustrated by studies of English and French Canadians in Quebec learning French and English respectively who start introducing ingroup phonological markers into the second language they are learning (Lambert and Tucker, 1972; Taylor, Meynard, and Rheault, 1977). This can be interpreted within our framework as an attempt to differentiate themselves from the ethnic group thereby establishing psycholinguistic distinctiveness.

Social identity theory is a dynamic perspective which also has the potential at least for considering ethnolinguistic *change*. In particular, a negative social identity would be expected to act as a motivating factor in social change as a means of attaining a more satisfactory social identity; a dominant group, which has satisfactory conditions for its ethnolinguistic identity would desire to maintain the *status quo*. There are ample examples, however, of ethnic groups in low status positions for whom a subordinate power position does not seem to provide sufficient motivation in and of itself to initiate changes in the social structure. Instances of this have been traditionally the Bantus in South Africa, minority groups in the United States, *Gastarbeiters* in West Germany, some immigrant groups in Britain, and isolated German and Italian groups in Brazil (Heye, 1979). The emphasis here is on *perceived* rather than actual conditions and we are concerned with conflicts which exist psychologically for the groups involved (Deutsch, 1973). That is, the emphasis is on: '. . . the perception of deprivation, people may be subjectively deprived with respect to their expectations even though an observer might not judge them to be in want'. (Gurr, 1970, p. 24) or vice-versa. A positive ethnic identity is achieved then to the extent that group members can make social comparisons with respect to relevant ethnic outgroups in their favour. However, should social comparisons with an ethnic group on valued dimensions result in a negative ethnic identity for ingroup members, Tajfel and Turner (1979) propose that the latter will adopt one or more specified strategies to achieve a more positive self-concept. One of these, upward mobility, will be argued to be an 'individualistic' strategy aimed at a disidentification with the erstwhile ethnic category, whereas the other strategies, such as social creativity and social competition, are considered more 'group-oriented' given that they imply individuals are attempting to achieve a positive ethnic group distinctiveness. Most of the strategies and their tactics can be seen to have important linguistic correlates* and these will be discussed below together with some of the conditions considered most likely to bring about their occurrence.

4.1.1 Individual mobility and group assimilation: linguistic strategies

This strategy refers to that whereby individuals wish to pass out of the group which is causing them so much comparative discomfort into a more positively valued one, usually the dominant ethnic collectivity. To this end, they will attempt to acquire or at least aspire towards the characteristics (physical and or psychological) of this other group and thereby secure for themselves a more adequate social identity. This strategy is most likely to be used by group members possessing a negative ethnic identity when intergroup boundaries are perceived as soft and permeable (see section 4.2.2 below) and when objections raised by either ingroup or outgroup for so doing are not considered strong. An important tactic for individual upward mobility in such a situation is of course a convergence towards the linguistic characteristics *believed* typical of the ethnic outgroup (Beebe, 1981; Thakerar, Giles, and Cheshire, in press) and hence the attenuation of the ingroup's speech markers (Giles, Scherer, and Taylor, 1979).

Large numbers of the ingroup acting in assimilationist terms (see Olmedo, 1979; Richardson, 1967; Taft, 1979) can give rise to collective consequences finding expression in the so-called 'erosion' or even 'death' of the ingroup language; such a process

*Previous discussions of the area of language and ethnicity by us and our colleagues, particularly as they relate to self-oriented and group-oriented strategies (for example, Bourhis, 1979; Giles, 1978, 1979; Giles, Bourhis and Taylor, 1977), were guided by an earlier version of social identity theory (Tajfel, 1974). In this present chapter, we prefer to base our approach on Tajfel and Turner (1979).

might be more appropriately termed 'language suicide' (Denison, 1977) in accord with social identity principles. Albo (1979) has studied the effects of group assimilation on two subordinate collectivities in the Andes. As the subordinate ethnic groups attempt to assimilate into the dominant Spanish-speaking group, their ethnic languages become restricted to certain domains of usage. This results in the languages lacking neologisms for technical advances, etc., since Spanish words are used instead to denote prestige. For example, the Spanish word is adopted for a modern kitchen whereas the ingroup word is used for a traditional kitchen, and Spanish words are preferred for telling the date or time while native numerals are allowed for counting sheep. The frequency of borrowing of Spanish words varies with topic; for example, only 11 per cent of borrowed words for a theme such as 'fear of spirits' but over 40 per cent borrowed Spanish words in discussions of politics or modern medicine. Thus, impoverishment of the subordinate groups' languages is likely to reach a stage where discussion in their ethnic languages will be impossible on certain topics. This so-called 'atrophication' is therefore a result of the subordinate groups' attempts to assimilate into the dominant Spanish-speaking group.

The strategy of upward mobility is not always ultimately a successful means for attaining a more satisfactory social identity. Indeed, rather than producing the desired effect, it may instead lead to anomie and a loss of cultural distinctiveness for those individuals who still value their ethnic group membership and see language as an important dimension of it. Thus, acquiring another ethnic group's speech style can lead sometimes to 'subtractive bilingualism' for an ethnic group with an inadequate social identity (Lambert, 1974, 1979, 1980). Further, the dominant group frequently does not fully accept the subordinate group even after it has attempted to assimilate as this in turn diminishes their own psycholinguistic distinctiveness. J. Ross (1979, p. 8) states that:

> An enlightened majority may find the policy of co-opting such individuals could offer significant payoffs in increasing social stability and more effective social control. However, in most cases the majority will deny the opportunity of full assimilation to upwardly mobile minority group members. Reasons for doing so range from a desire to preserve the sanctity of the social order to an attempt to limit access to elite and sub-elite positions.

Such a strategy of maintaining linguistic differentiation could be achieved by one or other of the following means. First, the dominant group could refuse to perceive linguistically assimilated individuals as sounding correct and properly spoken. In other words, however much the individual objectively sounds as indistinguishable from the dominant group the latter may nevertheless perceive them to sound 'ethnic' if they have other cues to use (such as name, or skin colour; see F. Williams, Whitehead, and Miller, 1971). Second, if linguistic assimilation amongst ethnic minorities occurs with such levels of proficiency and numbers that it dilutes the dominant group's cultural distinctiveness, powerful members of the dominant group may respond by upwardly diverging away (Giles and Powesland, 1975) from these passers and thereby create a new standard for comparison. In such circumstances, subordinate groups may find the language or prestige dialect of the dominant group an ever-shifting target to pursue. Elias (1978) has observed the same type of behavioural changes in a documentation of interclass rivalry in late seventeenth-century France (compare Ullrich, 1971). He comments that (1978, pp. 100–1):

> there is ample evidence to show at this period customs, behaviour, and fashions from the court are continuously penetrating the upper middle classes, where they are imitated and more or less altered in accordance with the different social situation. They thereby lose, to some extent, their character as means of distinguishing the upper class. They are somewhat devalued. This compels those above to further refinement and development of behaviour. And from this mechanism – the development of courtly customs, their dissemination downward, their slight social deformation, their devaluation as marks of distinction, the constant movement in behaviour patterns through the upper class receives part of its motivation. What is important is that in this change, in the inventions and fashions of courtly behaviour, which are at first sight perhaps chaotic and accidental, over extended time spans certain directions or lines of development emerge. These include, for example, what may be described as an advance of the threshold of embarrassment and shame, as 'refinement', or as 'civilization'. A particular social dynamism triggers a particular psychological one, which has its own regularities.

In any case, individuals who attempt to pass into the dominant group are often stigmatized as 'cultural traitors' by other members of their own group who value their ingroup identification very highly, and the former are accorded uncomplimentary linguistic labels by the latter (Khleif, 1979a; Kochman, 1976; Lukens, 1979). Nevertheless, it is possible that individuals might wish not to pass into the dominant ethnic collectivity but aspire to use their ethnic speech markers to enable them to qualify for membership of some *other* social category which would provide them with a more satisfactory group identity (G. Williams, 1979). A Welshman's accent in English for example might promote his chances of acceptance into working-class categories and hence his use of it would reflect his differentiation from others in class rather than in ethnic terms (Taylor and Giles, 1979).

Individual mobility then is quite a personal strategy in the sense that the original group's status remains unaltered, and such a lack of identification if widespread enough can act so as to blur group boundaries even further, decrease ingroup cohesiveness, and reduce the potential for collective action. When assimilation is not successful, and acceptance by the dominant group not complete, the group may reject this strategy as a means for attaining status parity and seek this instead through other forms of collective action. J. Ross (1979, p. 8) suggests that the subordinate ethnic group may at some point find that '. . . assimilation cannot be a solution to an increasingly intolerant enforced status deprivation. Increasingly, an alternative is sought in minority organization and political action. If individuals cannot escape minority status, they may seek to return to group life for the purpose of altering the group's inferior status through collective behaviour.' It might therefore be expected that assimilation would be one of the first strategies members of a subordinate group might adopt, but that it will be followed by other group strategies aimed to redefine the group on its own terms rather than being defined by the dominant group (Guillaumin, 1972; J. Ross, 1979). This of course would represent a definite psychological development for group members (Tajfel, 1978a).

4.1.2 *Strategies of psycholinguistic distinctiveness*

According to the schema of Tajfel and Turner (1979), we might expect to find that there are at least two strategies of positive differentiation possible to subordinate ethnic group members along linguistic lines, namely social creativity and social competition.

Social creativity. Social creativity refers to those strategies which attempt a redefinition of different elements of the comparison between subordinate and dominant ethnic groups. In contrast to the previous, individual mobility strategy, which implied an abandonment of the ethnic group, the present strategies are aimed at protecting the group's identity and restoring its positive distinctiveness. In this sense, they are considered 'group-oriented' even though these solutions, as opted for by individuals, may not actually alter the objective relationship existing between ethnic ingroup and outgroup on subordinate–dominant dimensions. It is thought likely that these strategies will be adopted by individuals possessing a negative ethnic identity either when intergroup boundaries are perceived as virtually impermeable or when there are severe social sanctions imposed by significant others in the ingroup for those not acting in accord with their ethnic group membership. In other words, social creativity strategies, of which there are at least three, should be adopted when individuals find it impossible to leave their ethnic group and identification with it is unavoidable.

The first of these strategies refers to an avoidance of 'painful' comparisons with the outgroup which is responsible for their negative ingroup image. Where there is a lack of comparability between ingroup and outgroup, evaluative deficiencies should be diluted and an inadequate identity less apparent. This can be achieved by individuals selecting other subordinate ethnic groups with which they can make favourable comparisons. For instance, Asian immigrants in Britain might compare themselves with the West Indian group and gain a more positive cultural identity from this comparison since (amongst other things) they have a distinct language whereas West Indians rely only on a distinctive dialect or accent for their ethnolinguistic differentiations. Instead, however, intergroup comparability may be avoided by fostering the intensity of *intra* group comparisons (see J. A. Williams and Giles, 1978). For example, a person with high occupational status might tend to make far more comparisons on this dimension with other individuals within his or her ethnic group rather than with ethnic outgroup members. However, the degree to which people can be successful by this means depends on how well-insulated the group is from the need for intergroup comparisons. In some social contexts, the group may be able to isolate itself to such a degree that daily interactions are predominantly with members of the same social group. 'When this group happens to have its own strongly integrated norms traditions, values and functions, a "negative" self-image elicited in comparisons with other groups need not by any means become the central focus of an individual's identity' (Tajfel, 1978c, p. 13).

Research on Asians and West Indians in Britain has indicated that the former tend to internalize their inferior status in white society to a lesser degree than do West Indians because of the stronger traditions (including linguistic and cultural) of the Asian community which may serve to strengthen further individual ties with it (Milner, 1975). This 'cultural isolation' (see Lanigan, 1970) is likely to be somewhat precarious, and successive generations will probably be subject to increasing pressures and influences from the surrounding society and culture (Tajfel, 1978c). Hence, given close proximity of the ethnic groups in contact, such a state of non-comparability is not feasible and other social creativity strategies need to be undertaken.

The second social creativity strategy refers to an attempt to change the values of the ingroup characteristics in a more positive direction such that negative ingroup comparisons are much reduced; the example *par excellence* is, of course, the 'Black is beautiful'-type slogans which included both verbal and non-verbal behaviours (see Drake, 1980; Kochman, 1976). Again, language assumes significance to the extent that the often-termed 'inferior', 'substandard' or 'minority' language, dialect or slang of ethnic ingroup are no longer stigmatized but are proudly heralded within that group as symbols of cultural pride (Lefevre, 1978). Needless to say, these circumstances promote tendencies of language retention and dialect maintenance within the ethnic ingroup (Ryan, 1979). An intriguing instance of alteration of existing linguistic dimensions of comparison, but this time by the dominant group, is the changes of Swahili made by the Boers in Kenya resulting in a new dialect, Kisetla (Muthiani, 1979). The dominant group, by altering the subordinate group's language, defined the situation via language as one in which they became superior and more powerful. The indigenous population were in no position to enforce a 'standard' form of their language, but rather in many instances adopted the outgroup's form of their own ethnic language.

The third social creativity strategy refers to a tendency to compare the ingroup with the outgroup on some new dimensions.

The resurrection of Hebrew in Israel (Fellman, 1974; Seckbach, 1974), the revival of Panjabi in Pakistan (Pandit, 1978), and the modernization, standardization and planning of varieties of language (Fishman, 1974; Griffen, 1980; Pool, 1979; Rubin and Jernudd, 1971) can sometimes be considered instances of such a stragegy. In Canada for instance, Ukranian nationalists replaced letters of the Russian alphabet with new 'Ukranian' ones to emphasize the distinctiveness of Ukranian (Anderson, 1979). However, as a study by Lemaine (1966) shows, strategies of social creativity involve several stages at which the subordinate group may experience difficulties. Having recognized their inferiority on existing dimensions of comparison, they have to introduce new dimensions of comparison on which they perceive themselves to be superior and must then struggle to have them recognized and legitimized. Thus for example, the revival of Welsh and Catalan and many other ethnic minority languages, have not automatically led to their recognition in various quarters such as government.

Social competition. Social competition refers to the strategy adopted by certain individuals who wish to reverse the perceived status of ingroup and outgroup on valued dimensions (Turner, 1975). Such a strategy of direct competition is viewed as taking place when group members (a) strongly identify with their ethnic group membership, and (b) intergroup comparisons are still active (and perhaps despite previous attempts at social creativity) or have become so. One set of determinants, besides proximity and perceived similarity, considered by Tajfel and Turner (1979) as crucial in fostering the latter so-called 'insecure social comparisons' is the awareness of cognitive alternatives to the groups' statuses. That is, for example, when subordinate group members are aware that their inferiority is based on unfair advantages and is *illegitimate* (Coser, 1956; Merton, 1968; Tajfel, 1978a) as well as believing that status differences are potentially changeable and *unstable* (Caddick, 1978; Turner and Brown, 1978), between-group comparisons will become more active than quiescent.

A large number of situational factors may induce an awareness of cognitive alternatives amongst subordinate group members to their inferiority with respect to members of the dominant group. Indeed, some of the aforementioned strategies may stimulate the group to see such cognitive alternatives to the *status quo*. Taylor suggests in his cyclic theory of intergroup relations (see Taylor and Giles, 1979) that it is in the interests of the dominant group to allow some subordinate members to pass into the dominant group if they have the necessary qualifications, such as education, or speech patterns; the intergroup structure is thereby seen as legitimate but a *little* unstable. Nevertheless some sufficiently qualified members of the subordinate group may not be admitted into the dominant group whereas assimilated individuals who have been, may not be *fully* accepted if their ethnic group membership is clear to the dominant group. It is these very individuals who then may come to see the intergroup situation as illegitimate and may return to their original group to instigate group action by the subordinate group against the existing status hierarchy.

Another possibility is that groups making comparisons with other subordinate collectivities undergoing successful ethnic revivals and redefinitions may come to see cognitive alternatives to their own low status positions. Admittedly, some ethnic revivals may be caused not so much by power or status discrepancies but by an idealized return to a 'vague nostalgia and an undefined ideology' as a reaction to the conditions of life in the twentieth century (Glazer, 1954) – 'what the son wishes to forget the grandson wishes to remember' (Bender and Kayiwada, 1968). However, through intercultural comparisons, another subordinate group may seize on this and other redefinitions as evidence of increasing instability, and be catalyzed into redefining their position economically, linguistically and culturally in new and more positive terms. For example, the revival of Welsh or the strengthening of the position of the French in Quebec may trigger other groups through intercultural comparisons to see their own subordinate position as unstable. Thus ethnic language revival in one place may catalyse ethnic rebirth in other places for different reasons. Tajfel (1978c) relates revival of ethnic groups worldwide (see also Fishman, 1977) to the increasing interdependence of different groups, economically and politically. Groups are also becoming increasingly aware of this interdependence, for example through the spread of the mass media, and this will tend to lead to an increased need for differentiation amongst themselves in order to maintain psychological distinctiveness. It also means subordinate groups are more likely to become aware of other groups' successful positive differentiation, which may catalyze their own ethnic group and language revival (as above).

One further factor mediating these intergroup comparisons might be the more pervasive spread of ideologies stressing 'common humanity' through human rights movements. Other factors likely to influence a subordinate group's perception of its position in the status hierarchy include some of the sociostructural factors discussed earlier (section 3.2) such as urbanization, industrialization, etc. G. Williams (1979, p. 63) argued that during periods of economic growth, the almost universal rise in the standard of living results in a tendency to emphasize class action, and regard ethnic stratification as legitimate: 'On the other hand, under conditions of stagnation there is a tendency to view economic relations in terms of a zero-sum game and to envisage competition for scarce resources between regions, ethnic groups etc.' These different but interrelated factors have their effect through stimulating a group to see their present status position as illegitimate or unstable – in other words, the group perceives cognitive alternatives to the pervading status structure.

To reiterate, factors which promote ethnic identification (to be discussed in section 4.2) and insecure interethnic comparisons (for example, the awareness of cognitive alternatives) will lead subordinate group members to challenge the superiority of the dominant group and initiate strategies of social competition. Examples of linguistic competition (or psycholinguistic distinctiveness) abound cross-nationally (for instance, in Spain, France, Sri Lanka, India) where individuals incite civil disobedience on behalf of their beleaguered languages. This can be illustrated by the Welsh language group's fight for representation in the media and education. Not only do group members simply wish to revalue their old speech characteristics and also create new ones for private use in their own ingroup domains, but they move to have these recognized as just as acceptable in more formal, public contexts. In this sense, people will wish to accentuate their ingroup speech markers (Bourhis and Giles, 1977; Bourhis et al., 1979; Taylor and Royer, 1980) and actively diverge away from where they believe the linguistic characteristics of an outgroup speaker to be in social encounters (see Thakerar, Giles, and Cheshire, in press).

Not only have we here the seeds of potential social conflict but also the possibility of ethnolinguistic and social changes as dominant groups are unlikely to ignore actions which do not simply increase the status of the subordinate group but also by implication threaten their own valued distinctiveness. Indeed, it would appear that the awareness of cognitive alternatives amongst the dominant group (for example, that their superiority is illegitimate and unstable; see Turner and R. J. Brown, 1978) makes them likely candidates for adopting reciprocal strategies of social creativity and competition in order to restore their positive ethnic identity. Further R. J. Brown (1978a) suggests an extension of the notion of illegitimacy to include cases where the dominant group see its superiority as illegitimately small. This might come about through comparisons with other dominant groups (for example colonial powers) since the interparty system is obviously not simply a two-party one. In such circumstances, derogatory language (Husband, 1977), abrasive verbal humour and oppressive policies will be aimed at the socially creative and competitive measures of the subordinate group by their dominant counterparts (for further discussion, see Giles, 1978).

4.2 Factors influencing the salience of ethnic identification

By adopting certain derivations from social identity theory to the area of language and ethnicity, we have seen how the social psychological processes of categorization, identification, comparison and positive differentiation can lead group members to seek a positive self-concept. The possible speech strategies in this regard have been referred to as the accentuation, maintenance and attenuation of ethnic speech markers, and redefinition of and social competition on linguistic dimensions. In this vein, we would argue that the differences reported in the literature in the use of different language strategies across a vast array of ethnic groups as well as a great deal of heterogeneity within many of these as well could be afforded some conceptual clarity. Obviously, the conditions for the choice of different strategies by the different groups requires further empirical attention, particularly in view of Turner and Brown's (1978) finding that a high status group, perceiving its position as both illegitimate and unstable, adopts strategies of creativity rather than direct competition. However, as the accentuation and attenuation of ethnic speech markers appears to depend in part on the strength of an individual's ethnic identification, we shall now proceed to extend social identity theory in a modest way so as to explore some of the situational and personal factors affecting the salience of a person's ethnic belongingness. These factors, which include the concepts of perceived ethnolinguistic vitality and perceived group boundaries, as well as notions concerning multiple group memberships will allow us towards the end of this chapter to propose even more precisely the conditions under which members of an ethnic group will wish to accentuate or attenuate their distinctive ethnolinguistic styles.

4.2.1 *Perceived ethnolinguistic vitality*

A social psychological approach to intergroup behaviour in general, and language and ethnicity in particular, should take into account individuals' cognitive representations of the sociostructural forces operating in interethnic contexts. To this end, and as an initial exploratory attempt to systematize the different *objective* structural conditions operating between different ethnic groups, Giles, Bourhis and Taylor (1977) compiled a taxonomy of so-called 'ethnolinguistic vitality' variables. It was argued that the more of these sociostructural factors a particular group had in its favour, the more vitality it is said to have and consequently the more likely it will survive and thrive as an active collective entity in interethnic contexts. Conversely, it was argued that ethnolinguistic minorities which have little or no group vitality would eventually cease to exist as distinctive collectivities (see Bourhis, 1979).

The most important sociostructural variables which are considered to determine ethnolinguistic vitality can be subsumed under status, demographic and institutional support factors. *Status* factors include economic, political, social, sociohistorical and language status variables (see Hinnenkamp, 1980). *Demographic* factors are those relating to the distribution of the group (national territory, concentration and population) and those relating to numbers (absolute number, birth rate, mixed marriages, immigration, emigration) (see Joy, 1978; Mougeon, 1977). *Institutional support* factors include representation of the ethnic group in mass media, education, government, industry, religion and culture. These factors are suggested as being influential in determining the overall vitality of the group – that is, members' strength of identification with the group and group solidarity, and the likelihood that group members and outsiders will continue to regard the group as a distinctive ethnolinguistic entity (Mougeon and Canale, 1978; Roberts and Williams, 1980). Thus the more a group has economic and political control over its own destiny, high social status, a strong tradition and history which is a source of pride to the group, and an ethnic speech style which is highly valued (or even of international status), the more potential the group is likely to have for survival as a distinct ethnolinguistic entity. Similarly, the greater the concentration of the ethnic group in its own territory, the higher the ethnic birth rate and the absolute number of the group, and the lower the incidence of mixed marriages and emigration, and immigration of outgroup members, the more potential the ethnic group has for survival as a distinct ethnolinguistic entity. Finally, the more institutional support the ethnic group has through representation in mass media, education, government, and in international bodies, etc. the more potential the group is likely to have for survival as a distinct ethnolinguistic entity.

To illustrate the above, consider the case of (upper middle-class, male) Anglo-Americans as an example of a group with high vitality. This group has high economic status and control, as well as high social status and although the group's traditions are of more recent conception than those of many ethnic groups, its history is a source of pride to the majority of its members, and its language enjoys high status throughout the world. The group has a high absolute number of members who are strongly concentrated in its own territory. Outgroup partners in mixed marriages and immigrating groups tend to assimilate into the Anglo-American group and emigrating members tend to maintain strong links with 'the folks back home'. Further, the group and its language are fully articulated in the mass media, education, government, etc. and in addition, its language is a primary medium of international affairs. In contrast, the Swedish-speaking group in Finland would appear to be an example of a group with fewer of the sociostructural factors in their favour, and would be expected to have lower vitality, that is, less potential for survival as a separate ethnolinguistic collective (Liebkind, 1979). Although generally Swedish is a language of fairly high status, in Finland, Swedish-speaking Finns show a readiness to converse in Finnish as soon as ability permits, even when the majority of those present are Swedish-speaking (Grönroos, 1978). The low prestige of Swedish in Finland is reflected in the low retention rate of Swedish in mixed marriages. It also results in a large proportion of the lower class members of the group shifting to Finnish for upward social mobility (Miemois, 1978), undermining further the minority group identity. Demographic factors do not seem to militate in favour of the group's vitality either. There is a fairly high rate of emigration to Sweden, a lower birth-rate in the Swedish-speaking group compared with the Finnish-speaking group, and members are spread around the country in various 'communes'; 15 per cent of the group live in bilingual or Finnish-speaking communes, with the concomitant likelihood of language shift and low institutional support for the Swedish language. Although the language has status as an offi- cial language as well as representation in the Swedish-speaking communes, overall the demographic variables are not favourable for the survival of the group (Leibkind, 1979). These two examples serve to illustrate how sociostructural factors may influence the vitality of an ethnic group with the possibility of characterizing it objectively as being relatively high or low on this dimension (see also Bourhis, 1979; Clément, 1980).

Giles, Bourhis, and Taylor (1977) drew a distinction between such objectively measured vitality and that perceived to be the case by the ingroup itself. While in many cases there may be considerable overlap between objective and subjective measures of vitality, in other contexts (as will be argued below) there may be little correspondence. Thus, attention has been focused recently more theoretically on *perceived* rather than actual, objective vitality as a mediator of interethnic behaviour and second language acquisition (Giles and Byrne, 1980) and, also in like fashion, we have been concerned with exploring empirically the dimensions of ethnic groups' perceptions of ingroup and outgroup vitalities (Bourhis, Giles, and Rosenthal, 1981). Hence, it has been proposed that the higher a subordinate group perceives its vitality to be, the more likely its members will accentuate their ethnolinguistic features in interethnic encounters when they are aware of cognitive alternatives to the existing interethnic status hierarchy. Dominant group members, when they perceive cognitive alternatives to their superiority are also more likely to respond more vigorously by accentuating their own, or creating new, speech forms if they perceive the subordinate group's vitality to be high (Giles, 1978, 1979).

It has been suggested that a dominant ethnic group may have an interest in maintaining the low vitality of a subordinate group in order to provide contrast, and increase the vitality of the dominant group (see Kramarae (1981) for a discussion of men's interest in maintaining 'women's speech' according to vitality principles). Hence if the dominant ethnic group percieves that the

subordinate ethnic group's vitality is increasing, then it is suggested that the dominant group will implement strategies to
undermine the subordinate group's vitality on certain dimensions; given the dominant group's control over many different
spheres in society, it has some scope for so doing. For instance, it
may overtly relinquish economic control and cultural division of
labour while covertly maintaining the inequalities of the system,
which may be revealed, for example, through the distribution of
different ethnic groups in the wage structure. In addition, it may
be able to present and support a biased view of the history of the
different groups, with emphases on its own historical achieve-
ments, neglecting those of the other ethnic groups in the
society. The dominant ethnic group's speech style may be presented as the 'norm' from which other styles deviate, the latter
being characterized as 'substandard', 'restricted' or 'inappropriate' for certain spheres of activity, such as education, the media,
government, etc. Indeed, through the exclusive use of the
dominant group's ethnic speech style in these areas, it will be
perpetuated as the norm and so, by limiting the functional
spheres of the subordinate speech styles, these may atrophy,
maintaining the linguistic status hierarchy. The dominant group
may emphasize through the media the 'national identity' (deriving from that of the dominant group), so that minority ethnic
groups' attempts to gain recognition or representation are seen as
a threat to the nation as a whole (see Husband, 1979). Control of
the economic, socializing, media system, etc. by the dominant
group also mean that it has control of the ideologies perpetuated
in the society, and consequently over the potential for survival of
other ethnic groups in the society. As Williams (1979, p. 63) has
stated:

> A major ingredient of the legitimisation process (of the minority
> ethnic group language, etc.) is the expression of an ideology wherein
> the minority language is viewed as an irrational allegiance of a
> traditionally-oriented population unarticulated to mass society and
> the State. The tendency for members of the minority language
> groups to reject the minority language is largely a result of this
> process.

It has been suggested that the dominant ethnic group has at its
disposal a variety of strategies by means of which it can manipulate subordinate ethnic groups' perceptions of their own groups'
vitalities. Hence, the dominant group has powerful mechanisms
for maintaining its superior position in the social structure. The

possibility of use of such strategies highlights the necessity for considering not only the sociostructural factors influencing the ethnic group's survival potential, but also the group's *perception* of its own position, that is, the psychological representation of these sociostructural factors. Hence, we propose that high perceived ingroup vitality acts so as to increase the situational salience of ethnic identification for group members and thereby bolsters the likelihood of their accentuating their ethnic speech markers in interethnic contexts where insecure social comparisons are operating in search of a positively valued psycholinguistic distinctiveness.

4.2.2 *Perceived group boundaries*

Another set of factors affecting the situational strength of ethnic identification relate to individuals' perceptions of their ethnic boundaries. Group boundaries are based on discontinuities in interactions between individuals (Merton, 1968; Weber, 1964). There is frequently, therefore, a coincidence of group and language boundaries and in these cases language can play an important role in the maintenance of the group boundaries. However, boundaries are maintained not by a lack of interaction across them but by the continuation of interactions of a particular kind. Interactants define the situation as one in which the boundaries are relevant and interact accordingly. Since group identity is embedded in group boundaries any blurring of them will influence the individual's identification with the group: '. . . all margins are dangerous. If they are pulled this way or that the shape of the fundamental experience is altered. Any structure of ideas is vulnerable at its margins.' (Douglas, 1966, p. 121). F. Ross (1979) suggests that group boundaries can be characterised in terms of three dimensions; distinctiveness, strength and value. *Distinctiveness* refers to the ease with which members and non-members can be identified, that is, to the clarity of cues associated with group membership, such as dress style, physiognomy, speech style, etc. with those stimuli offering the greatest intergroup contrast being most likely to become incorporated into the view each group has of the other (Campbell, 1967). If there are unambiguous distinguishing features associated with group membership then interactions between members of the two groups are likely to be very consistent, and this 'visibility' will make intergroup discrimination more likely, and more intense when it does occur

(Allen and Wilder, 1975; McGuire *et al.*, 1978; Sherif and Sherif, 1956).

Strength refers to the cross-situational relevance of the particular group membership. Some situations are perceived by most individuals in terms of their ethnic group membership while concurrently most situations are perceived by some individuals in this manner. The degree to which members of a group see that group as relevant to a wide range of situations is defined as the strength of the group boundaries.

Value refers to the extent to which group attributes, such as language, are generally accepted as positive or negative within the group. This will be related to the evaluation of the group from without, such that if an ethnic group and its speech style are of high social status then the ethnic group membership is likely to be highly valued by its members. Clearly all of these dimensions are closely linked to the concept of ethnolinguistic vitality. Indeed, one of the features of an ethnic group contributing to its vitality may be the clarity of criteria associated with the group membership, and thus the distinctiveness of an ethnic group's boundaries and its vitality are closely interrelated. Similarly, if an ethnic group has high vitality, it is more likely to be seen as relevant to a wider range of situations, that is, vitality and the strength of group boundaries are also interrelated. Finally, the status factor influencing the vitality of an ethnic group will also influence the value of the group to its members.

The effects of these three dimensions is assumed to be additive resulting in the overall 'hardness' of the group boundaries: 'clarity' in F. Ross's (1979) terms. While a number of scholars have discussed the salience of group boundaries with a view to strong ones being an optimal state for an ethnic group (see, for example, Banton, 1978; Khleif, 1979b; Paulston and Paulston, 1980), our emphasis lies as it did with ethnolinguistic vitality at the cognitive representational level. In this vein, Giles (1979) proposed a distinction between perceived hard versus soft ingroup boundaries, as members of the same ethnic group often perceive their group boundaries differently and hence as a consequence act differently in interethnic encounters. Hence, the harder the ethnic group boundaries are perceived to be, the more strongly ingroup members will identify with the group and the more likely ethnolinguistic differentiation will occur in between-group settings. Perceived hard boundaries enable a group to differentiate more clearly between their own and other ethnic groups thus allowing a clearer and more secure sense of identity and a more firmly established set of norms (see McKirnan and Hamayan, 1980).

An important factor contributing to the perceived hardness–softness of group boundaries is the degree to which individuals can move in and out of their membership groups (R. Brown, 1965; Dahrendorf, 1970; see also section 4.1.1). If the group boundaries are relatively 'closed' or impermeable and are linguistically perceived to be so, then they are also likely to be harder with the individuals being likely to identify more closely with that group than with others where boundaries are perceived as softer and more 'open' (Blau, 1964; Weber, 1964). The link between the 'closedness' and hardness of group boundaries is the distinctiveness of the cues to group membership. If membership of a particular group is determined by ascribed or inherited characteristics (such as sex, skin or colour) then the group will be highly distinctive and the group boundaries will be perceived as harder; where this is the case the group boundaries will be relatively closed and members of the group will be less able to leave it. In contrast, if membership is determined more on the basis of acquired or achieved characteristics (such as education, speech and dress style) then members of the group will be less distinctive, the group boundaries will correspondingly be softer, and members will be more able to leave the group; that is, group boundaries will be relatively open (Germani, 1966; Linton, 1936). In such a case, the more likely it is that emigration from the ethnic group will occur, and the lower the ethnolinguistic vitality of the group is likely to be.

Ethnolinguistic groups will vary in the degree to which their ethnic group boundaries are open or closed, since the linguistic criteria for ethnic group membership vary from being largely ascribed to being largely achieved. That is, linguistic criterial attributes vary in being mainly a function of paternity or patrimony respectively (see section 2.2; Fishman, 1977). Although an individual's first language is primarily ascribed at birth, the subsequent dialect, accent or speech style adopted is more a matter of choice (Ryan, 1979); for instance the degree to which an individual accentuates or attenuates the ethnic speech style. For example, while the Scots and Welsh ethnic groups are relatively open (intralingual markers as criteria for membership), the French and English Canadian groups in Quebec are relatively more closed (first language as more or less criterial for membership). It may be more difficult for members of the latter groups to move out of their ethnic group and it is therefore suggested that these individuals may tend to identify more closely with the group. That is, the more closed the boundaries of the ethnic group, the more likely its members are to act in terms of their ethnic group membership in a wider range of situations.

Giles (1979) suggested that members of an ethnic group will alter their linguistic and non-linguistic boundaries (see Smolicz, 1979) so as to maintain or to assume a high level of overall perceived boundary hardness. For example, if an ethnic group softens its linguistic boundaries because the group for economic reasons needs to communicate with another ethnic group, the members may harden their non-linguistic boundaries (see notion of 'ethnic affirmation' in this regard, in Yang and Bond, 1980). Alternatively, if an ethnic group senses that its non-linguistic boundaries are softening, and for example, members are being lost through intermarriage, then the group may attempt to harden its linguistic boundaries in an effort to counteract this trend. The outgroup will be expected to respond to these activities of the ingroup, since changes in one group's boundaries will affect the other's. In the example above, the outgroup may also react to the increase in intermarriage between the two groups by hardening its linguistic boundaries, thereby forcing the ingroup's boundaries to harden whether it wishes this or not. Therefore, group members will perceive the overall hardness of their boundaries in relation to those of another group through social comparison and will then act accordingly; often this may take the linguistic form of accentuating or attenuating ingroup speech markers. (For a discussion of the hardening of linguistic boundaries when both linguistic and non-linguistic boundaries are perceived to be soft, see Giles, 1979.)

In sum then, the perception of hard and closed ethnic boundaries facilitates (i) categorization of self and others into clearly defined ethnic collectivities, (ii) the establishment of a concrete set of group norms guiding interethnic behaviour, and (iii) a strong sense of ethnic identification.

4.2.3 *Multiple-group membership**

Implicit in the foregoing was the assumption that ethnic group

*In considering the influence of multiple-group membership on ingroup identification, group boundaries and linguistic differentiation, this section owes much to F. Ross (1979).

membership may *not* be salient in every social interaction between members of different ethnic groups (see McGuire *et al.*,
1978). Individuals are members of many different social groups,
each of which contribute in varying degrees to the individual's
self concept (Tajfel, 1974); some therefore are more central than
others. In general, however, the very fact that an individual is a
member of more than one group will influence the nature of the
group boundaries and the individual's personal attachment to a
particular group in at least four ways (F. Ross, 1979); see
Zavalloni (1973, 1975) for a technique for measuring an individual's multiple identities and strengths of identification with
different membership groups.

First, an individual may be a member of several social groups
which overlap in their spheres of influence. Perhaps not surprisingly, this suggests that the presence of other social groups with
which individuals *strongly* self-identify means that any one group
may make less stringent demands on individuals' behaviour than
if they belonged to fewer groups. Similarly, the greater the proportion of a particular group which possesses high multiple group
memberships, the less influence the group will be able to exert
over its members' behaviour with the situational variables leading an individual to act in terms of a particular group membership
having to be more intense. For example, an individual may be a
Welsh, middle-class, elderly executive female and could identify
to varying degrees with these social categories. In interaction
with a young working-class English male, she may define the
situation differently in terms of one or more of her group identities. Here multiple group membership is seen, in effect, as
reducing the hardness of the group boundaries, as each of her
membership groups will tend to have a less pervasive influence
in their common spheres of influence; that is, the strength of the
group boundaries has been reduced. This person is therefore less
likely to define the situation in interethnic terms and to respond
by linguistically accentuating speech markers of her *ethnic* group.

Second, individuals in interaction are less likely to respond in
interethnic terms if they share several group memberships and
differ only ethnically (Coser, 1956; Evans-Pritchard, 1940;
Simmel, 1955). In this cognitively complex situation, individuals
may tend to act in terms of a simple psychological dichotomy,
based either on their shared group memberships or on their different ethnic group membership (R. J. Brown and Turner, 1979).
Thus, if two individuals from different ethnic groups both iden-

tify with the same religious, occupational, racial, sex and age groups, then the ethnolinguistic differences between the individuals may have to be more salient for them to define the situation in interethnic terms than if they shared fewer common membership groups. Thus Christian members of different tribes in Nigeria were observed to celebrate Christian festivals together, their shared religious affiliations being more salient than their distinct ethnic backgrounds on these occasions (Salamone and Swanson, 1979).

Third, the social identity which each membership group provides for the individual may be inadequate. A membership which is of low social status will tend to provide a less positive sense of identity than will a membership group of higher social status (Tajfel, 1978c; Turner, 1975a). Consequently, the individual may tend to be less attached to the membership groups which are of low social status than to those of higher social status, and a hierarchy might be seen as developing within the individual's membership groups relating to how much they contribute to the individual's self-concept. The position of any one of the membership groups in this 'hierarchy' will depend on the group's status and hence will relate to the group's vitality and the hardness of its boundaries. However, the notion of status congruence (for example, Hughes, 1945; Sampson, 1968) predicts that individuals will attempt to equilibriate any status differences they possess in order to achieve an *overall* congruent social status. According to the axioms of upward mobility and equilibriation, individuals will try to raise a low social status until it is of equivalent rank to their higher social statuses thereby achieving status equilibrium and congruence. However, in order to do this, and given that social statuses derive from group memberships, individuals may have to raise the low status of that *membership group*. Where there are sufficient group members with incongruent statuses, and where the social system leading to a particular group's inferior rank is seen as illegitimate and unstable, social change is possible (see J. A. Williams and Giles, 1978). However, if the system is seen as legitimate and stable, in other words there are few cognitive alternatives to the low status group membership, then the status incongruence may be minimized by individuals emphasizing their higher status group memberships at the expense of their lower status ones. In this situation, the more the non-ethnic membership groups contribute to the individual's sense of a positive identity, the higher the threshold may be for the individual to act in terms of ethnicity which may provide a *relatively* less adequate sense of identity. In some cases, an individual may belong to social groups which are all of high social status or all of low social status; in the latter case, the individual is likely to have an inadequate sense of social identity. An example might be an individual who was old, female, uneducated and who self-identified as a member of the lower social classes and a subordinate ethnic group such as Mexican-Americans in the United States. The position of such an individual has been characterized as 'double (or multiple) jeopardy' (see Sebastian and Ryan, in press).

Fourth, while the above notion concerns the general consensus of the status of a particular group in the social stratification system, the status of the individual *within* a particular group may also be worthy of consideration. Previously, within-group status has been considered as a factor influencing *intra*group interactions, with group status being the influential factor in intergroup situations (see, for example, Hartley, 1951). However, it is suggested that if an individual is of low status within a group, then he/she is less likely to see the situation in terms of this group, or act as a representative of this group than a person of higher intragroup status. Therefore, if an individual has a low status position within one membership group but enjoys higher status within another membership group, the individual will be more attached to the group within which he/she enjoys a high status position (Blau, 1964) and will consequently be more likely to act linguistically in terms of this group. Support for this proposition comes indirectly from an investigation of Greek immigrants' language attitudes in Montreal which showed that higher status members of the ethnic community (such as those representing the ethnic group in local government) were more involved with and more active in maintaining ethnic group identity than were lower status members (Smith, Tucker, and Taylor, 1977). Edwards (1977) also proposed that often the most active instigators and supporters of bilingual education (in the ethnic group language and an official language) are the high status members of the ethnic group, acting as representatives of the group. However, he suggests that frequently these individuals are not reflecting the desires and needs at the grassroots level of the community. Here are found the (lower status) majority of the ethnic group whose main concern is often for their children to assimilate culturally and linguistically into the mainstream culture so as to facilitate their socioeconomic advancement.

In this section, it has been argued that ethnic boundaries will be influenced by the multiple group memberships of any member, and by the adequacy of the sense of social identity which the different group memberships provide for the individual. Thus it is proposed generally that the more positive and secure the individual's sense of ethnic identity compared with those deriving from the individual's other membership groups, the more likely it is that the individual will value highly the ethnic group membership, the lower the threshold will be for defining interactions in interethnic terms, and the more likely it is that individuals will differentiate ethnolinguistically from outgroup members in interethnic contexts.

5 Propositions

The social psychological approach adopted by us in the area of language and ethnic relations has included aspects of social identity theory as well as the related concepts of perceived ethnolinguistic vitality, perceived group boundaries and multiple group membership. Consideration of these elements allows an integration of them all by means of a set of propositions which goes some way towards answering our original question: who in an ethnic group uses which language strategy, when and why? We propose therefore that *individuals are more likely to define an encounter with an outgroup person in interethnic terms and to adopt strategies for positive linguistic distinctiveness when they:*

1 identify strongly with their ethnic group which considers language an important dimension of its identity;
2 make insecure interethnic comparisons (for example, are aware of cognitive alternatives to their own group's status position);
3 perceive their ingroup to have high ethnolinguistic vitality;
4 perceive their ingroup boundaries to be hard and closed;
5 identify strongly with few other social categories;
6 perceive little overlap with the outgroup person in terms of other social category memberships;
7 consider that the social identities deriving from other social category memberships are relatively inadequate;
8 perceive their status within the ethnic group to be higher than their intragroup status in their other social category memberships.

While these eight conditions are thought to specify when accentuation of existing, and the creation of new, ethnic speech markers is most likely to occur, their corollaries (low vitality, open boundaries, etc.) are naturally enough likely to locate the conditions necessary for the attenuation of ethnic ingroup speech forms and linguistic assimilation with the outgroup.

There may well be further conditions which would stimulate the adoption of strategies for positive linguistic differentiation. For example, where there is incompatibility between the internal and external criteria of membership, as in the case of an illegitimate member of a group (Breakwell, 1979), the individual may attempt to resolve this conflict by accentuating relevant dimensions of group identity, such as the ethnic speech style, in order to appear a 'good' member. Thus while the above propositions may not cover all possible conditions contributing towards positive linguistic differentiation, we believe they encapsulate the most important factors and make sense of an otherwise unstructured understanding of language and ethnic relations as well as contributing to our understanding of the social psychological factors promoting and impeding native-like acquisition of a second language (Giles and Byrne, 1980; Hildebrandt and Giles, 1980).

6 Conclusion

In this chapter, we have argued that language has at least four psychological roles in relation to ethnicity, in that a certain speech style or language is often a necessary attribute for membership of a particular ethnic group, a salient cue for interethnic categorization, an important aspect of ethnic identity, and the ideal medium for facilitating intragroup cohesion. These different aspects of the language–ethnicity relationship have resulted in language being considered a highly emotive and *central* dimension of the ethnicity experience around which interethnic conflicts often arise. Ethnic group membership has been viewed here as a subjective phenomenon and the definition adopted is a social psychological one, in other words, those individuals who identify themselves as belonging to the same ethnic category.

We have classified previous approaches to language and ethnicity as being primarily 'sociolinguistic', 'sociological' and 'communication breakdown'. The first provides a linguistic taxonomy of ethnic markers in the speech of groups with the same language while the second relates the phenomenon of 'language erosion' to sociostructural factors such as radical, political, social or economic changes. The third focuses on how and why interethnic communication may be perceived to break down, relating this to factors such as the salience of language to ethnic identity and interethnic differences in sociocultural and linguistic norms. These approaches have clearly made valuable contributions but problems in the field, such as wide variations in interethnic situations, language strategies and attitudes to the ingroup's language, have made generalized predictions from one ethnic context to another difficult. However, we hope to have shown that our social psychological approach can clarify the empirical and theoretical confusion by identifying common processes underlying diverse speech strategies and language attitudes as well as taking into account sociostructural influences on the groups as perceived by their members. Arguably, this perspective is the best equipped currently to explore the important question of who uses which language strategies, when and for what purpose.

More specifically, our (admittedly embryonic) approach has had an intergroup orientation relying on social identity theory, the concepts of perceived ethnolinguistic vitality and perceived group boundaries, and notions of multiple group memberships. Social identity theory with its emphasis on group identification and social comparison defined some of the important psychological conditions necessary for individuals to search for a positive self-concept and indicated the possible strategies ethnic group members may adopt to attain a more positive ethnolinguistic distinctiveness. The possible speech strategies included in this regard were the accentuation or attenuation of ethnic speech markers, and the redefinition and creation of, and social competition on, linguistic dimensions. Social identity theory was the framework to which all the other elements related with these specifying more precisely some of the personal and situational factors enhancing the salience of ethnic identification for group members. Hence, a high perceived ingroup vitality, hard and closed perceived ingroup boundaries as well as the lack of identification with few other non-ethnic, social categories were some of the important factors considered by us as increasing the salience of ethnic identification for individuals. An integration of the various elements of our approach allowed us by means of a set of propositions to specify the conditions under which speakers would most likely wish to accentuate their ethnolinguistic varieties, and those under which they would most likely be prone to lose or attentuate them.

Needless to say, we consider empirical exploration along the lines of our theoretical propositions with different factions of a wide variety of ethnic groups an absolute necessity. Indeed, as yet, little research has been directed at the concepts of perceived vitality (see however, Bourhis, Giles, and Rosenthal, 1981) and the effects of multiple group memberships on perceived group boundaries and the language strategies an ethnic group adopts. Moreover, attention should be focused upon elucidating far more precisely *which* linguistic strategies are adopted when by both dominant and subordinate groups; linguistic and acoustic research in this direction could usefully incorporate and expand the sociolinguistic approach (see section 3.1). Furthermore, while we agree – and hope to have shown – with F. Ross (1979) that a multiple group membership perspective is an essential development of social identity theory, we should also in a similar vein focus our theoretical energies on the important issue of ethnic relations not being simply *two*-party affairs but more commonly manifest in complex, multiethnic contexts. In other words, many societies are composed of an array of subordinate minorities often hierarchically arranged, who compete not only with the dominant group(s) but also among themselves. While we have attempted to underline the value of this approach for comprehending the dynamics of language and ethnicity, we are not blind to the fact that no single perspective as currently defined is capable of capturing a complete picture of all the processes involved. We see our approach not as an alternative but as a complement to those outlined earlier in section 3. Nevertheless, to return to our starting point, a social psychological orientation derives part of its value from incorporating two different but interrelated perspectives on speech; as a dependent variable reflecting the interethnic situation and changes in it, and simultaneously as an independent variable defining, redefining and maintaining interethnic relations (Giles, Hewstone, and St Clair, in press; Smith, Giles, and Hewstone, 1980; Taylor and Giles, 1979). In these ways, the approach not only highlights the central and dual functions of speech in ethnic relations, but may also be highly applicable to an analysis of the role of language in *any* intergroup context (between the sexes, ages, religions, and occupational groups, etc.).

REFERENCES

Adam, B. (1978), Inferiorisation and 'Self Esteem', *Social Psychology*, **41**, 47–53.

Adorno, T. W., Frenkel-Brunswik, E., Levinson, D. J., and Sanford, R. N. (1950), *The Authoritarian Personality*, New York, Harper.

Albo, X. (1979), The future of the oppressed languages in the Andes, in W. C. McCormack and S. A. Wurm (eds.), *Language and Society*, The Hague, Mouton Press.

Allen, V. L. and Wilder, D. A. (1975), Categorisation, belief similarity, and group discrimination, *Journal of Personality and Social Psychology*, **32**, 971–7.

Allen, V. L. and Wilder, D. A. (1979), Group categorisation and attribution of belief similarity, *Small Group Behaviour*, **110**, 73–80.

Allport, F. H. (1924), *Social Psychology*, New York, Houghton Mifflin.

Allport, F. H. (1962), A structuronomic conception of behaviour: individual and collective, *Journal of Abnormal and Social Psychology*, **64**, 3–30.

Allport, G. W. (1954), *The Nature of Prejudice*, Cambridge, Mass., Addison-Wesley.

Allport, G. W. and Postman, L. (1947), *The Psychology of Rumour*, New York, Holt.

Amir, Y. (1969), Contact hypothesis in ethnic relations, *Psychological Bulletin*, **71**, 319–42.

Anderson, A. B. (1979), The survival of ethnolinguistic minorities: Canadian and comparative research, in H. Giles and B. St Jacques (eds.), *Language and Ethnic Relations*, Oxford, Pergamon Press.

Apfelbaum, E. and Herzlich, C. (1971), La théorie de l'attribution en psychologie sociale, *Bulletin de Psychologie*, **24**, 961–76.

Aronson, E. (1976), *The Social Animal*, 2nd edition, San Francisco, Freeman.

Asch, S. E. (1952), *Social Psychology*, New Jersey, Prentice Hall.

Ashely-Montagu, M. F. (ed.) (1968), *Man and Aggression*, New York, Oxford University Press.

Ashmore, R. D. and Del Boca, F. K. (1976), Psychological approaches to understanding intergroup conflict, in P. Katz (ed.), *Towards the Elimination of Racism*, New York, Pergamon, 73–124.

Ashmore, R. D., Turner, F., Donato, D. A., and Nevenglosky, T. (1973), *How White Americans View the Concept of Black Power*, unpublished manuscript.

Avigdor, R. (1953), Etude expérimentale de la génèse des stéréotypes, *Cahiers Internationaux de Sociologie*, **14**, 154–68.

Baldwin, J. and McConville, M. (1977), *Negotiated Justice*, London, Martin Robertson.

Bales, R. F. and Strodtbeck, F. L. (1951), Phases in group-problem solving, *Journal of Abnormal and Social Psychology*, **46**, 485–95.

Banks, W. C. (1976), White preference in blacks: a paradigm in search of a phenomenon, *Psychological Bulletin*, **83 (vi)**, 1179–86.

Banton, M. (1978), A theory of race and ethnic relations: rational choice (Research Unit on Ethnic Relations, University of Bristol), *Working Papers on Ethnic Relations*, **8**.

Baron, R. A. and Byrne, A. (1977), *Social Psychology*, 2nd edition, London, Allyn and Bacon.

Barth, F. (1969), *Ethnic Groups and Boundaries: The Social Organisation of Culture Difference*, Boston, Little, Brown and Company.

Bāskauskas, L. (1977), Multiple identities: adjusted Lithuanian refugees in Los Angeles, *Urban Anthropology*, **6**, 141–54.

Bass, B. M. and Dunteman, G. (1963), Biases in the evaluation of one's own group, its allies and opponents, *Journal of Conflict Resolution*, **7**, 16–20.

Batstone, E., Boraston, I., and Frenkel, S. (1977), *Shop Stewards in Action*, Oxford, Blackwell.

Beebe, L. (1981), Code-switching in a Thai community, *International Journal of the Sociology of Language*, in press.

Bender, G. I. and Kayiwada, G. (1968), Hansen's law of third generation return and the study of American religio-ethnic groups, *Phylon*, **39**, 360–70.

Berger, C. R. (1979), Beyond initial interaction: uncertainty, understanding and the development of interpersonal relationships, in H. Giles and R. N. St Clair (eds.), *Language and Social Psychology*, Oxford, Blackwell.

Berger, P. L. and Luckmann, T. (1967), *The Social Construction of Reality*, London, Allen Lane.

Berkowitz, L. (1962), *Aggression: A Social Psychological Analysis*, New York, McGraw-Hill.

Berkowitz, L. (1972), Frustrations, comparisons and other sources of emotion arousal as contributors to social unrest, *Journal of Social Issues*, **28**, 77–91.

Berkowitz, L. (1974), Some determinants of impulsive aggression: role of mediated associations with reinforcements for aggression, *Psychological Review*, **81**, 165–76.

Best, D. L., Smith, S. C., Graves, D. J., and Williams, J. E. (1975), The modification of racial bias in preschool children, *Journal of Experimental Child Psychology*, **20**, 193–205.

Billig, M. G. (1972), *Social Categorisation and Intergroup Relations*, unpublished PhD thesis, University of Bristol.

Billig, M. G. (1973), Normative communication in a minimal intergroup situation, *European Journal of Social Psychology*, **3**, 339–43.

Billig, M. G. (1976), *Social psychology and intergroup relations*, European Monographs in Social Psychology, No 9, London, Academic Press.

Billig, M. G. (1978), *Fascists: A social psychological view of the National Front*, European Monographs in Social Psychology, No 15, London, Academic Press.

Billig, M. G. and Tajfel, H. (1973), Social categorisation and similarity in intergroup behaviour, *European Journal of Social Psychology*, **3**, 27–52.

Blake, R. R. and Mouton, J. S. (1961a), Reactions to intergroup competition under win-lose conditions, *Management Science*, **7**, 420–35.

Blake, R. R. and Mouton, J. S. (1961b), Loyalty of representatives to ingroup positions during intergroup conflict, *Sociometry*, **24**, 177–84.

Blake, R. R. and Mouton, J. S. (1962), The intergroup dynamics of win–lose conflict and problem-solving collaboration in union–management relations, in M. Sherif (ed.), *Intergroup Relations and Leadership*, New York, Wiley, chapter 5, 94–140.

Blau, P. M. (1964), *Exchange and Power in Social Life*, New York, John Wiley and Sons.

Bogardus, E. S. (1925), Measuring social distance, *Journal of Applied Sociology*, **9**, 299–308.

Bogardus, E. S. (1928), *Immigration and Race Relations*, Boston, D. C. Heath.

Boswell, D. A. (1974), *An Empirical Study of Some Theoretical Components of Racial Bias in Young Children*, master's thesis, Wake Forest University, North Carolina.

Bourhis, R. Y. (1979), Language and ethnic interaction, in H. Giles and B. St Jacques (eds.), *Language and Ethnic Relations*, Oxford, Pergamon.

Bourhis, R. Y. and Giles, H. (1977), The language of intergroup distinctiveness, in H. Giles (ed.), *Language, Ethnicity and Intergroup Relations*, London, Academic Press.

Bourhis, R. Y., Giles, H., Leyens, J. P., and Tajfel, H. (1979), Psycholinguistic distinctiveness: language divergence in Belgium, in H. Giles and R. N. St Clair (eds.), *Language and Social Psychology*, Oxford, Blackwell.

Bourhis, R. Y., Giles, H., and Rosenthal, D. (1981), Notes on the Construction of a 'Subjective Vitality Questionnaire' for Ethnolinguistic Groups. *Journal of Multilingual and Multicultural Development*, in press.

Boyanowsky, E. O. and Allen, V. L. (1973), Ingroup norms and self-identity as determinants of discriminatory behaviour, *Journal of Personality and Social Psychology*, **25**, 408–18.

Bragga, G. (1979), International languages; concept and problems, *International Journal of the Sociology of Language*, **22**, 27–49.

Brand, E. S., Ruiz, R. A., and Padilla, A. M. (1974), Ethnic identification and preference: a review, *Psychological Bulletin*, **81**, 860–90.

Breakwell, G. (1979), Woman: group and identity?, *Women's Studies International Quarterly*, **2**, 9–17.

Brein, M. and David, K. H. (1971), Intercultural communication and the adjustment of the sojourner, *Psychological Bulletin*, **67**, 215–30.

Brewer, M. B. (1979), Ingroup bias in the minimal intergroup situation: a cognitive–motivational analysis, *Psychological Bulletin*, **86**, 307–24.

Brewer, M. B. and Silver, M. (1978), Ingroup bias as a function of task characteristics, *European Journal of Social Psychology*, **8**, 393–400.

Brigham, J. C. (1971), Ethnic stereotypes, *Psychological Bulletin*, **86**, 15–38.

Brown, P. and Fraser, C. (1979), Situational determinants of speech, in K. Scherer and H. Giles (eds.), *Social Markers in Speech*, Cambridge, Cambridge University Press.

Brown, R. (1965), *Social Psychology*, London, Collier-Macmillan.

Brown, R. J. (1978a), Divided we fall: an analysis of relations between sections of a factory work-force, in H. Tajfel (ed.), *Differentiation Between Social Groups: Studies in the Social Psychology of Intergroup Relations*, London, Academic Press.

Brown, R. J. (1978b), *The Role of Similarity in Intergroup Relations*, Paper presented to BPS Conference: The Social Psychology of Intergroup Relations, Bristol, November 1978.

Brown, R. J. (1978c), *Competition and Co-operation between Similar and Dissimilar Groups*, unpublished PhD dissertation, University of Bristol.

Brown, R. J. and Deschamps, J.-C. (1980/81), Discrimination entre individus et entre groupes, *Bulletin de Psychologie*, **34**, 185–95.

Brown, R. J. and Turner, J. C. (1979), The criss-cross categorisation effect in intergroup discrimination, *British Journal of Social and Clinial Psychology*, **18**, 371–83.

Bruner, J. S. (1957), On perceptual readiness, *Psychological Review*, **64**, 123–52.

Bruner, J. S. (1973), *Beyond the Information Given: Studies in the Psychology of Knowing* (ed. J. M. Anglin), New York, Norton.

Bruner, J. S., Goodnow, J. J., and Austin, G. A. (1956), *A Study of Thinking*, New York, Wiley.

Bruner, J. S. and Klein, G. S. (1960), The functions of perceiving: new look retrospect, in B. Kaplan and S. Wapner (eds.), *Perspectives in Psychological Theory: Essays in Honour of Heinz Werner*, New York, International Universities Press.

Bruner, J. S. and Perlmutter, H. V. (1957), Compatriot and foreigner: a study of impression formation in three countries, *Journal of Abnormal and Social Psychology*, **55**, 253–60.

Bruner, J. S. and Potter, M. C. (1964), Interference in visual recognition, *Science*, **144**, 424–5.

Bruner, J. S. and Rodriguez, J. S. (1953), Some determinants of apparent size, *Journal of Abnormal and Social Psychology*, **48**, 585–92.

Brunswik, E. (1947), *Systematic and Representative Design of Psychological Experiments with Results in Physical and Social Perception*, Berkeley, California, University of California Press.

Brunstein, E. and McRae, A. V. (1962), Some effects of shared threat and prejudice in racially mixed groups, *Journal of Abnormal and Social Psychology*, **64**, 257–63.

Buss, A. R. (1978), Causes and reasons in attribution theory: a conceptual critique, *Journal of Personality and Social Psychology*, **36**, 1311–21.

Byrne, D. (1971), *The Attraction Paradigm*, New York, Academic Press.

Byrne, D. and McGraw, C. (1964), Interpersonal attraction toward negroes, *Human Relations*, **17**, 201–13.

Byrne, D. and Wong, T. J. (1968), Racial prejudice, interpersonal attraction and assumed dissimilarity of attitudes, *Journal of Abnormal and Social Psychology*, **65**, 246–53.

Caddick, B. F. J. (1978), *Status, Legitimacy and the Social Identity Concept in Intergroup Relations*, unpublished PhD thesis, University of Bristol.

Campbell, D. T. (1958), Common fate, similarity and other indices of the status of aggregates of persons as social entities, *Behavioural Science*, **3**, 14–25.

Campbell, D. T. (1965), 'Ethnocentric and other altruistic motives, *Nebraska Symposium on Motivation*, 283–301.

Campbell, D. T. (1967), Stereotypes and perception of group differences, *American Psychologist*, **22**, 812–29.

Caprio, R. J. (1972), Place utility, social obsolescence and qualitative housing change, *Proceedings of the Association of American Geographers*, **4**, 14–19.

Cartwright, D. (1979), Contemporary social psychology in historical perspective, *Social Psychology Quarterly*, **42**, 82–93.

Chapman, L. J. (1967), Illusory correlations in observational report, *Journal of Verbal Learning and Verbal Behaviour*, **6**, 151–5.

Charters, W. W. and Newcomb, T. M. (1952), Some attitudinal effects of experimentally increased salience of a membership group, in G. E. Swanson *et al.* (ed.), *Readings in Social Psychology*, New York, Holt.

Christie, R. and Cook, P. (1958), A guide to the published literature relating to the authoritarian personality through 1956, *Journal of Psychology*, **45**, 171–99.

Clark, K. B. and Clark, M. P. (1947), Racial identification and preference in negro children, in T. M. Newcomb and E. L. Hartley (eds.), *Readings in Social Psychology*, New York, Holt, 169–78.

Clément, R. (1980), Ethnicity, contact and communicative competence in a second language, in H. Giles, W. P. Robinson and P. M. Smith (eds.), *Language: Social Psychological Perspectives*, Oxford, Pergamon.

Clyne, M. (1979a), Factors promoting migrant language maintenance in Australia, in P. R. de Lacy and M. E. Poole (eds.), *Mosaic or Melting Pot*, Sydney, Harcourt Brace Jovanovich Group.

Clyne, M. (1979b), Communicative competences in contact, *ITL*, **43**, 17–37.

Clyne, M. (1981), Culture and discourse structures, *Journal of Pragmatics*, **5**, 61–6.

Coffman, T. L. (1979), *Cross-cultural Trauma Without Moving Abroad*, Paper presented at 87th annual convention of the American Psychology Association, Duke University, Durham, North Carolina.

Cohn, N. (1967), *Warrant for Genocide*, New York, Harper.

Collett, P. (1971), Training Englishmen: the nonverbal behaviour of Arabs. An experiment on inter-cultural communication, *International Journal of Psychology*, **6**, 209–15.

Commins, B. and Lockwood, J. (1979), The effects of stress differences, favoured treatment and equity on intergroup comparisons, *European Journal of Social Psychology*, **9**, 218–9.

Cook, S. W. (1962), The systematic analysis of socially significant events, *Journal of Social Issues*, **18 (2)**, 66–84.

Cooper, J. B. and McGaugh, J. L. (1963), *Integrative Principles of Social Psychology*, Cambridge, Massachusetts, Schenkman.

Coser, L. A. (1956), *The Functions of Social Conflict*, London, Routledge and Kegan Paul.

Dahrendorf, R. (1970), The origins of inequality, in E. O. Laumann, P. M. Siegel and R. W. Hodge (eds.), *The Logic of Social Hierarchies*, Chicago, Markham.

de la Zerda, N. and Hopper, R. (1979) Employment interviewers' reactions to Mexican American speech, *Communication Monographs*, **46**, 126–34.

Denison, N. (1977), Language death or language suicide?, *International Journal of the Sociology of Langauge*, **12**, 13–22.

Deschamps, J.-C. (1977), *L'Attribution et la Catégorisation Sociale*, Bern, Peter Lang.

Deschamps, J.-C. (1978), La perception des causes du comportement, in W. Doise, J.-C. Deschamps and G. Mugny (eds.), *Psychologie Sociale Expérimentale*, Paris, Armand Colin.

Deutsch, M. (1973), *The Resolution of Conflict: Constructive and Destructive Processes*, Newhaven and London, Yale University Press.

Deutsch, M. and Collins, M. E. (1951), *Inter-racial Housing*, Minneapolis, University of Minneapolis Press.

Deutscher, I. (1966), Words and deeds: social science and social policy, *Social Problems* **13**, 235–54.

De Vos, G. (1975), Ethnic pluralism: conflict and accommodation, in G. de Vos and K. Romanucci-Ross (eds.), *Ethnic Identity: Cultural Continuity and Change*, Palo Alto, California, Mayfield.

De Vries, J. (1979), Demographic approaches to the study of language and ethnic relations, in H. Giles and B. St Jacques (eds.), *Language and Ethnic Relations*, Oxford, Pergamon Press.

Diab, L. N. (1970), A study of intra-group and intergroup relations among experimentally produced small groups, *Genetic Psychology Monographs*, **82**, 49–82.

Dion, K. L. (1973), Cohesiveness as a determinant of ingroup–outgroup bias, *Journal of Personality and Social Psychology*, **28**, 163–71.

Dion, K. L. (1979), Intergroup conflict and intra-group cohesiveness, in W. G. Austin and S. Worchel (eds.), *The Social Psychology of Intergroup Relations*, Monterey, California, Brooks/Cole.

Dion, K. L., Earn, B. M., and Yee, P. H. N. (1978), The experience of being a victim of prejudice: an experimental approach, *International Journal of Psychology*, **13**, 197–214.

Dixon, B. (1977), *Catching Them Young, Sex, Race and Class in Children's Fiction*, London, Pluto Press.

Doise, W. (1969a), Intergroup relations and polarisation of individual and collective judgements, *Journal of Personality and Social Psychology*, **12**, 136–43.

Doise, W. (1969b), Les strategies de jeu à l'intérieur et entre des groupes de nationalité différente, *Bulletin de CERP*, **18**, 13–26.

Doise, W. (1971), Die experimentalle Untersuchung von Beziehungen zwischen Gruppen, *Zeitschrift Experimentalle-Angewandte Psychologie*, **18**, 151–89.

Doise, W. (1978), *Groups and Individuals: Explanations in Social Psychology*, Cambridge, Cambridge University Press.

Doise, W., Csepeli, G., Dann, H.-D., Gouge, G. C., Larsen, K., and Ostell, A. (1971), *Intergroup Relations – Preliminary Report*, Report from the 3rd European Summer school for Experimental Social Psychology, Konstanz, 4–31 July 1971.

Doise, W., Csepeli, G., Dann, H.-D., Gouge, G. C., Larsen, K., and Ostell, A. (1972), An experimental investigation into the formation of intergroup representations, *European Journal of Social Psychology*, **2**, 202–4.

Doise, W., Deschamps, J.-C., and Meyer, G. (1978), The accentuation of intra-category similarities, in H. Tajfel (ed.), *Differentiation Between Social Groups*, London, Academic Press.

Doise, W. and Sinclair, A. (1973), The categorisation process in intergroup relations, *European Journal of Social Pscyhology*, **3**, 145–57.

Doise, W. and Weinberger, M. (1973), Représentations masculines dans différentes situations de rencontres mixtes, *Bulletin de Psychologie*, **26**, 649–57.

Dollard, J., Doob, L. W., Miller, N. E., Mowrer, O. H., and Sears, R. R. (1939), *Frustration and Aggression*, New Haven, Yale University Press,

Dorian, N. C. (1980), Linguistic lag as an ethnic marker, *Language in Society*, **9**, 33–41.

Douglas, A. (1957), The peaceful settlement of industrial and intergroup disputes, *Journal of Conflict Resolution*, 1, 69–81.

Douglas, A. (1962), *Industrial Peacemaking*, New York, Columbia University Press.

Douglas, M. (1966), *Purity and Danger: An Analysis of Concepts of Pollution and Taboo*, New York, Praeger.

Drake, G. F. (1980), The social role of slang, in H. Giles, W. P. Robinson and P. Smith (eds.), *Language: Social Psychological Perspectives*, Oxford, Pergamon Press.

Dreger, R. M. and Miller, K. S. (1960), Comparative psychological studies of negroes and whites in the US, *Psychological Bulletin*, 57, 361–402.

Dreger, R. M. and Miller, K. S. (1968), Comparative psychological studies of negroes and whites in the US, 1959–1965, *Psychological Bulletin*, Monograph Supplement 70.

Druckman, D. (ed.) (1977), *Negotiations: Social-Psychological Perspectives*, London, Sage.

Druckman, D. (1978), Boundary role conflict: negotiation as dual responsiveness, chapter 5 in I. W. Zartman (ed.), *The Negotiation Process: Theories and Applications*, London, Sage.

Duncan, B. L. (1976), Differential social perception and attribution of intergroup violence: testing the lower limits of stereotyping of Blacks, *Journal of Personality and Social Psychology*, 34, 590–8.

Durkheim, E. (1938), *The Rules of Sociological Method*, edited by G. E. Catlin, translated by S. A. Solovy and P. H. Mueller, Chicago, University of Chicago Press.

Dustin, D. S. and Davis, H. P. (1970), Evaluative bias in group and individual competition, *Journal of Social Psychology*, 80, 103–8.

Dutton, D. G. and Lennox, V. L. (1974), The effect of prior 'token' compliance on subsequent inter-racial behaviour, *Journal of Personality and Social Psychology*, 29, 65–71.

Eastman, C. M. (1974), Ethnicity and the social scientist: phonemes and distinctive features, *African Studies Review*, 17, 29–38.

Edwards, J. R. (1977), Ethnic identity and bilingual education, in H. Giles (ed.), *Language Ethnicity and Intergroup Relations*, London, Academic Press.

Ehrlich, H. J. (1973), *The Social Psychology of Prejudice*, New York, Wiley.

Eiser, J. R. (1979), *Cognitive Social Psychology*, London McGraw-Hill.

Eiser, J. R. and Stroebe, W. (1972), *Categorisation and Social Judgement*, European Monographs in Social Psychology, No 3, London, Academic Press.

Eiser, J. R., Van der Pligt, J., and Gossop, M. R. (1979), Categorisation, attitude and memory for the source of attitude statements, *European Journal of Social Psychology*, 9, 243–51.

Elias, N. (1978), *The Civilizing Process*, New York, Urizen Books.

Evans-Pritchard, E. E. (1940), *The Nuer*, London, Oxford University Press.

Feagin, J. R. (1970), Home defense and the police: black and white perspectives, *American Behavioural Scientist*, **13**, 717–26.

Feinstein, M. H. (1980), Ethnicity and topicalization in New York City English, *International Journal of the Sociology of Language*, **26**, 15–24.

Fellman, J. (1974), The academy of the Hebrew language, *International Journal of the Sociology of Language*, **1**, 95–103.

Ferguson, C. K. and Kelley, H. H. (1964), Significant factors in over-evaluation of own group's products, *Journal of Abnormal and Social Psychology*, **69**, 223–8.

Feshbach, S. and Singer, R. (1957), The effects of personal and shared threats upon social prejudice, *Journal of Abnormal and Social Psychology*, **54**, 411–16.

Festinger, L. (1950), Informal social communication, *Psychological Review*, **57**, 271–82.

Festinger, L. (1954), A theory of social comparison processes, *Human Relations*, **7**, 117–40.

Festinger, L. (1957), *A Theory of Cognitive Dissonance*, Stanford, Stanford University Press.

Festinger, L., Pepitone, A., and Newcomb, T. (1952), Some consequences of de-individuation in a group, *Journal of Abnormal and Social Psychology*, **47**, 382–9.

Festinger, L., Schachter, S., and Back, K. W. (1950), *Social Pressures in Informal Groups: A Study of a Housing Community*, New York, Harper.

Fiedler, F. E. (1967), The effect of inter-group competition on group member adjustment, *Personnel Psychology*, **20**, 33–44.

Fishman, J. A. (1972), *Language and Nationalism*, Rowley, Massachusetts, Newbury.

Fishman, J. A. (ed.) (1974), *Advances in Language Planning*, The Hague, Mouton.

Fishman, J. A. (1977), Language and ethnicity, in H. Giles (ed.), *Language Ethnicity and Intergroup Relations*, London, Academic Press.

Fishman, J. A. and Giles, H. (1978), Language in society, in H. Tajfel and C. Fraser (eds.), *Introducing Social Psychology*, Harmondsworth, Middlesex, Penguin.

Frank, B. (1978), *The Politics of Legitimacy*, London, Routledge and Kegan Paul.

Germani, G. (1966), Social and political consequences of mobility, in N. J. Smelser and S. M. Lipsett (eds.), *Social Structure and Mobility in Economic Development*, London, Routledge and Kegan Paul.

Giles, H. (1977), *Language, Ethnicity and Intergroup Relations*, London, Academic Press.

Giles, H. (1978), Linguistic differentiation in ethnic groups, in H. Tajfel (ed.), *Differentiation Between Social Groups*, London, Academic Press.

Giles, H. (1979), Ethnicity markers in speech, in K. Scherer and H. Giles (eds.), *Social Markers in Speech*, Cambridge, Cambridge University Press.

Giles, H. and Bourhis, R. Y. (1975), Linguistic assimilation: West Indians in Cardiff, *Language Sciences*, **38**, 9–12.

Giles, H. and Bourhis, R. Y. (1976), Voice and racial categorisation in Britain, *Communication Monographs*, **43**, 108–14.

Giles, H., Bourhis, R. Y., and Taylor, D. M. (1977), Towards a theory of language in ethnic group relations, in H. Giles (ed.), *Language, Ethnicity and Intergroup Relations*, London, Academic Press.

Giles, H. and Byrne, J. L. (1980), An intergroup approach to second language acquisition, *Revista de Educación*, **265** (in press).

Giles, H., Hewstone, M., and St Clair, R. N. (in press), Cognitive structures and a social psychology of language: new theoretical models and an overview, in H. Giles and R. N. St Clair (eds.), *Recent Advances in Language Communication and Social Psychology*, Hillsdale, New Jersey, Erlbaum.

Giles, H., Llado, N., McKirnan, D. J., and Taylor, D. M. (1979), Social identity in Puerto Rico, *International Journal of Psychology*, **14**, 185–201.

Giles, H. and Powesland, P. F. (1975), *Speech Style and Social Evaluation*, London, Academic Press.

Giles, H., Scherer, K., and Taylor, D. M. (1979), Speech markers in social interaction, in K. Scherer and H. Giles (eds.), *Social Markers in Speech*, Cambridge, Cambridge University Press.

Giles, H., Taylor, D. M., and Bourhis, R. Y. (1977), Dimensions of Welsh identity, *European Journal of Social Psychology*, **7**, 29–39.

Giles, H., Taylor, D. M., Lambert, W. E., and Albert, G. (1976), Dimensions of ethnic identity: an example from Northern Maine, *Journal of Social Psychology*, **100**, 11–19.

Glazer, N. (1954), Ethnic groups in America: from national culture to ideology, in M. Berger, T. Abel, and C. Page (eds.), *Freedom and Control in Modern Society*, New York, Van Nostrand.

Goldman, M., Stockbauer, J. W., and McAuliffe, T. G. (1977), Intergroup and intragroup competition and co-operation, *Journal of Experimental Social Psychology*, **13**, 81–8.

Goodman, M. E. (1946), Evidence concerning the genesis of inter-racial attitudes, *American Anthropologist*, **48**, 624–30.

Goodman, M. E. (1952), *Race Awareness in Young Children*, Cambridge, Massachusetts, Addison-Wesley.

Goodman, M. E. (1964), *Race Awareness in Young Children*, New York, Collier Books.

Grayshon, M. C. (1980), Social grammar, social psychology and linguistics, in H. Giles, W. P. Robinson, and P. Smith (eds.), *Language: Social Psychological Perspectives*, Oxford, Pergamon Press.

Greenberg, B. S. and Atkins, C. K. (1978), *Learning about Minorities from*

Television, Paper presented to the Minorities and Communication Division, Association for Education in Journalism Annual Convention.

Gregor, A. J. and McPherson, D. A. (1966), Racial preference and ego-identity among white and Bantu children in the Republic of South Africa, *Genetic Psychology Monographs*, **73**, 217–53.

Gregor, A. J. and McPherson, D. A. (1968), Racial attitudes among white and negro children in a deep south standard metropolitan area, *Journal of Social Psychology*, **68**, 95–106.

Griffen, T. D. (1980), Nationalism and the emergence of a new standard Welsh, *Language Planning and Language Problems*, **4**, 187–94.

Grönroos, M. (1978), Suomenruotsalaiset ja heidän kielensä (The Swedish-speaking Finns and their language), in N. Ahlberg (ed.), *Kultuuir-identileetin ongetmia: Soumen kultuurivähemmistöt*, The Finnish National Commission for UNESCO, Publication Series No 14.

Groves, W. E. and Rossi, P. H. (1970), Police perceptions of a hostile ghetto: realism or projection, *American Behavioural Scientist*, **13**, 727–44.

Guboglo, M. (1979), Linguistic contacts and elements of ethnic identification, in W. C. McCormack and S. A. Wurm (eds.), *Language and Society*, The Hague, Mouton.

Guillaumin, C. (1972), *L'Idéologie Raciote: Génèse et Language Actuel*, Paris, Mouton.

Gumperz, J. J. (1978), The conversational analysis of inter-ethnic communication, in E. L. Ross (ed.), *Inter-ethnic Communication. Proceedings of the Southern Anthropological Society*, Atlanta, Georgia.

Gurr, T. R. (1970), *Why Men Rebel*, Princeton, Princeton University Press.

Hall, E. T. (1966), *The Hidden Dimension*, Garden City, New York, Doubleday Books.

Hamilton, D. L. (1976), Cognitive biases in the perception of social groups, in J. S. Carroll and J. W. Payne (eds.), *Cognition and Social Behaviour*, Hillsdale, New Jersey, Erlbaum.

Hamilton, D. L. (1978), Who is responsible? Towards a *social* psychology of responsibility attribution, *Social Psychology*, **41**, 316–28.

Hamilton, D. L. and Gifford, R. K. (1976), Illusory correlations in inter-personal perception: a cognitive basis of stereotypic judgements, *Journal of Experimental Social Psychology*, **12**, 392–407.

Hancock, I. F. (1974), Identity, equality and standard language, *Florida FL Reporter*, Spring/Fall, 49–52, 101–2.

Harbin, S. P. and Williams, J. E. (1966), Conditioning of colour connotations, *Perceptual and Motor Skills*, **22**, 217–18.

Harding, J. and Hogrefe, R. (1952), Attitudes of white department store employees towards negro co-workers, *Journal of Social Issue*, **8**, 18–28.

Harding, J. B., Proshansky, H., Kutner, B., and Chein, I. (1969),

Prejudice and ethnic relations, in G. Lindzey and E. Aronson (eds.), *The Handbook of Social Psychology*, Volume 5, Reading, Massachusetts, Addison-Wesley.

Harris, R. McL. (1979), Fever of ethnicity: the sociological and educational significance of the concept, in P. R. de Lacy and M. E. Poole (eds.), *Mosaic or Melting Pot*, Sydney, Harcourt Brace, Jovanovich Group.

Hartley, E. I. (1951), Psychological problems of multiple group membership, in J. H. Rohrer and M. Sherif (eds.), *Social Psychology at the Cross-roads*, New York, Harper.

Harvey, J. H. and Smith, W. P. (1977), *Social Psychology: An Attributional Approach*, St Louis, C. V. Mosby Co.

Harvey, O. J. (1956), An experimental investigation of negative and positive relations between small groups through judgemental indices, *Sociometry*, **19**, 201–9.

Hendrick, C., Bixenstine, V. E., and Hawkins, G. (1971), Race vs. belief similarities as determinants of attraction: a search for a fair test, *Journal of Personality and Social Psychology*, **17**, 250–8.

Hensley, V. and Duval, S. (1976), Some perceptual determinants of perceived similarity, liking and correctness, *Journal of Personality and Social Psychology*, **34**, 159–68.

Hewstone, M. and Jaspars, J. (1982), Intergroup relations and attribution processes, in H. Tajfel (ed.), *Social Identity and Intergroup Relations*, Cambridge, Cambridge University Press, and Paris, Editions de la Maison des Sciences de l'Homme.

Heye, J. (1979), Bilingualism and language maintenance in two communities in Santa Catarina, Brazil, in W. C. McCormack and S. A. Wurm (eds.), *Language and Society*, The Hague, Mouton.

Hildebrandt, N. and Giles, H. (1980), The English language in Japan: a social psychological perspective, *Japanese Association of Language Teachers Journal*, **2**, 63–87.

Hinde, R. A. (1979), *'Towards Understanding Relationships'*, European Monographs in Social Psychology, London, Academic Press.

Hinkle, S. and Schopler, J. (1979), Ethnocentrism in the evaluation of group products, in W. G. Austin and S. Worchel (eds.), *The Social Psychology of Intergroup Relations*, Monterey, California, Brooks/Cole.

Hinnenkamp, V. (1980), The refusal of second language learning in inter-ethnic context, in H. Giles, W. P. Robinson, and P. M. Smith (eds.), *Language: Social Psychological Perspectives*, Oxford, Pergamon Press.

Holt, G. (1973), Inversion in black communication, in T. Kochman (ed.), *Rappin' and Stylin' Out: Communication in Urban Black America*, University of Illinois Press.

Homans, G. C. (1961), *Social Behaviour: Its Elementary Forms*, London, Routledge and Kegan Paul.

Hornstein, H. A. (1972), Promotive tension: the basis of prosocial behaviour from a Lewinian perspective, *Journal of Social Issues*, **28**, 191–218.

Hornstein, H. A. (1976), *Cruelty and Kindness: A New Look at Aggression and Altruism*, Englewood Cliffs, New Jersey, Prentice-Hall.

Hraba, J. and Grant, C. (1970), Black is beautiful: a re-examination of racial identification and preference, *Journal of Personality and Social Psychology*, **16**, 398–402.

Hudson-Edwards, A. (1980), Sociolinguistic reflexes of Jewish identification, *International Journal of the Sociology of Language*, **26**, 41–74.

Hughes, E. C. (1945), Dilemmas and contradictions of status, *American Journal of Sociology*, **50**, 353–4.

Husband, C. (ed.) (1975), *White Media and Black Britain*, London, Arrow Books.

Husband, C. (1977), News, media, language and race relations: a case study in identity maintenance, in H. Giles (ed.), *Language Ethnicity and Intergroup Relations*, London, Academic Press.

Husband, C. (1979), Social identity and the language of race relations, in H. Giles and B. St Jacques (eds.), *Language and Ethnic Relations*, Oxford, Pergamon Press.

Huston, T. L. (ed.), (1974), *Foundations of Interpersonal Attraction*, New York, Academic Press.

Irle, M. (1975), *Lehrbuch der Sozialpsychologie*, Göttingen, Hogrefe.

Israel, J. and Tajfel, H. (eds.) (1972), *The Context of Social Psychology*, London, Academic Press.

Jahoda, G., Thomson, S. S., and Bhatt, S. (1972), Ethnic identity and preferences among Asian immigrant children in Glasgow, *European Journal of Social Psychology*, **2**, 19–32.

Janssens, L. and Nuttin, J. R. (1976), Frequency perception of individual and group successes as a function of competition, coaction and isolation, *Journal of Personality and Social Psychology*, **34**, 830–6.

Jaspars, J. M. F. (1978), The nature and measurement of attitudes, in H. Tajfel and C. Fraser (eds.), *Introduction to Social Psychology*, Harmondsworth, Middlesex, Penguin.

Jaspars, J. M. F. and Hewstone, M. (1981), Cross-cultural interaction, social attribution and intergroup relations, in S. Bochner (ed.), *Cultures in Contact: Studies in Cross-cultural Interaction*, Oxford, Pergamon Press.

Johnson, D. W. (1967), Use of role reversal in intergroup competition, *Journal of Personality and Social Psychology*, **7**, 135–41.

Jones, E. E. and Gerard, H. B. (1967), *Foundations of Social Psychology*, New York, Wiley.

Joy, R. J. (1978), *Les Minorités des Langues Officielles au Canada*, Montreal, C. D. Howe.

Kahn, A. and Ryen, A. H. (1972), Factors influencing the bias towards one's own group, *International Journal of Group Tensions*, **2**, 33–50.

Kalin, R. and Marlowe, D. (1968), The effects of intergroup competition, personal drinking habits and frustration in intra-group co-operation, *Proceedings of 76th Annual Convention APA*, **3**, 405–6.

Kalin, R. and Rayko, D. (1980), The social significance of speech in the job interview, in R. N. St Clair and H. Giles (eds.), *The Social and Psychological Contexts of Language*, Hillsdale, New Jersey, Erlbaum.

Kardiner, A. and Ovesey, L. (1951), *The Mark of Oppression*, New York, Norton.

Katz, D. and Braly, K. R. (1933), Racial stereotypes of one hundred college students, *Journal of Abnormal and Social Psychology*, **28**, 280–90.

Katz, D. and Braly, K. R. (1935), Racial prejudice and racial stereotypes, *Journal of Abnormal and Social Psychology*, **30**, 175–93.

Katz, P. A. (1976), *Towards the Elimination of Racism*, New York, Pergamon.

Kelley, H. H. and Thibaut, J. W. (1969), Group problem solving, in G. Lindzey and E. Aronson (eds.), *The Handbook of Social Psychology, Volume IV*, Reading, Massachusetts, Addison-Wesley.

Kennedy, J. and Stephan, W. (1977), The effects of co-operation and competition on ingroup–outgroup bias, *Journal of Applied Social Psychology*, **7**, 115–30.

Khleif, B. B. (1979a), Insiders, outsiders and renegades: towards a classification of ethnolinguistic labels, in H. Giles and B. St Jacques (eds.), *Language and Ethnic Relations*, Oxford, Pergamon Press.

Khleif, B. B. (1979b), Language as an ethnic boundary in Welsh–English relations, *International Journal of the Sociology of Language*, **20**, 59–74.

Khubchandani, Lachman, M. (1979), Language planning processes for pluralistic societies (a critical review of the Indian scene), *Language Problems and Language Planning*, **2**, 141–61.

Kiernan, V. G. (1972), *The Lords of Human Kind: European Attitudes to the Outside World in the Imperial Age*, Harmondsworth, Middlesex, Penguin Books.

Kirscht, J. P. and Dillehay, R. C. (1967), *Dimensions of Authoritarianism*, Lexington, University of Kentucky Press.

Klimoski, R. J. (1978), Simulation methodologies in experimental research on negotiation by representatives, *Journal of Conflict Resolution*, **22**, 61–77.

Klineberg, O. and Zavalloni, M. (1969), *Nationalism nad Tribalism among African Students*, Paris, Mouton.

Kloss, H. (1966), German-American language maintenance efforts, in J. Fishman (ed.), *Language Loyalty in the United States*, The Hague, Mouton.

Kluckhohn, C. (1944), *Navaho Witchcraft*, Harvard University, Peabody Museum Papers, Volume 22, No 2.

Kochman, T. (1976), Perceptions along the power axis: a cognitive residue of inter-racial encounters, *Anthropological Linguistics*, **18**, 261–73.

Kochman, T. (1979), Boasting and bragging: 'black' and 'white',
    Sociolinguistic Working Papers, No 58, April.
Kramarae, C. (1981), *Women and Men Speaking: Frameworks for Analysis*,
    Rowley, Massachusetts, Newbury House.
Krech, D., Crutchfield, R. S., and Ballachey, E. L. (1962), *Individual in
    Society*, New York, McGraw-Hill.
Laferriere, M. (1979), Ethnicity in phonological variations and change,
    Language, **55**, 603–7.
Laishley, J. (1975), The image of blacks and whites in the children's
    media, in C. Husband (ed.), *White Media and Black Britain*, London,
    Arrow, pp. 69–89.
Lambert, W. E. (1974), Culture and language as factors in learning and
    education, in F. Aboud and R. D. Meade (eds.), *Cultural Factors in
    Learning*, Bellingham, Washington, Western Washington State
    College Press.
Lambert, W. E. (1979), Language as a factor in intergroup relations, in
    H. Giles and R. N. St Clair (eds.), *Language and Social Psychology*,
    Oxford, Blackwell.
Lambert, W. E. (1980), The social psychology of language: a perspective
    for the 1980s, in H. Giles, W. P. Robinson and P. Smith (eds.),
    Language: Social Psychological Perspectives, Oxford, Pergamon Press.
Lambert, W. E. and Tucker, G. R. (1972), *Bilingual Education in Children:
    The St Lambert Experiment*, Rowley, Massachusetts, Newbury House.
Lamy, P. (1979), Language and ethnolinguistic identity: the
    bilingualism question, *International Journal of the Sociology of Language*,
    20, 23–36.
Lanigan, R. L. (1970), Urban crisis: polarisation and communication,
    Central States Speech Journal, **21**, 108–16.
Le Bon, G. (1896), *The Crowd*, London, Unwin.
Lefevre, J. (1978), Dialect and regional identification: the case of
    Wallonia, *International Journal of the Sociology of Language*, **15**, 47–51.
Lemaine, G. (1966), Inégalité, comparaison et incomparabilité: Esquisse
    d'une théorie de l'originalité social, *Bulletin de Psychologie*, **20**, 185–97.
Lewis, G. (1979), A comparative study of language contact: the
    influence of demographic factors in Wales and the Soviet Union, In,
    W. C. McCormack and S. A. Wurm (eds.), *Language and Society*, The
    Hague, Mouton.
Lieberman, E. J. (1979), Esperanto and trans-national identity: the case
    of Dr Zamenhof, *International Journal of the Sociology of Language*, **20**,
    89–107.
Liebkind, K. (1979), The social psychology of minority identity: a case
    study of intergroup identification, *Research Reports*, Department of
    Social Psychology, University of Helsinki.
Lilli, W. (1975), *Soziale Akzentuierung*, Stuttgart, Kohlhammer.
Linton, R. (1936), *The Study of Man*, New York, Appleton-
    Century-Crofts.

Litcher, J. H. and Johnson, D. W. (1969), Changes in attitudes towards negroes of white elementary school students after use of multi-ethnic readers, *Journal of Educational Psychology*, **60 (ii)**, 148–52.

Lott, A. J. and Lott, B. E. (1965), Group cohesiveness as interpersonal attraction: a review of relationships with antecedent and consequent variables, *Psychological Bulletin*, **64**, 259–309.

Lukens, J. G. (1979), Inter-ethnic conflict and communicative distance, in H. Giles and B. St Jacques (eds.), *Language and Ethnic Relations*, Oxford, Pergamon Press.

Lyons, M. H. (1972), Race and ethnicity in pluralistic societies: a comparison of minorities in the UK and USA, *New Community*, **1**, 256–62.

McCarthy, J. and Yancey, W. (1971), Uncle Tom and Mr Charlie: metaphysical pathos in the study of racism and personal disorganisation, *American Journal of Sociology*, **76**, 648.

McClendon, M. J. (1974), Inter-racial contact and the reduction of prejudice, *Sociological Focus*, **7**, 47–65.

McDonagh, E. C. and Richards, E. S. (1953), *Ethnic Relations in the United States*, New York, Appleton-Century-Crofts.

McDougall, W. (1908), *Social Psychology*, London, Methuen.

McDougall, W. (1920), *The Group Mind*, Cambridge, Cambridge University Press.

McGuire, W. J., McGuire, C. V., Child, P., and Fujioka, T. (1978), Salience of ethnicity in the spontaneous self-concept as a function of one's ethnic distinctiveness in the social environment, *Journal of Personality and Social Psychology*, **36**, 511–20.

McGuire, W. J. and Padawer-Singer, A. (1976), Trait salience in the spontaneous self concept, *Journal of Personality and Social Psychology*, **33**, 743–54.

McGrath, J. E. (1966), A social psychological approach to the study of negotiation, in R. Bowers (ed.), *Studies on Behaviour in Organisations: A Research Symposium*, Athens, Georgia, University of Georgia Press, pp. 101–34.

McKillip, J., Dimiceli, A. J., and Luebke, J. (1977), Group salience and stereotyping, *Social Behaviour and Personality*, **5**, 81–5.

McKirnan, D. J. and Hamayan, E. V. (1980), Language norms and perceptions of ethnolinguistic group diversity, in H. Giles, W. P. Robinson, and P. M. Smith (eds.), *Language: Social Psychological Perspectives*, Oxford, Pergamon Press.

Macnamara, J. (1966), *Bilingualism and Primary Education*, Edinburgh, Edinburgh University Press.

Magenau, J. M. and Pruitt, D. G. (1979), The social psychology of bargaining, in G. M. Stephenson and C. J. Brotherton (eds.), *Industrial Relations: A Social Psychological Approach*, London, Wiley.

Malof, M. and Lott, A. J. (1962), Ethnocentrism and the acceptance of negro support in a group pressure situation, *Journal of Abnormal and Social Psychology*, **65**, 254–8.

Mann, J. F. and Taylor, D. M. (1974), Attribution of causality: role of ethnicity and social class, *Journal of Social Psychology*, **94**, 3–13.

Mercer, N., Mercer, E., and Mears, R. (1979), Linguistic and cultural affiliation amongst young Asian people in Leicester, in H. Giles and B. St Jacques (eds.), *Language and Ethnic Relations*, Oxford, Pergamon Press.

Merton, R. K. (1968), *Social Theory and Social Structure*, London Collier-Macmillan, 2nd edition.

Miemois, K. J. (1978), Changes in the structure of the Swedish-speaking population in Finland, 1950–1970, *Research Reports*, No 19, University of Helsinki, Research group for comparative sociology.

Milgram, S. (1974), *Obedience to Authority*, New York, Harper and Ross.

Milgram, S. and Toch, H. (1969), Collective behaviour: crowds and social movements, in G. Lindzey and E. Aronson (eds.), *The Handbook of Social Psychology*, Reading, Massachusetts, Addison-Wesley, Volume 4, 2nd edition.

Milner, D. (1973), Racial identification and preference in 'black' British children, *European Journal of Social Psychology*, **3**, 281–95.

Milner, D. (1975), *Children and Race*, Harmondsworth, Penguin Books.

Minard, R.'D. (1931), Race attitudes of Iowa children, *University of Iowa Student Characteristics*, **4**.

Minard, R. D. (1952), Race relationships in the Pocahontas coal fields, *Journal of Social Issues*, **25**, 29–44.

Morley, I. E. and Stephenson, G. M. (1969), Interpersonal and interparty exchange: a laboratory simulation of an industrial dispute at the plant level, *British Journal of Psychology*, **60**, 543–5.

Morley, I. E. and Stephenson, G. M. (1970a), Strength of case, communication systems and outcomes of simulated negotiations. Some social psychological aspects of bargaining, *Industrial Relations Journal*, **1**, 19–29.

Morley, I. E. and Stephenson, G. M. (1970b), Formality in experimental negotiations: A validation study, *British Journal of Psychology*, **61**, 383–4.

Morley, I. E. and Stephenson, G. M. (1977), *The Social Psychology of Bargaining*, London, Allen and Unwin.

Moscovici, S. (1972), Society and theory in social psychology, in J. Israel and H. Tajfel (eds.), *The Context of Social Psychology: A Critical Assessment*, European Monographs in Social Psychology, No 2, London, Academic Press.

Mougeon, R. (1977), French language replacement and mixed marriages: the case of the francophone minority of Welland, Ontario, *Anthropological Linguistics*, **19**, 368–77.

Mougeon, R. and Canale, M. (1978), Maintenance of French in Ontario: is education in French enough?, *Interchange*, **9**, 30–9.

Muhyi, I. (1952), *Certain Content of Prejudices Against Negroes Among White Children of Different Ages*, unpublished doctoral dissertation, Columbia University.

Muthiani, J. (1979), Sociopsychologial bases of language choice and use: the case of Swahili vernaculars and English in Kenya, in W. C. McCormack and S. A. Wurm (eds.), *Language and Society*, The Hague, Mouton.

Myers, A. (1962), Team competition, success and the adjustment of group members, *Journal of Abnormal and Social Psychology*, **65**, 325–32.

Newcomb, T. M. (1961), *The Acquaintance Process*, New York, Holt, Rinehard and Winston.

Nobles, W. W. (1973), Psychological research and the black self-concept: a critical review, *Journal of Social Issues*, **29 (i)**, 11–31.

Novak, D. W. and Lerner, M. J. (1968), Rejection as a consequence of perceived similarity, *Journal of Personality and Social Psychology*, **9**, 147–52.

Oakes, P. J. and Turner, J. C. (1980), Social categorisation and intergroup behaviour: does minimal intergroup discrimination make social identity more positive?, *European Journal of Social Psychology*, **10**, 295–301.

Olmedo, E. L. (1979), Acculturation: a psychometric perspective, *American Psychologist*, **34**, 1061–70.

Osgood, C. E. (1967), Cross-cultural comparability in attitude measurement via multi-lingual semantic differentials, in M. Fishbein (ed.), *Readings in Attitude Theory and Measurement*, New York, John Wiley.

Pandit, P. B. (1978), Language and identity: the Punjabi language in Delhi, *International Journal of the Sociology of Language*, **16**, 93–108.

Parkin, D. (1977), Emergent and stabilised multilingualism: poly-ethnic peer groups in urban Kenya, in H. Giles (ed.), *Language, Ethnicity and Intergroup Relations*, London, Academic Press.

Paulston, C. B. and Paulston, R. G. (1980), Language and ethnic boundaries, *Language Sciences*, **2**, 69–101.

Perret-Clermont, A. N. (1980), *Social Interaction and Cognitive Development in Children*, European Monographs in Social Psychology, London, Academic Press.

Pettigrew, T. F. (1958), Personality and socio-cultural factors in inter-group attitudes: a cross-national comparison, *Journal of Conflict Resolution*, **2**, 29–42.

Pettigrew, T. F. (1964), *A Profile of the Negro American*, Princeton, Van Nostrand.

Pettigrew, T. F. (1967), Social evaluation theory: convergencies and applications, *Nebraska Symposium on Motivation*, Nebraska, University of Nebraska Press.

Pettigrew, T. F. (1971), *Racially Separate or Together?*, New York, McGraw-Hill.

Pettigrew, T. F. (1978), Placing Adam's argument in a broader perspective: comment on the Adam paper, *Social Psychology*, **41**, 58–61.

Pool, J. (1979), Language planning and identity planning, *International Journal of the Sociology of Language*, **20**, 5–21.

Pruitt, D. G. and Kimmel, M. J. (1977), Twenty years of experimental gaming: critique, synthesis and suggestions for the future, *Annual Review of Psychology*, **28**, 363–92.

Pushkin, I. (1967), Personal communication.

Pushkin, I. and Veness, T. (1973), The development of racial awareness and prejudice in young children, in P. Watson (ed.), *Psychology and Race*, Harmondsworth, Middlesex, Penguin, pp. 23–42.

Rabbie, J. M. (1974), *Effects of Expected Intergroup Competition and Co-operation*, Paper presented to Annual Convention APA, New Orleans, August, University of Utrecht.

Rabbie, J. M., Benoist, F., Oosterbaan, H., and Visser, L. (1974), Differential power and effects of expected competitive and co-operative intergroup interaction on intragroup and outgroup attitudes, *Journal of Personality and Social Psychology*, **30**, 46–56.

Rabbie, M. J. and de Brey, J. H. C. (1971), The anticipation of intergroup co-operation and competition under private and public conditions, *International Journal of Group Tensions*, **1**, 230–51.

Rabbie, J. M. and Horwitz, M. (1969), Arousal of ingroup–outgroup bias by a chance win or loss, *Journal of Personality and Social Psychology*, **13**, 269–77.

Rabbie, J. M. and Huygen, K. (1974), Internal disagreements and their effects on attitudes towards in- and outgroup, *International Journal of Group Tensions*, **4**, 222–46.

Rabbie, J. M. and Wilkens, G. (1971), Intergroup competition and its effect on intragroup and intergroup relations, *European Journal of Social Psychology*, **1**, 215–34.

Reicher, S. D. (1982), The Determination of collective behaviour, in H. Tajfel (ed.), *Social Identity and Intergroup Relations*, Cambridge and Paris, Cambridge University Press and Editions de la Maison des Sciences de l'Homme.

Richardson, A. (1967), A theory and a method for the psychological study of assimilation, *International Migration Review*, **2**, 3–30.

Roberts, C. and Williams, G. (1980), Attitudes and ideological bases of support for Welsh as a minority language, in H. Giles, W. P. Robinson, and P. M. Smith (eds.), *Language: Social Psychological Perspectives*, Oxford, Pergamon Press.

Rogers, C. (1969), *Encounter Groups*, London, Penguin.

Rokeach, M. (1960), *The Open and Closed Mind*, New York, Basic Books.

Rokeach, M. (1968), *Reliefs, Attitudes and Values*, San Francisco, Jossey-Bass.

Rokeach, M. and Mezei, L (1966), Race and shared belief as factors in social choice, *Science*, **151**, 167–72.

Rokeach, M., Smith, P. W., and Evans, R. I. (1960), Two kinds of prejudice or one?, in M. Rokeach (ed.), *Open and Closed Mind*, New York, Basic Books.

Rosenberg, M. and Simmons, R. G. (1972), *Black and White Self-esteem: The Urban School Child*, Washington, DC, American Sociological Association.

Ross, F. (1979), *Multiple Group Membership, Social Mobility and Intergroup Relations: An Investigation of Group Boundaries and Boundary Crossing*, unpublished PhD thesis, University of Bristol.

Ross, J. A. (1979), Language and the mobilisation of ethnic identity, in H. Giles and B. St Jacques (eds.), *Language and Ethnic Relations*, Oxford, Pergamon Press.

Rothbart, M., Fulero, S., Jensen, C., Howard, J., and Birrell, P. (1978), From individual to group impressions: availability heuristics in stereotype formation, *Journal of Experimental Social Psychology*, **14**, 237–55.

Rubin, J. and Jernudd, B. H. (1971), *Can Language be Planned?*, Honolulu, East-West Center Books.

Rubin, J. Z. and Brown, B. R. (1975), *The Social Psychology of Bargaining and Negotiations*, New York, Academic Press.

Ryan, E. B. (1979), Why do low-prestige language varieties persist?, in H. Giles and R. N. St Clair (eds.), *Language and Social Psychology*, Oxford, Blackwell.

Ryan, E. B. and Carranza, M. A. (1977), Ingroup and outgroup reactions to Mexican American language varieties, in H. Giles (ed.), *Language Ethnicity and Intergroup Relations*, London, Academic Press.

Ryen, A. H. and Kahn, A. (1975), Effects of intergroup orientation on group attitudes and proxemic behavior, *Journal of Personality and Social Psychology*, **31**, 302–10.

St Claire, L. and Turner, J. C., *The Role of Demand Characteristics in the Minimal Group Paradigm*, University of Bristol, in preparation.

Salamone, F. A. and Swanson, C. H. (1979), Identity and ethnicity: ethnic groups and interactions in a multi-ethnic society, *Ethnic Groups*, **2**, 167–83.

Sampson, E. E. (1968), Status congruence and cognitive consistency, *Sociometry*, **26**, 146–62.

Sattler, J. (1973), Racial experimenter effects, in K. S. Miller and R. M. Dreger (eds.), *Comparative Studies of Blacks and Whites in the US*, New York, Seminar Press.

Sawyer, J. B. (1973), Social aspects of bilingualism in San Antonio, Texas, in R. W. Bailey and J. L. Robinson (eds.), *Varieties of Present-day English*, New York, Macmillan.

Scodel, A. and Austrin, H. (1957), The perception of Jewish photographs by non-Jews and Jews, *Journal of Abnormal and Social Psychology*, **54**, 278–80.

Scollon, R. and Scollon, S. B. K. (1979), Literacy as inter-ethnic communication: an Athabaskan case, *Sociolinguistic Working Papers*, No 59.

Sears, D. O. and Kinder, D. R. (1971), Racial tensions and voting in Los Angeles, in W. Z. Hirsch (ed.), *Los Angeles: Viability and Prospects for Metropolitan Leadership*, New York, Praeger, pp. 51–88.

Sebastian, R. J. and Ryan, E. B. (in press), The effects of speech cues on social evaluation and behaviour, in H. Giles and R. N. St Clair (eds.), *Recent Advances in Language, Communications and Social Psychology*, Hillsdale, New Jersey, Erlbaum.

Seckbach, F. (1974), Attitudes and opinions of Israeli teachers and students about aspects of modern Hebrew, *International Journal of the Sociology of Language*, 1, 105–24.

Secord, P. F. and Backman, C. W. (1964), *Social Psychology*, New York, McGraw-Hill.

Segalowitz, N. (1976), Communicative competence and nonfluent bilingualism, *Candaian Journal of Behavioural Science*, 8, 122–31.

Shaw, M. E. (1976), *Group Dynamics: The Psychology of Small Group Behaviour*, New Delhi, Teta McGraw-Hill, 2nd edition.

Sherif, M. (1936), *The Psychology of Social Norms*, New York, Octagon Books.

Sherif, M. (1951), A preliminary experimental study of inter-group relations, in J. H. Rohrer and M. Sherif (eds.), *Social Psychology at the Crossroads*, New York, Harper.

Sherif, M. (1967), *Group Conflict and Co-operation*, London, Routledge and Kegan Paul.

Sherif, M., Harvey, O. J., White, B. J., Hood, W. R., and Sherif, Carolyn, W. (1961), *Intergroup Conflict and Co-operation. The Robbers Cave Experiment*, Norman, Oklahoma, University of Oklahoma Book Exchange.

Sherif, M. and Sherif, C. W. (1953), *Groups in Harmony and Tension*, New York, Harper.

Sherif, M. and Sherif, C. W. (1956), *An Outline of Social Psychology*, New York, Harper, revised edition.

Sherif, M. and Sherif, C. W. (1969), *Social Psychology*, New York, Harper and Row.

Sherif, M., White, B. J., and Harvey, O. J. (1955), Status in experimentally produced groups, *American Journal of Sociology*, 60, 370–9.

Shomer, R. W. and Centers, R. (1970), Differences in attitudinal responses under conditions of implicitly manipulated group salience, *Journal of Personality and Social Psychology*, 15, 125–32.

Short, J. A. (1974), Effects of medium of communication on experimental negotiation, *Human Relations*, 27, 225–34.

Short, J. A., Williams, E., and Christie, B. (1976), *The Social Psychology of Telecommunications*, London, Wiley.

Shuy, R., Baratz, J., and Wolfram, W. (1969), *Sociolinguistic Factors in Speech Identification*, Research Project No. MH. 15048-01, Center for Applied Linguistics, Washington, DC.

Shuy, R. W. and Fasold, R. W. (eds.), *Language Attitudes: Current Trends and Prospects*, Washington, DC. Georgetown.

Simard, L. (1980), Intergroup communication, in R. C. Gardner and R. Kalin (eds.), *A Canadian Social Psychology of Ethnic Relations*, London, Methuen.

Simard, L. (1981), Cross-cultural interaction: potential invisible barriers, *Journal of Social Psychology*, in press.

Simard, L. and Taylor, D. (1973), The potential for bicultural communication in a dyadic situation, *Canadian Journal of Behavioural Science*, 5, 211–17.

Simmel, G. (1955), *Conflict and the Web of Group Affiliations*, London, Collier-Macmillan.

Simmons, R. (1978), Blacks and high self-esteem: a puzzle, *Social Psychology*, 41, 54–7.

Simpson, G. E. and Yinger, J. M. (1965), *Racial and Cultural Minorities*, New York, Harper and Row.

Skinner, M. R. (1979), The social psychology of intergroup conflict, in G. M. Stephenson and C. J. Brotherton (eds.), *Industrial Relations: A Social Psychological Approach*, London, Wiley.

Smith, P. M., Giles, H., and Hewstone, M. (1980), Sociolinguistics: a social psychological perspective, in R. N. St Clair and H. Giles (eds.), *The Social and Psychological Contexts of Language*, Hillsdale, New Jersey, Erlbaum.

Smith, P. M., Tucker, G. R., and Taylor, D. M. (1977), Language, ethnic identity and intergroup relations: one immigrant group's reaction to language planning in Quebec, in H. Giles (ed.), *Language Ethnicity and Intergroup Relations*, London, Academic Press.

Smolicz, J. J. (1979), *Culture and Education in a Plural Society*, Canberra, Curriculum Development Centre.

Sole, K., Marton, J., and Hornstein, H. A. (1975), Opinion similarity and helping: three field experiments investigating the bases of promotive tension, *Journal of Experimental Social Psychology*, 11, 1–13.

Stallybrass, O. (1977), Stereotype, in A. Bullock and O. Stallybrass (eds.), *The Fontana Dictionary of Modern Thought*, London, Fontana/Collins.

Stein, D. D. (1966), The influence of belief systems on interpersonal preference: a validation study of Rokeach's theory of prejudice, *Psychological Monographs*, 80, 8 (whole No 816).

Stein, D. D., Hardyck, J. A., and Smith, M. B. (1965), Race and belief: an open and shut case, *Journal of Personality and Social Psychology*, 1, 281–9.

Steiner, I. D. (1974), Whatever happened to the group in social psychology?, *Journal of Experimental Social Psychology*, 10, 94–108.

Stephan, W. (1977), Stereotyping: role of ingroup–outgroup differences in causal attribution of behaviour, *Journal of Social Psychology*, 101, 255–66.

Stephenson, G. M. (1978), Interparty and interpersonal exchange in negotiation groups, in H. Brandstatter, J. H. Davis, and H. Schuler (eds.), *Dynamics of Group Decisions*, London, Sage.

Stephenson, G. M. and Brotherton, C. J. (1975), Social progression and polarisation: a study of discussion and negotiation in groups of mining supervisors, *British Journal of Social and Clinical Psychology*, **14**, 241–52.

Stephenson, G. M., Kniveton, B. K., and Morley, I. E. (1977), Interaction analysis of an industrial wage negotiation, *Journal of Occupational Psychology*, **50**, 231–41.

Stroebe, W. (1979), The level of social psychological analysis: a plea for a more social social psychology, in L. H. Strickland (ed.), *Social Psychology – A Modern Perspective: Western and Soviet Points of View*, Oxford, Pergamon Press.

Sumner, G. A. (1906), *Folkways*, New York, Ginn.

Sussman, M. B. and Weil, W. B. (1960), An experimental study on the effects of group interaction upon the behaviour of diabetic children, *International Journal of Social Psychiatry*, **6**, 120–5.

Taft, R. (1979), The concept of social adaptation of migrants, in P. R. de Lacy and M. E. Poole (eds.), *Mosaic or Melting Pot*, Sydney, Harcourt Brace Jovanovich Group.

Tajfel, H. (1957), Value and the perceptual judgement of magnitude, *Psychological Review*, **64**, 192–204.

Tajfel, H. (1959), Quantitative judgement in social perception, *British Journal of Psychology*, **50**, 16–29.

Tajfel, H. (1963), Stereotype, *Race*, **V**, 3–14.

Tajfel, H. (1969a), Cognitive aspects of prejudice, *Journal of Social Issues*, **25**, 79–97.

Tajfel, H. (1969b), Social and cultural factors in perception, in G. Lindzey and E. Aronson (eds.), *Handbook of Social Psychology*, Volume 3, Cambridge, Massachusetts, Addison-Wesley.

Tajfel, H. (1972a), Experiments in a vacuum, in J. Israel and H. Tajfel (eds.), *The Context of Social Psychology: A Critical Assessment*, European Monographs in Social Psychology, No 2, London, Academic Press.

Tajfel, H. (1972b), Social categorisation. English ms of La catégorisation sociale, in S. Moscovici (ed.), *Introduction à la Psychologie Sociale*, Volume I, Paris, Larousse, Chapter 8, pp. 272–302.

Tajfel, H. (1973), The roots of prejudice: cognitive aspects, in P. Watson (ed.), *Psychology and Race*, Harmondsworth, Middlesex, Penguin Books, pp. 76–95.

Tajfel, H. (1974), Social identity and intergroup behaviour, *Social Science Information*, **13**, 2, 65–93.

Tajfel, H. (ed.), (1978a), *Differentiation Between Social Groups: Studies in the Social Psychology of Intergroup Relations*, London, Academic Press.

Tajfel, H. (1978b), Intergroup behaviour: individualistic perspectives, in H. Tajfel and C. Fraser (eds.), *Introducing Social Psychology*, Harmondsworth, Middlesex, Penguin.

Tajfel, H. (1978c), *The Social Psychology of Minorities*, Report No 38, Minority Rights Group, London.

Tajfel, H. (1978d), The structure of our views about society, in H. Tajfel and C. Fraser (eds.), *Introducing Social Psychology*, Harmondsworth, Middlesex, Penguin Books.

Tajfel, H. (1979), Individuals and groups in social psychology, *British Journal of Social and Clinical Psychology*, **18**, 183–90.

Tajfel, H. (ed.) (1982), *Social Identity and Intergroup Relations*, Cambridge, Cambridge University Press, and Paris, Editions de la Maison des Sciences de l'Homme.

Tajfel, H. and Billig, M. G. (1974), Familiarity and categorisation in intergroup behaviour, *Journal of Experimental Social Psychology*, **10**, 159–70.

Tajfel, H., Flament, C., Billig, M. G., and Bundy, R. F. (1971), Social categorisation and intergroup behaviour, *European Journal of Social Psychology*, **1**, 149–77.

Tajfel, H. and Turner, J. C. (1979), An integrative theory of intergroup conflict, in W. G. Austin and S. Worchel (eds.), *The Social Psychology of Intergroup Relations*, Monterey, California, Brooks/Cole.

Tajfel, H. and Wilkes, A. L. (1963), Classification and quantitative judgement, *British Journal of Psychology*, **54**, 101–14.

Tajfel, H. and Wilkes, A. L. (1964), Salience of attributes and commitment to extreme judgements in the perception of people, *British Journal of Social and Clinical Psychology*, **2**, 40–9.

Tannen, D. (1979), Ethnicity as conversational style, *Sociolinguistic Working Papers*, No 55.

Taylor, D. M. and Aboud, F. E. (1973), Ethnic stereotypes: is the concept necessary?, *Canadian Psychologist*, **14**, 330–8.

Taylor, D. M., Bassili, J. N., and Aboud, F. E. (1973), Dimensions of ethnic identity in Canada, *Journal of Social Psychology*, **89**, 185–92.

Taylor, D. M. and Brown, R. J. (1979), Towards a more social social psychology?, *British Journal of Social and Clinical Psychology*, **18**, 173–80.

Taylor, D. M. and Gardner, R. C. (1970a), Bicultural communication: a study of communicational efficiency and person perception, *Canadian Journal of Behavioural Science*, **2**, 67–81.

Taylor, D. M. and Gardner, R. C. (1970b), The role of stereotypes in communication between ethnic groups in the Philippines, *Social Forces*, **49**, 217–83.

Taylor, D. M. and Giles, H. (1979), At the crossroads of research into language and ethnic relations, in H. Giles and B. St Jacques (eds.), *Language and Ethnic Relations*, Oxford, Pergamon Press.

Taylor, D. M. and Guimond, S. (1978), The belief theory of prejudice in an intergroup context, *Journal of Social Psychology*, **105**, 11–25.

Taylor, D. M. and Jaggi, V. (1974), Ethnocentrism and causal attribution in a South Indian context, *Journal of Cross-Cultural Psychology*, **5**, 162–71.

Taylor, D. M., Meynard, R., and Rheault, E. (1977), Threat to ethnic identity and second language learning, in H. Giles (ed.), *Language Ethnicity and Intergroup Relations*, London, Academic Press.

Taylor, D. M. and Royer, L. (1980), Group processes affecting anticipated language choice in intergroup relations, in H. Giles, W. P. Robinson and P. M. Smith (eds.), *Language: Social Psychological Perspectives*, Oxford, Pergamon Press.

Taylor, D. M. and Simard, L. (1975), Social interaction in a bilingual setting, *Canadian Psychological Reviews*, 16, 240–54.

Taylor, D. M., Simard, L. M., and Papineau, D. (1978), Perceptions of cultural differences and language use: a field study in a bilingual environment, *Canadian Journal of Behavioural Science*, 10, 181–91.

Taylor, S. E., Fiske, S. T., Etcoff, N. L., and Ruderman, A. (1978), Categorical and contextual bases of person memory and stereotyping, *Journal of Personality and Social Psychology*, 36, 778–93.

Teplin, L. (1974), *Misonceptualisation as Artifact? A Multitrait–Multimethod Analysis of Inter-racial Choice and Interaction Methodologies Utilised in Studying Children*, Paper presented to annual meeting of the Society for the Study of Social Problems in Montreal.

Thakerar, J. N., Giles, H., and Cheshire, J. (in press), Psychological and linguistic parameters of speech accommodation theory, in C. Fraser and K. R. Scherer (eds.), *Social Psychological Dimensions of Langauge Behaviour*, Cambridge, Cambridge University Press.

Thibaut, J. W. and Kelley, H. H. (1959), *The Social Psychology of Groups*, New York, Wiley.

Thomas, K. (1971), *Religion and the Decline of Magic*, London, Weidenfeld and Nicolson, reprinted in 1973, Penguin Books.

Thurstone, L. L. (1931), The measurement of social attitudes, *Journal of Abnormal and Social Psychology*, 36, 249–69.

Trager, H. G. and Radke-Yarrow, M. (1952), *They Learn What They Live*, New York, Harper.

Trent, R. D. (1954), The colour of the investigator as a variable in experimental research with Negro subjects, *Journal of Social Psychology*, 40, 281–7.

Triandis, H. C. and Davis, E. E. (1965), Race and belief as shared determinants of behaviour intentions, *Journal of Personality and Social Psychology*, 2, 715–25.

Trudgill, P. (1974), *Sociolinguistics*, Harmondsworth, Middlesex, Penguin.

Tucker, G. R. and Gedalof, H. (1970), Bilinguals as linguistic mediators, *Psychonomic Science*, 20, 369–71.

Turner, J. C. (1975a), Social comparison and social identity: some prospects for intergroup behaviour, *European Journal of Social Psychology*, 5, 5–34.

Turner, J. C. (1975b), *Social Categorisation and Social Comparison in Intergroup Relations*, unpublished PhD thesis, University of Bristol.

Turner, J. C. (1978a), Social categorisation and social discrimination in the minimal group paradigm, in H. Tajfel (ed.), *Differentiation Between Social Groups: Studies in the Social Psychology of Intergroup Relations*, London, Academic Press.

Turner, J. C. (1978b), Social comparison, similarity and ingroup favouritism, in H. Tajfel (ed.), *Differentiation Between Social Groups: Studies in the Social Psychology of Intergroup Relations*, London, Academic Press.

Turner, J. C. (1978c), Social identification and intergroup behaviour: some emerging issues in the social psychology of intergroup behaviour, *Research Proposal*, University of Bristol.

Turner, J. C. (1980), Fairness or discrimination in intergroup behaviour? A reply to Braithwaite, Doyle and Lightbown, *European Journal of Social Psychology*, **10**, 131–47.

Turner, J. C. (1982), Towards a cognitive redefinition of the social group, in H. Tajfel (ed.), *Social Identity and Intergroup Relations*, Cambridge and Paris, Cambridge Unviersity Press and Editions de la Maison des Sciences de l'Homme.

Turner, J. C. and Brown, R. J. (1978), Social status, cognitive alternatives and intergroup relations, in H. Tajfel (ed.), *Differentiation Between Social Groups*, London, Academic Press.

Turner, J. C., Brown, R. J., and Tajfel, H. (1979), Social comparison and group interest in ingroup favouritismm *European Journal of Social Psychology*, **9**, 187–204.

Turner, J. C., Hogg, M., Oakes, P. J., and Smith, P. M. (in preparation), *Group Formation as a Process of Self-attitude Change: The Effects of Success and Failure on Group Cohesiveness*, University of Bristol.

Tversky, A. and Kahneman, D. (1973), Availability: a heuristic for judging frequency and probability, *Cognitive Psychology*, **5**, 207–32.

Ullrich, H. E. (1971), Linguistic aspects of antiquity: a dialect study, *Anthropological Linguistics*, **13**, 106–13.

Van Der Berghe, P. L. (1967), *Race and Racism*, New York, Wiley.

Van Knippenberg, A. and Wilke, H. (1979), Perception of Collegiens and Apprentis re-analysed, *European Journal of Social Psychology*, **9**, 427–34.

Vaughan, G. M. (1964a), The development of ethnic attitudes in New Zealand school-children, *Genetic Psychology Monographs*, **70**, 135–75.

Vaughan, G. M. (1964b), Ethnic awareness in relation to minority-group membership, *Journal of Genetic Psychology*, **105**, 119–30.

Vaughan, G. M. (1978a), Social change and inter-group preferences in New Zealand, *European Journal of Social Psychology*, **8**, 297–314.

Vaughan, G. M. (1978b), Social categorisation and intergroup behaviour in children, in H. Tajfel (ed.), *Differentiation Between Social Groups: Studies in the Social Psychology of Intergroup Relations*, London, Academic Press.

Veltman, C. J. (1979), New opportunities for the study of language shift, *Language Problems and Language Planning*, **3**, 65–75.

Vidmar, N. and McGrath, J. E. (1965), Role assignment and attitudinal commitment as factors in negotiation, *Technical Report No 3*, AFOSR Contract AF49 (638) 1291, Department of Psychology, University of Illinois, Urbana.

Walton, R. E. (1969), *Interpersonal Peacemaking: Confrontations and Third-Party Consultation*, Reading, Massachusetts, Addison-Wesley.

Walton, R. E. and McKersie, R. B. (1965), *A Behavioural Theory of Labor Negotiations: An Analysis of a Social Interaction System*, New York, McGraw-Hill.

Ward, S. H. and Braun, J. (1972), Self-esteem and racial preference in black children, *American Journal of Orthopsychiatry*, **42 (iv)**, 644–7.

Warr, P. B. (1973), *Psychology and Collective Bargaining*, London, Hutchinson.

Weber, M. (1964), *From Max Weber: Essays in Sociology*, edited and translated by H. H. Gerth and C. W. Mills, New York, Oxford University Press.

Weinstein, B. (1979), Language strategists: redefining political frontiers on the basis of linguistic choices, *World Politics*, **31**, 345–64.

White, M. J. (1977), Counter-normative behaviour as influenced by de-individualizing conditions and reference group salience, *Journal of Social Psychology*, **103**, 75–90.

Wicker, A. W. (1969), Attitudes versus actions: the relationship of verbal and overt behavioural responses to attitude objects, *Journal of Social Issues*, **25**, 41–78.

Wicklund, R. A. and Brehm, J. W. (1976), *Perspectives on Cognitive Dissonance*, Hillsdale, New Jersey, Erlbaum.

Wilder, D. A. (1978), Reduction of intergroup discrimination through individuation of the outgroup, *Journal of Personality and Social Psychology*, **36**, 1361–74.

Williams, F., Whitehead, J. L., and Miller, L. M. (1971), Ethnic stereotyping and judgments of children's speech, *Speech Monographs*, **38**, 166–70.

Williams, G. (1979), Language group allegiance and ethnic interaction, in H. Giles and B. St Jacques (eds.), *Language and Ethnic Relations*, Oxford, Pergamon Press.

Williams, J. A., and Giles, H. (1978), The changing status of women in society: an inter-group perspective, in H. Tajfel (ed.), *Differentiation Between Social Groups*, London, Academic Press.

Williams, J. E. (1964), Connotations of colour names among Negroes and Caucasians, *Perceptual and Motor Skills*, **19**, 721–31.

Williams, J. E. (1970), Connotations of racial concepts and color names, in M. L. Goldschmid (ed.), *Black Americans and White Racism*, New York, Holt, Rinehart and Winston.

Williams, J. E. and Morland, J. K. (1976), *Race, Color and the Young Child*, Chapel Hill, University of North Carolina Press.

Williams, J. E. and Morland, J. K. (1979), Comment on Banks's 'white preferences in blacks: a paradigm in search of a phenomenon', *Psychological Bulletin*, **86 (i)**, 28–32.

Williams, J. E., Morland, J. K., and Underwood, W. L. (1970), Connotations of colour names in the US, Europe and Asia, *Journal of Social Psychology*, **82**, 3–14.

Williams, J. E. and Roberson, J. K. (1967), A method of assessing racial attitudes in pre-school children, *Educational and Psychological Measurement*, **27**, 671–89.

Wilner, D. M., Walkley, R. P., and Cook, S. W. (1952), Residential proximity and intergroup relations in public housing projects, *Journal of Social Issues*, **8**, 45–69.

Wilson, W., Chun, N., and Kayatani, M. (1965), Projection, attraction, and strategy choices in intergroup competition, *Journal of Personality and Social Psychology*, **2**, 432–35.

Wilson, W. and Kayatani, M. (1968), Intergroup attitudes and strategies in games between opponents of the same or of a different race, *Journal of Personality and Social Psychology*, **9**, 24–30.

Wilson, W. and Robinson, C. (1968), Selective intergroup bias in both authoritarians and non-authoritarians after playing a modified Prisoner's Dilemma Game, *Perceptual and Motor Skills*, **27**, 1051–8.

Wilson, W. and Wong, J. (1968), Intergroup attitudes towards co-operative versus competitive opponents in a modified Prisoner's Dilemma Game, *Perceptual and Motor Skills*, **27**, 1059–66.

Wilson, W. C. (1963), Development of ethnic attitudes in adolescence, *Child Development*, **34**, 247–56.

Wittgenstein, L. (1953), *Philosophical Investigations*, Oxford, Blackwell.

Wolff, H. (1959), Intelligibility and inter-ethnic attitudes, *Anthropological Linguistics*, **1**, 34–41.

Wolfram, W. (1973), Sociolinguistic aspects of assimilation: Puerto Rican English in East Harlem, in R. W. Shuy and R. W Fasold (eds.), *Language Attitudes: Current Trends and Prospects*, Washington, DC, Georgetown.

Worchel, S. (1979), Co-operation and the reduction of intergroup conflict: some determining factors, in W. G. Austin and S. Worchel (eds.), *The Social Psychology of Intergroup Relations*, Monterey, California, Brooks/Cole.

Worchel, S., Andreoli, V. A., and Folger, R. (1977), Intergroup co-operation and intergroup attraction: the effect of previous interaction and outcome of combined effort, *Journal of Experimental Social Psychology*, **13**, 131–40.

Worchel, S., Axsom, D., Ferris, F., Samaha, C., and Schweitzer, S.

(1978), Factors determining the effect of intergroup co-operation on intergroup attraction, *Journal of Conflict Resolution*, **22**, 429–39.

Worchel, S., Lind, E. A., and Kaufman, K. (1975), Evaluations of group products as a function of expectations of group longevity, outcome of competition, and publicity of evaluations, *Journal of Personality and Social Psychology*, **31**, 1089–97.

Wrightsman, L. S. (1977), *Social Psychology*, Belmont, Wadsworth, 2nd edition.

Yaffe, Y. and Yinon, Y. (1979), Retaliatory aggression in individuals and groups, *European Journal of Social Psychology*, **9**, 177–86.

Yang, K. S. and Bond, M. H. (1980), Ethnic affirmation in Chinese bilinguals, *Journal of Cross-Cultural Psychology*, **11**, 411–25.

Zavalloni, M. (1973), Social identity: perspectives and prospects, *Social Science Information*, **12**, 65–92.

Zavalloni, M. (1975), Social identity and the recoding of reality: its relevance for cross-cultural psychology, *International Journal of Psychology*, **10**, 197–217.

Zimbardo, P. (1969), The human choice: individuation, reason and order versus de-individuation, impulse and chaos, in W. J. Arnold and D. Levine (eds.), *Nebraska Symposium on Motivation*, Lincoln, University of Nebraska Press.

Zirkel, P. A. and Moses, E. G. (1971), Self-concept and ethnic group membership among public school students, *American Educational Research Journal*, **8**, 253–65.

INDEX

actions, collective, 6, 8, 35, 62, 105,
 158–62, 222
Adam, B., 136
Adorno, T. W., 10–11, 12–13, 106
aggression, 11–12, 113; displacement
 of, 105, 159
Allen, V. L., 54–5, 56–7, 79
Allport, F. H., 8, 9, 33–5, 40, 65
Allport, G. W., 10–11, 59–60, 62,
 112, 148–9, 156, 166
altruism, 39, 57–8, 88, 97
Asch, S. E., 10, 29, 34–6, 54
Ashmore, R. D., 114–15, 117, 140,
 142
assimilation, group, 204, 207–8,
 219–22, 226, 239, 241
attitudes, individual, 13, 30, 48, 100;
 changes in, 91–3; development of,
 13, 18, 102, 117, 118–31; negative,
 106–7, 112; positive, 88;
 self-attitude, 38–40, 87, 91–3, 96,
 131–7
attitudes, intergroup, 2, 21, 57, 74,
 94; changes in, 50, 68, 75, 91–2, 99,
 114, 141; negative, 10–11, 18, 21,
 28–9, 31, 48, 73, 89, 93–4, 97,
 102–3, 125–6, 213; positive, 49,
 85–7, 89, 93–5, 110, 142; racial, 9,
 18–19, 53, 61–2, 102–4, 108–9,
 112–14, 123–6, 141–2
attraction, 17, 39, 48–9; intergroup,
 73, 77, 86–7, 95–6; interpersonal,
 11, 53–4, 58, 59–63, 71, 86–7,
 88–90; intragroup, 77
attribution theory, 30, 92–3, 159,
 165–6
authoritarian personality, concept of,
 10–11, 12, 28–9, 34, 106–9, 140

Bales, R. F., 182
Banks, W. C., 133–5

bargaining, intergroup, 1, 3, 14, 21–2,
 43, 73, 177–90; bargaining
 relationships, 170, 171–7, 178,
 181–8, 195; costs of, 168, 189;
 definition, 168–9, 174; outcomes,
 22, 169–70, 177, 179–81, 185
bargaining, interpersonal, 13, 21, 43,
 168–70, 171–7, 178, 180–1, 183,
 186–7, 190–8
bargaining, intragroup, 188
Barth, F., 201
Batstone, E., 186–7, 194
belief congruence theory, 1, 16, 34,
 47–59, 64
Berkowitz, L., 34
bias: ingroup, 50, 66–7, 68–9, 71–5,
 77, 79–82, 85, 90–1, 93–4, 151;
 race, 128
Billig, M. G., 24, 45, 55–6, 76–8, 105,
 110–11, 141, 161
Blake, R. R., 69–71, 188
Bogardus, E. S., 9, 104
Boraston, I., 186–7, 194
Bourhis, R. Y., 229, 231
Boyanowsky, E. O., 54–5
Braly, K. R., 9
Brewer, M. B., 71, 79, 81, 94
Brotherton, C. J., 180–1
Brown, R. J., 16, 42, 79, 81–2, 193,
 228
Bruner, J. S., 154, 157
Buss, A. R., 166
Byrne, D., 53, 54

Cartright, D., 8–9
categorization, 2, 19–20, 37, 51, 87,
 88–9, 97–8, 100, 217; criteria for,
 80, 94, 96; and discrimination,
 75–84; effects of, 17, 24–7, 55–6,
 87, 110; function of, 149–53;
 interethnic, 23, 57, 206, 207, 236;